T0351225

ELEMENTAL POWERS FOR WITCHES

About the Author

Frater Barrabbas Tiresius is a practicing ritual magician who has studied magic and the occult for more than forty years. He believes that ritual magic is a discipline whose mystery is unlocked by continual practice and by occult experiences and revelations. Frater Barrabbas believes that traditional approaches should be balanced with creativity and experimentation, and that no occult or magical tradition is exempt from changes and revisions.

Over the years, he found that his practical magical discipline was the real source for all of his creative efforts. That creative process helped him build and craft a unique and different kind of magical system, one quite unlike any other yet based on common Wiccan practices. So, despite its uniqueness, this magical system is capable of being easily adapted and used by others.

Frater Barrabbas is also the founder of a magical order called the Order of the Gnostic Star, and he is an elder and lineage holder in the Alexandrian tradition of Witchcraft. Visit his blog at fraterbarrabbas.blogspot.com.

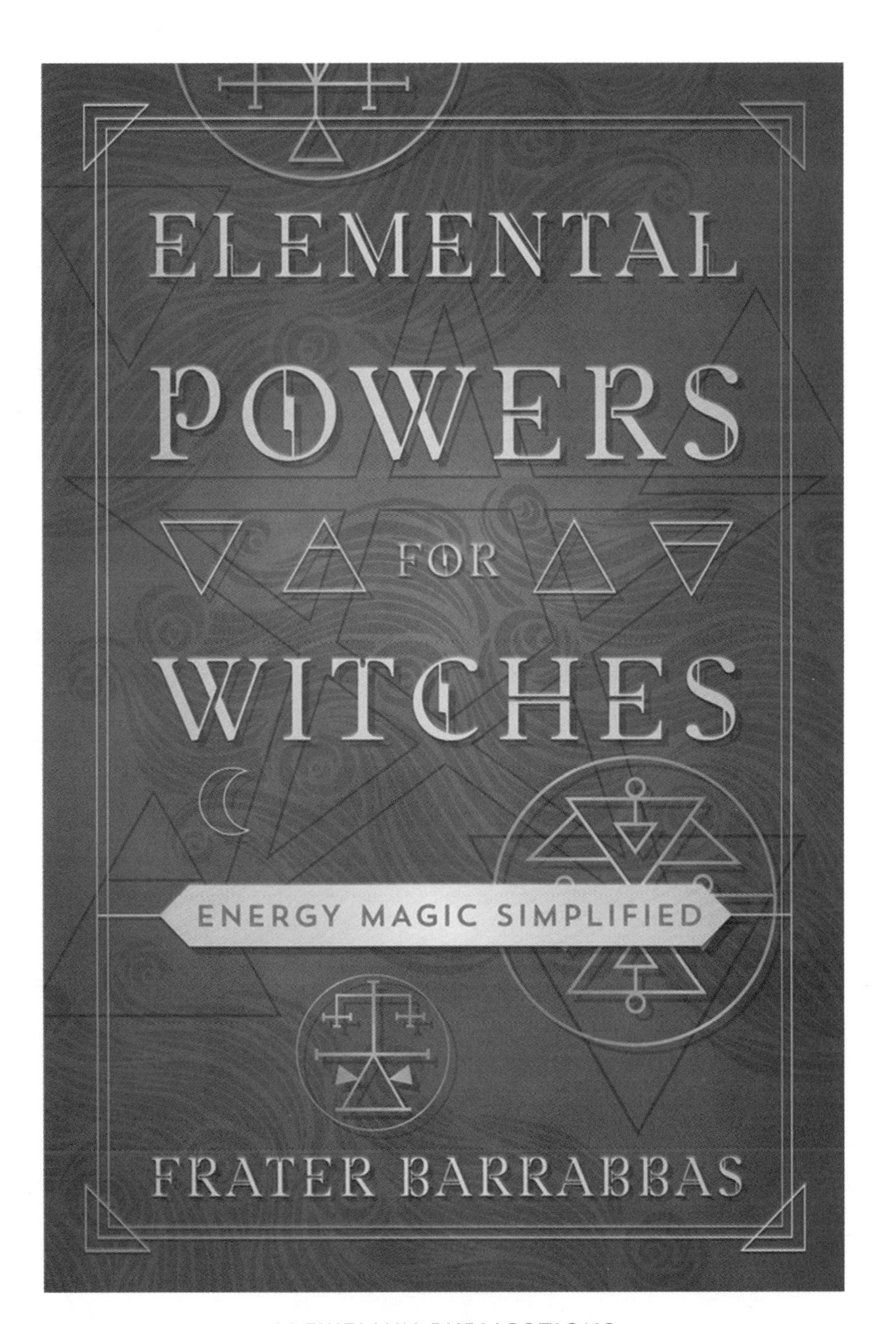

LLEWELLYN PUBLICATIONS
WOODBURY, MINNESOTA

First Edition
First Printing, 2021

Book design by Samantha Peterson
Cover design by Kevin R. Brown
Editing by Laura Kurtz
Interior illustrations by Keith Ward

Library of Congress Cataloging-in-Publication Data
Names: Barrabbas, Frater, author.
Title: Elemental powers for witches : energy magic simplified / Frater Barrabbas.
Description: First edition. | Woodbury, Minnesota : Llewellyn Worldwide, Ltd, 2021. | Includes bibliographical references and index. | Summary: "A more formalized book on elemental magic for witches and Pagans"—Provided by publisher.
Identifiers: LCCN 2021043434 (print) | LCCN 2021043435 (ebook) | ISBN 9780738768670 | ISBN 9780738768793 (ebook)
Subjects: LCSH: Magic. | Witchcraft. | Four elements (Philosophy)—Miscellanea.
Classification: LCC BF1621 .B365 2021 (print) | LCC BF1621 (ebook) | DDC 133.4/3—dc23
LC record available at https://lccn.loc.gov/2021043434
LC ebook record available at https://lccn.loc.gov/2021043435

Llewellyn Publications
A Division of Llewellyn Worldwide Ltd.
2143 Wooddale Drive
Woodbury, MN 55125-2989
www.llewellyn.com

Printed in the United States of America

Other Books by Frater Barrabbas

Spirit Conjuring for Witches (Llewellyn, 2017)

Magical Qabalah for Beginners (Llewellyn, 2013)

Forthcoming Books by Frater Barrabbas

Talismanic Magic for Witches

ACKNOWLEDGMENTS

This book is dedicated to Sarah, Joseph, Keith, and Scott—new and old friends who influenced and inspired the writing of this book. Also, to my wife, Joni, who taught me how to write books, and Lynxa, my feline muse.

I also want to thank all of the people in the medical field in the world who are engaged in fighting the coronavirus that is scourging our planet. You are the heroes of our age.

Mayakovsky: "Do you know what magic is? Energy capable of making this shithole world one fractional speck less unbearable ..."
The Magicians, season 2, episode 12: "Ramifications"

NOTE BY THE AUTHOR

This book, *Elemental Powers for Witches,* is the companion for the 2017 book *Spirit Conjuring for Witches* and was written with this idea in mind. Some of the methodologies and information contained in *Spirit Conjuring* will dovetail with information presented in this book. What I wanted to do, though, was limit the amount of repetition between these two works and also to write them so that a person could purchase one or the other and find it complete and ready for use. Therefore, what I did was to write *Elemental Powers* only with the information needed to work with the energy and information models of magic. While combining the two books together and using rituals from either to build a more comprehensive system of magic is both expected and encouraged, it won't be necessary.

Some of the contents in *Spirit Conjuring* that won't be repeated in this work are associated with the topics of the Godhead Assumption, the Rose Ankh device and Vortex ritual, and the more extensive discussions about basic meditation practices and trance techniques. These subjects are more important with spirit conjuring than they are with magical energy workings.

Conversely, I will need to repeat the topics about the eight-node magic circle, the four spirals, and the visualization techniques that would be used to see energy fields. Other subjects that are very necessary are the techniques of grounding and centering using the ascending and descending waves, since dealing with latent energy in the body is important in both conjuring and energy workings. Additionally, going over the lunation cycle will be important in energy workings as they are in conjuring, so I will be repeating them in this book as well. What I have to repeat will be in a different context, so it is my hope that this will be enough to make these subjects unique instead of redundant.

FRATER BARRABBAS

CONTENTS

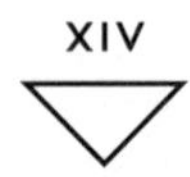

Chapter One

WHAT ARE MAGICAL POWERS?

> There are more things in heaven and earth, Horatio,
> Than are dreamt of in your philosophy [science]
>
> —WILLIAM SHAKESPEARE,
> *HAMLET* ACT I, SCENE 5, 167–168

A study of the ancient Witches of antiquity and even those who were infamously noted in the Witch trials during the Renaissance showed women who had magical powers. Yet those magical powers came not from their own abilities or devices but were gifted to them through divine genetics, or patronage with a god, a familiar spirit, or the Devil himself. These powers were considered supernatural and only supernatural beings could wield supernatural powers. Unless a Witch had a divine parent or two, she did not have any intrinsic power within herself. Until the modern age, the basic rule of thumb in Witchcraft was that she had to get them from some other source, such as a demigod, faery, or demon.

Something happened in the interval between the Middle Ages and the twentieth century—that something was the belief in the specialized powers inherent in human beings. The famous person in the eighteenth century who changed this whole perspective was Franz Anton Mesmer; his technique of Mesmerism appeared to suggest that the human mind and the individual body had more going on than what had been previously believed. While Mesmerism was something of a passing fad, it led to all kinds of new perspectives on the possibility of human potential. In addition, the mystical arts of the East became increasingly accessible to the reading and traveling public, thus opening the public's mind through such organizations as the Theosophical Society.

Such studies brought to the public imagination the seemingly limitless possibilities of kundalini yoga, paranormal mind states, and the power of meditation and yoga to contain and discipline the mind. These abilities fascinated many people in the West, and they certainly had quite an impact on the magic practiced later by Witches and Pagans. By the second half of the twentieth century, wide variations on these ideas and practices became a part of the core magical practices of many traditions of Witchcraft and Paganism. We will examine this passage of ideas in greater detail in chapter 3.

I find it curious that the Witches of the Renaissance needed to have a supernatural helper to perform their feats of magical power but modern Witches found their own power in their bodies and in group magical workings where that power could be amplified. Both perspectives, however, are still active in Western magic today. Through this evolution of thought, magic became an operation centered in the body instead of something borrowed from a spirit. I was very much a part of that work in the early years (in the 1970s) of the Witchcraft movement and learned a great deal through experimentation and personal development. Even so, based on the Gardnerian Book of Shadows, the Witches Dance was the means to generating magical energy from the body. We believed that the more people who gathered together to work Witchcraft, the greater the overall magical power that would be generated.

Additionally, the rituals and magical lore from the Golden Dawn became available to practically anyone who was interested, so a separate system for working with magical energy became available. I was also interested in those rituals and sought to somehow harness them using a basic Witchcraft methodology. I found that the group magical practices of Wiccan covens were limited, and I wasn't particularly handy with herbal lore or attracted much to folk magic. There also wasn't a magical lodge in my small midwestern town and I found the Golden Dawn material too staid for my creative impulses. Instead, I found a way to build a kind of ritual magic based on Witchcraft but also including the patterns of Golden Dawn ceremonial magic.

What I produced was a hybrid methodology based on the teachings of my Alexandrian coven and vetted by the senior members of that group. Ceremonial magicians decried my work and many Witches thought that it was too ceremonial—but it was really neither of them. Still, this methodology worked really well and allowed me to build a whole system of magic. This book contains a more up-to-date variation of those rituals that I devised many years ago.

Witches and other magical practitioners who had a taste for ceremonial magic but didn't have the patience to master it or the desire to work a separate magical system saw a lot of value in what I had produced. They found it useful then and many still find it useful today. The hybrid nature of this methodology did make it a bit idiosyncratic, since it was mixing the lore of my Alexandrian coven with the lore of ceremonial magic. There were and are differences in my magical system from the traditional way of doing things in ceremonial magic; but they do fit within the practices and beliefs of Witchcraft.

Magical powers are basically whatever a Witch or magician projects into the world, either on themselves or on the material world around them. The methods and techniques, while quite different, have the same basic foundation. They are a system of beliefs and practices that make the phenomena of magic plausible, accessible, and richly empowering. While some will believe and see magical powers as energy, others will see them as spirits who aid them in their workings. In my opinion, they can be both simultaneously instead of being one or the other. They are just different views and perspectives of the same thing.

In the magical energy work I have developed, I see these spirits as ones of power who are more emotional and energetic than intellectual—they are energies and spirits. This means that conjuring these spirits is similar to generating a magical force. It is quite different than performing an evocation, since the Witch is using the spirit to empower her or him to effect something in the material world. Because these spirits are close to the earth, they can be easily summoned just by calling them with intention. Whichever way one defines magical powers, there are methods for organizing and effectively generating them. In short, there is a myriad of ways to perform this magic, and all of them work, more or less. What I have produced is just one of many.

The rationale for performing slightly more complex and structured rituals is that they become more easily objectified by a greater number of people. The ritual structures that I use are not difficult nor overly complex; in fact, they are quite simple. What might seem complex is whenever these simple ritual structures are assembled together to formulate a magical working. I understand that not everyone will find working this kind of magic to be satisfying. Others will think that if they really want to practice ceremonial magic, they will invest themselves in the Golden Dawn lore or pick up a grimoire and study it. Some people find this style of magic useful because it allows them to practice more advanced ritual workings in the same space and using the same tools they already have without the need to commit to a ceremonial regimen. Some will this find attractive with my hybrid system of magic; others likely will not find it interesting at all.

My reading audience are those Witches and Pagans who are attracted to creativity yet not daunted by complexity. These are people who won't like the regimented approach to ceremonial magic and the requirement for retooling and even rethinking the kind of magic they wish to perform. They approach magic as an artistic endeavor. They like the theatric approach to rituals but find long-winded dialogs and complexity for its own sake to be boring. They like to experience magical energies through their bodies, but they also like summoning spirits of power and purpose and getting a thrill out of directly experiencing them.

There are really two tracks occurring in this work simultaneously. The first track is the most direct and simplistic: it uses the basic approach to summon the element-based spirits and engages them in the energy working. The second track is more elaborate and involves working with the element-based spirits in a more traditional manner that is closest to a formal evocation. I will make suggestions to embellish the workings and to include other elements from external sources, such as traditional grimoires, to enhance the esthetics of the working. A practitioner could therefore work this proposed system of magic with only the essential components and get the same results as someone who added the magical seals, talismans, and barbarous words of evocation, and then made offerings to the spirits. How you approach these workings is clearly your own choice. I will, however, facilitate both approaches and recommend neither one.

Traditional Witches and Pagans will find much to like in this system, and also those who are self-made Witches and Pagans who follow no tradition. Yet it is the people who want to craft their own magical system with unlimited creative vectors who will find this work to be compelling and helpful. I believe that there is something of value in this work that practically any Witch or Pagan will find useful, even if it is nothing more than cherry-picking ideas and ritual structures.

Because I expect that my reader has a basic understanding of Witchcraft and Pagan magic and an already established practice, I feel that this book better serves the intermediate level practitioner rather than being an instructive guide for the beginner. There are plenty of beginner books or websites for the novice to peruse and study, so I don't think that they will be lacking in materials. It does take a while to develop a regular practice and establish a magical discipline, depending on how much time the student puts into it. Once that step is accomplished then the beginner becomes an experienced practitioner, and it is at that stage where a book such as this would become important.

Why Use Elaborate Rituals Harnessing Magical Powers?

One of the most difficult discussions that any author can have with the reading public is to get people to accept doing something different from what they have been doing. The old adage "if it works, why try to fix it?" comes into play in these kinds of arguments. For some people, change is a friend; to others, it is an enemy to be avoided and practically despised. Our opinions are backed up by our feelings about what is right or wrong. So when I deliver the message that Witches and Pagans should consider alternatives to harnessing and using magical powers, it might be met with some resistance. There are reasons for this perspective, so I do understand what some might think or feel, but all I ask is that my readers consider my words and see if what I am saying is constructive and useful.

Witchcraft magic has a reputation for being a simplistic but effective methodology. It is likely driven by intense emotional energies such as outrage, anger at injustice, or a passion for something to change, whether individual, local, or in the world at large. The passion for this thing drives the process, so it can lead to impulsive workings done at the moment with whatever is at hand. Witchcraft can therefore appear to be wild, exotic, like a fierce and sudden rain storm. While such workings can be repeated, the initial working is truly unique and not repeatable because it is so much in the moment.

If we use the art of analogy to make some comparisons to this kind of magic and life in general, would we ever do anything that way when we are, say, buying a house, a car, making a career change, relocating to another town or state, taking a vacation, getting married, divorced, or some other critical decision? These kinds of life changes, however mundane, would require some planning, perhaps even a methodical and practical approach if we want to be assured (as much as possible) of success.

While I am not saying anything negative about this kind of approach to Witchcraft magic, I have found that planning, researching, building tools, and using ritual workings to do this kind of magic might give one a greater chance at a successful outcome. Correspondingly, I have found that working unplanned, unstructured, and impulsive works of magic—although immediately gratifying—has about as much chance of success as anything else in life done in this manner; hit or miss, with an emphasis on miss. That's my opinion, for certain, and my MO is to be methodical when it comes to working magic; but I have been around and seen enough to at least have a well-established opinion.

Another good analogy is humanity's use of fire. By itself, fire can very useful or incredibly dangerous to anyone who handles it. The best case for getting the most out of fire is to carefully develop and manage it and to use a fair amount of caution in all things having to do with it. Learning the proper procedures for starting and using fire, not to mention extinguishing it, and steadfastly following them will ensure a safe and productive use. Doing crazy and hazardous things with fire in an uncontrolled manner will probably produce more harm than good and could unleash a truly destructive conflagration. I tend to treat magic in a similar manner that I treat the use of fire. It might be considered by some practitioners as overkill, but when I do magic, it generally has a positive outcome, although not always what I expect.

Rituals and spells are what produce and drive magical powers. It starts with our passion and desire aligned with our intention, but we typically generate, amplify, and express magical powers using some kind of ritual or spells. We feel the power through our emotions, but we typically don't bother to examine it while we are doing magic. As I pointed out, planning and being methodical in life produces greater success in our endeavors, and so too in magic. We can just perform the magical rite or spell, get it out of our system and exteriorize it into the world, and hope that it makes something happen. Or, we can take a more elaborate approach and build rituals that will generate the exact power that we need, imprint it, and send it out to do our bidding with a greater certainty that something approaching our intention will occur.

Whether consisting of one or many individuals, Witchcraft magical workings has as its foundation the magic circle with its four directional wards. There is an implicit middle point in the center, making a total of five points that can be used for building rituals that generate and project energy. We can add other structures to these five points, and in the magic that I work, we will certainly do that; but we are using what is already established. I am not seeking to suggest a completely different environment and foundation than the one you are already using. I am just adding to the basic five points, and by doing so introducing a whole new methodology to work Witchcraft magic.

While the structures of this methodology might seem elaborate, even bordering on the ceremonial side, they are nested right in the foundation that you already possess. They are simply an extension to what you already know and practice. All that I require is that you take the steps to develop a new method for working with magical powers, one that will make you far more effective in your magical work than you are currently. The reason I can say this is that following these steps will make you more aware of your magic in a structured manner than you have ever been aware. That will make quite a difference, as you shall see.

My basic rationale for this approach is that by using ritual structures to build up ritual workings, you are putting together a system that is repeatable, somewhat controllable, and able to be shared or worked by one or more practitioners. Additionally, by characterizing and categorizing the magical energies, you will be able define the kind of power that you want to deploy in a given magical working so that it matches your expected outcome. Therefore, what I am offering is repeatability, a method that can be shared with others, and precision regarding the projected magical powers. While it is impossible for me (or anyone) to guarantee the results of any magic worked in this manner, I can at least say that the probability of success is considerably higher and more consistent by engaging in magic in an ordered and organized manner.

Examining the Odd Nature of Magic and Energies

One thing that I can state without any equivocation is that magic is subtle and almost imperceptible to most people when it is working. I am sure my readers already know this to be true. Once the drama of the ritual event is completed and the magic is unleashed things appear to get quiet. Even experienced magicians have to perform some kind of objective examination of the apparent results produced by their magical workings in order to judge them as being successful. Often the results are not very obvious even when completely successful, and it is important to critically weigh whether a successful outcome was achieved due exclusively to magic or simply by chance.

I believe that successful forms of magic bend the inherent probabilities of a desired outcome to the advantage of the practitioner; but the mechanism used to produce that effect is much debated. If something is likely improbable then unless there is a lot of activity to make it probable using both magical and mundane efforts, the fact that magic is performed to enhance the possibilities will not in any way help it to be achieved. That would make impossible objectives practically beyond the reach of nearly all magical operations. A simple rule to follow is that if a desired outcome is unachievable without the use of magic then it is probably unachievable even with the use of magic.

Because magical operations are subtle and at times, nearly imperceptible, then magical powers are also very subtle and not easily subjected to one's objective analysis. When you talk to practitioners, however, they will passionately talk about how *powerful* a magical working was, or how they could tangibly sense and feel the *energy* that was being generated by their magical working.

Some ceremonial magicians will say that their wand is *powerful* and their magical tools, having been made of costly and rarefied materials, have an awesome *energy* capable of producing forces that can be tangibly felt. Others who are so attuned will readily agree. Still, other people who are neither knowledgeable nor experienced will either consider such talk to be nonsense or they will confuse it with what is being hyped in the media about super paranormal powers. This is all magical gossip, of course, and a simple stick picked up in the woods will have just as much impact to the wielder as a costly jeweled wand.

What is happening here is much more fundamental, but is often greatly amplified through the practitioner's emotions and bodily triggers. Talented or trained individuals can and do feel the magical powers that they wield and others can feel them too, or not. The question that should be asked is whether or not this energy is real, imaginary, or metaphorical.

Since I am writing a book about using magical powers to perform and practice magic, you could assume that I do believe that they exist and have some kind of reality. That is true, but often things are not as clear and straightforward as we would like them to be. What I have found is that the term *energy* used in magical operations is not something that could be identified as occurring within the electromagnetic spectrum. In fact, it is my opinion that magical energy is not some mysterious energy unknown to science that will be discovered some day in the future.

What I do believe is that this phenomenon is integral to consciousness itself, and that as intelligent beings, we partake of this multifold and complex shared reality where perceived bodily energies do externally manifest; that there is a unified energy that appears to invest and connect all living things and that disembodied conscious entities independently live within that sphere. I have referred to it as the domain of spirit, but I could also call it the domain of magical energy as well. In my hypothesis, all of these phenomena exist within the world of individual and collective consciousness. In fact, I believe that magic seems to function as a subtle, disembodied, conscious being itself, and that my impressions of this phenomenon would indicate that it is wholly a thing that exists within individual and the collective consciousness simultaneously.

Therefore, I would state that magical energy, which can be alternatively called an energy or a power, is a metaphorical phenomenon that exists wholly within the sphere of consciousness. It is both subjectively within our minds and also is shared through our conscious collective. It is a persistent thing that has been a part of humanity since the dawn of human consciousness. It can and does have a real and tangible effect on the material world we live in, immersed as we are in a sphere of consciousness. As a universal metaphor that can be found in all cultures throughout time, it functions as if it were both a force resident within the living body and as a distinct and separate force that pervades our world, connecting everyone and everything within it. It can and typically is personified, given names and qualities, and characterized in some manner, as we shall see.

What this means is that magical energy or whatever it has been called (and the names are quite numerous in the world and throughout the ages) appears to be a force that is generated within the body of the magician that reaches a triggering level of intensity where a more universal source is accessed, focused and used for specific magical purposes. There are a number of clues that would seem to indicate that various magical energies are not restricted to operating just within the bodies of those who have performed exercises to generate them. We will examine those clues when we discuss how magical energy is generated and released, and how it specifically affects the body of the person who is generating it. Yet it would seem that the apparent reality of this energy cannot be defined as something measurable by science and therefore would function as an objective phenomenon based on physical laws.

What Science Says About Bodily Energy and Powers

Science has measured and determined the actual energy that a human body produces or the energy associated with the firing of a single neuron. Body energy is produced and maintained by a biological process called metabolism, which consists of complex and life-sustaining biochemical reactions. The actual thermal body heat associated with warm blooded animals is caused by an internal respiration, which is the oxidation of carbohydrates. There is the catabolic breaking down of compounds ingested or breathed into the body, and the anabolic building up or synthesizing of compounds needed for the maintenance of life.

The combination of mechanical (muscle-based) energy and the catabolic chemical reactions deep in the body establish a thermal signature that typically produces about the same amount of energy as a 100-watt incandescent light bulb when the body is at rest.[1] However, a warm-blooded animal expends most of the thermal energy (80 to 90 percent) generated on maintaining a constant body temperature. Other than allowing for the maintenance of life and the mechanical use of muscles, there is not much left to use for miraculous paranormal effects such as levitation or knocking down buildings. Human beings are left with their mental ingenuity and collective work efforts to build pyramids and cities, and terraform the planet. However mundane it might seem, that is remarkable all by itself.

The other source of energy is found in the nervous system. A single neuron can generate a rapid pulse of around 40 to 80 millivolts, so a whole brain can contain a lot of pathways simultaneously lit with millions of micro voltages, but

---

1. Wei Lang Mok, "Power of a Human," *The Physics Factbook*, accessed May 17, 2020: https://hypertextbook.com/facts/2003/WeiLiangMok.shtml.

it doesn't amount to the energy of a single car battery.[2] If we are looking at the power to dramatically change or affect living things or material objects directly by some bodily-based energy, we will have to look at other kinds of resources than the body or the nervous system. The human body as a power source of miraculous material transformations is limited by the fact that it produces such a small amount of overall energy, and nearly all of that is used to maintain life, establish cognition, and allow for physical activity.

Whether of yoga, pranayama, sitting meditation, the martial arts, spiritual healing, magic, and/or many others, many practitioners will note that stimulating the body and the mind within these various techniques is the starting point and the key to unleashing subtle and somewhat paranormal forces that can and do change us and the world in some fashion. Yet all of these techniques have a common basis—consciousness itself. They also have a common focus: regulating, monitoring and modifying the breathing cycle, and sometimes incorporating some kind of repetitive movement and visualization. However, the mere fact that all of these metaphysical disciplines are not only surviving in a scientifically objective and secular world, they are in fact thriving is representative of some kind of truth. The only way that this can be explained is that these diverse methodologies and techniques are working in an area of the mind that is not as restrictive as hardcore scientific objectivity.

Consciousness is still an evasive and mysterious phenomenon that has resisted qualitative and quantitative analysis. We still don't really know what consciousness actually is. But we can note that much of our subjective world, both as individuals and as a collective group, appears to give evidence that there is much more going on in our minds and in our world than objective science seems to accept as fact. At some point, it would seem that science and mysticism will meet eye to eye, and at that topical place and point in time, great revelations will finally be determined. Until that time arrives, we can work magic using magical *energy* as our hypothetical base with a certain confidence that we will be able to change ourselves and the world around us in some manner, whether great or small. We will have to accept this phenomenon as subjective and anecdotal, but real nonetheless.

---

2. Carl Zimmer, "You're a Dim Bulb (And I mean that in the best possible way)," *Discover,* accessed May 17, 2020: https://www.discovermagazine.com/mind/youre-a-dim-bulb-and-i-mean-that-in-the-best-possible-way.

You are probably wondering what exactly I mean when I say that magical phenomena are embodied in the collective consciousness. Since neuroscience has pretty much debunked the whole concept of an unconscious mind that acts as a separate and at times contrasting force and intelligence within our brains, we need to respect this fact when talking about the mind and consciousness.[3] There is a part of our brain that handles lower autonomous bodily functions, but that cannot be equated with an unconscious mind as defined by old-school psychology.

Our awareness could be described as a narrow focus operating within our conscious being, and often there is much in our conscious minds that we are not focusing on or is part of our ongoing current awareness. It is still part of our conscious mind, but we are not actively focusing our awareness on it. The same could said about a collective unconsciousness, as proposed by Jung. If there is no real unconscious mind, there cannot be a collective unconscious mind either.

What there is, in fact, are a lot of contextual beliefs, assumptions, archetypes, media personalities, myths, traditions, and stories bound up by a shared language and a culture. We may not be aware of everything occurring in this domain of collective or social consciousness, but we are powerfully affected by it. On a certain level, it is the glue that connects together the various experiences or narratives of being human in a specific place and time. It can unite us not only as a species but as living beings in the universe at large. This is the domain where I believe magic exists and thrives; where paranormal powers reside; where spirits live; and where individual beings can grow, evolve, and contribute to the collective. It is also the place where a kind of collective conscious energy can be found.

Universal Magical Energy and Magical Workings

While it is logical and seemingly factual to state that there is some kind of energy operating within the consciousness of individual human beings, it might seem a bit of a stretch to also propose that there is a collective energy or a kind of source for all of these individual phenomena. If magical energy can be attributed directly to physical and mental stimulation and it is generated in

---

3. John A. Bargh and Ezequiel Morselle, "The Unconscious Mind" at the US National Library of Medicine, National Institute of Health, accessed May 17, 2020: https://www.ncbi.nlm.nih.gov/pmc/articles/PMC2440575/.

the human nervous system, it would seem to be difficult to propose that this energy has any basis outside of the body.

There are quite a number of culturally-based metaphysical beliefs in such a unified energy field and personal experiences also seem to agree with these mystical theories. While some of the magicians I have talked to over the years have told me about experiences that led them to conclude that there is some kind of overall energy source, others have said quite the opposite. I would include myself as one of those individuals who has experienced magical energy both on an individual basis as well as demonstrating that there is some kind of unified source. I have said previously that there are clues that this phenomenon does in fact exist, and now is the time to state them. All of these clues are subjective, of course, and could be interpreted differently depending upon your point of view.

When I am working magic and using what I believe are magical energies to achieve my objective, I go through a process of stimulating my mind and body to generate the triggers for this phenomenon to manifest. It is, as said earlier, a combination of movement, breath control, visualization, and sensitive bodily stimulation that begins the process. Before I can start, I have to shed the mental baggage and the mind-state of the mundane world and its cares so I can be freed to experience these states unencumbered.

Through a combination of controlled breathing, visualization, and movement I will become aware of an energy coursing through my body. It is quite tangible, since I can not only feel it coursing through my body, but I can sometimes even vaguely see it projecting from my hands or the magical tool that I am wielding. However, when this perceived energy reaches a certain stable and excited state, I will feel greatly exhilarated, inspired, empowered, and capable of accomplishing nearly anything. It is a euphoric state of consciousness, but it is also a phenomenon that makes me feel as though I am connected to everyone and everything. I perceive it both within myself and in my environment.

The connection between the energy in the body and the universal energy is triggered by something that I call resonance. Resonance is where a vibration of energy in a single body is amplified by other bodies or the surrounding area. A good example of this phenomenon is singing in a tiled steam room in a gym. The tones will be echoed, but one tone will seem to be greatly amplified and fill the whole room when compared to the others. I used to get a kick out of finding that tone when in concrete or tiled rooms. What causes that amplification is the resonance of sound, but I believe that magical energy does the same thing. We experience an in-pouring of energy when our exhilarated senses achieve a certain level of vibration, and the resultant triggering of resonance causes that experience of in-pouring energy that amplifies what we were initially experiencing.

When I project this energy, I can feel it leaving my body and moving into the world at large; but I also sense that I am partaking of a larger field of energy residing outside my body. When the magical operation is completed, I don't feel tired and depleted as one would expect. Instead, it feels as though I have a larger quantity of energy in my body than I had started with, and I typically have to *ground* that energy or remove it from my body in some fashion to achieve a state of equilibrium.

To recap: when I engage with magical energy, I feel connected to everything. I experience this magical energy both within me and outside of my body. I can see and feel this energy in the magic circle and other people who are there with me can feel it and sometimes see it, too. When I project this energy into something inanimate I can both see and feel that it has been changed, or *charged* as I would call it. I have performed healings where I have projected this energy into another person and they can feel the energy pass into them. Most importantly, I feel as though this energy has been drawn from a much larger, seemingly inexhaustible source. I am left with a large surplus of energy that I have to dispense with in order to return to normal consciousness.

Connecting with this energy makes me feel as though I have tapped into something that is much greater and vaster than what my own body might generate on its own. I believe that these various things that I consistently experience would indicate that this energy is both internal and external to myself and that there is a kind of overall pervading source to this energy that I can tap into when required. Also, when I engage with this energy it causes me to undergo a kind of universal consciousness, which is a very transcendental experience.

All of these phenomena appear to agree with the numerous cultural beliefs in a universal metaphysical power variously called chi, qi, prana, kundalini, the vital or life force, and even the numinous presence of deity (hand of God) even when no deity is detected. All of these mystical systems are variously different, but they would seem to be defining the same kind of human experience. It is just a matter of culture, language, and belief that makes them different, but they are proposing the same basic type of universal energy.

What I propose in this book is that you can tap these energies and use them to subtly and even dramatically change yourself and the world both from an external material standpoint as well as individually from a conscious standpoint. There are certain structures, techniques, and exercises (rituals) that you would need to practice so that this energy would become physically apparent and fully realized. Other practices and techniques would allow you to proficiently use this energy to change yourself and your material circumstances. While there are a number of magical models or theories that seek to help explain and encapsulate the phenomenon of magic, the model that this book will be focusing on is what I would call the *energy model* of magic; particularly, an expanded energy model that goes beyond what is typically practiced in the world of Western Magic and Modern Witchcraft in particular.

Chapter Two

FOUR ELEMENTS AND THE ENERGY MODEL OF MAGIC

> If you want to find the secrets of the universe, think in terms of energy, frequency, and vibration.
>
> —Nikola Tesla

Now that we have defined the basics about the nature of magical energy, we can focus on the energy model of magic and the four elements. We can look at the model to determine the structure and approach to rituals and we can define the basic qualities of magical energies. This is a traditional approach to defining magical energies and it is the one that I use, but it is not the only approach.

The energy model of magic states that all magical phenomena are produced by the generation and manipulation of energy. This model would seem to be limited because it only focuses on magical energy, but it is not separate from the other models. We are looking at it alone for a moment to examine the nature of magic according to this model, and we will be using it in combination with other models to produce a broader magical context. This combined approach will produce more interesting insights and speculation about energy and how it is exclusively used in magic.

A practical approach to magic would include all of the models of magic and much more, since there is a great deal that is not thoroughly understood about the phenomena of magic. It helps sometimes to isolate a single quality within a complex process in order to facilitate a greater understanding of it.

Some of the other models of magic would be the spirit model (covered in my other work, *Spirit Conjuring for Witches*), the psychological model, and the information model. We will be covering the energy model in this book as well as the information model since they function in tandem to produce and project magical energies in order to complete a magical working.

I might add that many practitioners of magic who use the energy model, such as myself, tend to perceive it as an analogy for electricity. Such a model will use terms such as: power, forces, colored lights, polarity, resonance, vibes, intensity, bolts, sparks, wave-forms, emitting, magnetic, electrical, charging, loading, compressing, short-circuiting, zapping, and blasting. These terms are used at some point in the many lively discussions about energy-based magic. All of them seem to describe a very physical phenomena that is mindless and easily applied to any methodology, one that is harmless and utilitarian as long as it is controlled.

We have already discussed this issue that magical energy is a metaphor, and these are just additional descriptive qualities used to describe something that resides wholly in consciousness. We should, however, keep in mind that magical energy does seem to have some kind of physical qualities regarding the physical body and the central nervous system. Some of these terms are important for qualifying magical energy and will be discussed later, particularly the concepts of drawing lines of force, polarity, resonance, the qualities of electrical and magnetic charging or loading things or people, the qualities of circulation (circuitry), blockages, projecting, compression, exteriorization, and grounding.

While the analogy to electricity appears to define and qualify the phenomena of magical energy, it would also be misleading to say that such analogies are more than actual qualifying labels. Magical energy is not mindless and autonomous, nor can it be easily applied to any ritual mechanism or methodology; it cannot be turned off and on like an electric appliance. As long as we understand the limits of models and metaphors when describing a complex process, we can avoid the mistake of thinking that models and metaphors *are* what they seek to describe.

Models are maps and they are imperfect representations of reality. We should never confuse the map for the reality it describes. Another useful point is that human nature often uses terms and ideas based on technology and science to explain conscious phenomena. Comparing the mind to a computer, the cosmos to a clockwork, the perception of reality to spectacles, and magical energy to electricity is where poetic license starts and science ends—these are metaphors. In some cases, these metaphors might be very misleading if taken literally.

However, one overriding factor in the various concepts and ideas around the phenomenon of magical energy is the symbolic joining of opposites to create a holistic formulation that can be experienced and used to cause transformative change. As I have stated previously the experience of magical energy fully-realized produces a feeling of interconnection with all things, a form of euphoric union. What exemplifies this holism is the reduction in the mind of opposites to form a union. Therefore, when symbolic and experiential objects are polarized in the mind through a specific focus, what is released in the process when they are joined is magical energy.

We are talking here about natural and conceptual or symbolic opposites, such as male and female, light and darkness, day and night, flesh and mind, material and spiritual, matter and anti-matter, and all of the various symbols associated with classical and obvious opposites, called syzygies. By focusing on one of a pair intensely followed by the other, and then keeping the two both intensely focused together in the mind and joining them into a synthesis through the imagination, a release of energy occurs. The resultant state is one of a heightened experience of transcendental consciousness. This is particularly true when the chosen opposites are significant and personally charged with meaning.

Another aspect of magical energy that I need to bring up is that it has characteristics and qualities that are quite outside of the metaphor of electricity. Magical energy also assumes the forms of mythical animals, totems, personalities, and spirits. Since visualization is important to conceptualizing magical energy, the full poetic effect of various metaphors, myths, and beliefs pervade the qualities and various divisions of this conscious force. What this means is that magical energy has many faces and personalities that allow the practitioner to use it in a selective and concise manner, and it also facilitates the important factor of visualization in the acquisition and projection of these powers. It would also be apparent that magical energy is in fact a sentient, conscious, living energy—it has a spiritual quality as well.

Four Elements as Magical Energies

Magical energy is also categorized as consisting of four basic elements, joining together to form a fifth: the unified and undifferentiated source. These elements are the age-old elements of fire, air, water, and earth, with spirit functioning as the unifying quintessence. They are polarized as opposites, too, such as fire to water, or earth to air. These four elements represent specific occult qualifiers for the undifferentiated and universal force. Each element has a specific quality represented in physical terms and qualifications. They also have spiritual attributes as well, represented by the four archetypal beings of salamanders, sylphs, undines, and gnomes, or the four elemental kings.

The archetypal symbols of these four elements, united with the fifth of spirit, are encapsulated by the ancient star-form known as the pentagram. It is this symbol that is used to help generate and banish the qualified energy of one or more of the four elements and the polarized quality of spirit (creative and receptive). Any ritual (in the Western magical tradition) that would generate one of these four elements and spirit would likely use the pentagram as a magical device, drawing it in the air with a magical tool.

The four elements represent the basic metaphorical model of the energy model of magic, but that is just the starting point. An extended energy model would include other and more articulated representations of magical energy, and these would take the basic four elements and combine them with themselves or with other symbolic characteristics to produce more differentiated energy qualities.

In this manner, the four elements would be combined together to produce sixteen elementals (element as base and qualifier), forty qualified powers (four elements as the base and ten number-based symbolic attributes as the qualifier), twenty-eight talismanic elementals (four elements as the base and seven planetary attributes as the qualifier), forty-eight zodiacal elementals (four elements as the base and twelve zodiacal attributes as the qualifier), and the 256 doubled elementals (elemental as the base and an elemental as the qualifier). The possibilities are nearly endless, but they are all based on the symbolic number four, the base number for the elements.

While elementals might be an energy quality that is recognized by many occultists, being a combination of a base and qualifying element, the qualified powers are much more obscure, so I should define them more explicitly before we move forward. A qualified power is an element charged or qualified by one of the ten attributes of the deity as determined by the ten mystical numbers (one through ten) of the Pythagoreans. That makes it ten by four, or forty different types of qualified energies. The four aces and thirty-six pip cards of the tarot are direct correspondences, so are the thirty-six zodiacal decans and the four elemental kings. Each of these energy constructs has a very specific kind of magical energy. I have found them very useful in magical workings. The sixteen elementals would correspond to the sixteen court cards in the tarot.

We will be focusing on only the four elements and their derivatives in this book—the sixteen elementals and the forty qualified powers. I have given examples of the other base-element systems of power since they are all linked together in the system of energy magic, but they are not used to work magic in this book.

One of the most important repositories for all of the symbols, archetypes, and qualities of the four elements is to be found in the lesser arcana of the tarot. The fifty-six cards of the lesser arcana represent all of the various symbolic correspondences for the elements in the energy model of magic. In this particular case the court cards represent the sixteen elementals and the pip cards (including the four aces) represent the forty qualified powers. These forty qualified powers consist of the four elemental kings and the thirty-six astrological decans. Specifics of the elementals are covered in chapter 7 and the qualified powers in chapter 8.

The practitioner who makes use of the energy model of magic can use the symbols, images, and personalities corresponding to these 56 cards to help qualify and more deeply define the energies that he or she would make use of in rituals that generate magical energies. Thus, the tarot is an important repository of the visual images and qualities of magical energy. We will examine these important analogies of magical energy later in this work.

Symbolic Link

Generating magical energy is one of the tasks of this kind of magic, but imprinting that energy with a message or a goal is just as important. If a magician generates a great deal of magical energy yet does not give it a purpose or a goal when it is released, it will just dissipate. Forging a symbolic link that can be used to characterize and imprint the purpose of the magical energy before exteriorizing it will give it a concretely defined goal and an objective. This is one of the important topics that we will be discussing in this work in chapter 9 on Sigils.

Imprinting magical energy with just one's internalized desire might suffice for many simple forms of energy magic. However, the art of developing that desire and clarifying it as well as giving it a symbolic character and applying that graphic design to a piece of parchment or a metal disc, which can be employed in a ritual, will ensure that the magical imprinting is reliably potent and complete.

Crafting a symbolic design that can be drawn on paper, wood, or metal is a magical technology known as sigil magic. A sigil becomes the emblem for the results that the Witch seeks to achieve, and it acts as a symbolic link both clarifying and reducing the objective to single graphic design. It is charged like any magical tool and then it is used to imprint the magical energy when that force is compressed to a focal point just before exteriorization. Sigil magic employs the information model of magic. We will be covering this type of magic and how to employ it with the energy model to ensure that a magical objective is clearly defined and realized in chapter 9.

Rituals that are used to generate attributes and qualities of the elements and their derivatives will use the pentagram and other magical devices to build up magical energies within the confined space of the consecrated magic circle. Then the Witch will imprint those energies with a symbolic link representing her desire and release them into the mundane world to fulfill their objective.

A simple form for generating magical power is to be found in the Witches' dance that is used to raise energy and also to exteriorize it to fulfill a given objective. A more concise mechanism is to be found in the ritual structures of the pyramid and the octagon, the pylon, the eight-node magic circle, and the invoking and exteriorizing spirals. Included are techniques for breath control and guided visualization, as well as physical exercises; postures; movement; and the use of resonance, compression, and exteriorization.

Sigils are crafted and charged to symbolically represent the target of a working and they are used to imprint the energy generated and collected in the magic circle. All of these ritual structures and physical techniques are joined together to create a magical repertoire of ritual lore that can greatly enhance a Witch's ability to be psychically empowered and to impact the material world around her. These methodologies not only use the technology of the energy model of magic but also greatly expand it to new and endless possibilities.

Symbols, Devices, and Tools

When talking about magic, I have a specific nomenclature that I stick to when discussing symbols, devices, and tools. I will refer to symbols, but then talk about devices and then refer to it as a tool. Let me define these terms now before we get too far down the magical rabbit hole.

Magical symbols are numerous in the practice of magic and are used in a significant manner in the extended energy model. Let us consider the symbol of the pentagram. We have already explained that the symbol of the pentagram has many meaningful layers attached to it, representing as it does the four elements and spirit. That is the magical symbol. However, when I draw it in the air using a dagger or a wand while visualizing it in front of me, it is a device. A symbol becomes a device when it is drawn in the air or somehow visualized. If I were to have a pentagram etched on a metal disc or plate then it becomes a tool, which means it is now a physical object that I can manipulate.

Practical Energy Magic

We will also consider what to do when the use of empowered magic fails to produce the results that the Witch desires to achieve. This happens more often than not, and sometimes the problem is caused by either internal or external cross-purposes that short-circuit the magical working.

Perhaps the most singular cause for a failed working besides the obvious—insufficient mundane actions or attempting something that is highly improbable—would be what is called being at cross-purposes. Maybe we desire something that we don't actually want, or we are not taking into account internal or even external obstacles. Sometimes we are our own worst enemies, and we can unknowingly put up an obstacle and keep something desirable or needed from happening.

Divination is an important tool to recognize when we are at cross-purposes or when someone is crossing us. When this is revealed as the cause for failure, the energy model of magic can supply us with a ritual technique to *uncross* ourselves and thereby clear the way for us to achieve our goals.

We should also examine the most practical elements of working magic and how it can be done in such a manner that would tilt things in our favor. There is an art and a science to assembling a magical working that will be successful, and anyone who is contemplating working empowered magic to achieve their desires should understand the methods for getting the best results. Still, nothing is ever guaranteed in life and in magic, so sometimes the magic that we work won't produce the results that we are expecting. Examining failed workings is actually even more important and instructive than ignoring them and focusing on just the ones that are successful.

The use of magical energy to *charge* or embody objects with that energy will also lead to ideas about storing this energy, transporting it, and applying it to other situations or people. This magical technology is called talismanic magic or the use of magically charged or *consecrated* objects. While classical talismanic magic uses both planetary and astrological symbolism as well as an active awareness of the celestial domain of the earth to imbue and qualify objects with their characteristics, energy magic can do the same with elementals and qualified powers. This mechanism can give the practicing Witch many opportunities to engage with magically empowered objects.

Other Aspects of Energy Magic

Since the four elements are also perceived as domains in themselves, the Witch can also discover (by divination or just by feelings) certain geographic locations and special places that naturally house a reservoir of these energies, thereby empowering everything that such a domain might materially contain. A Witch can visit such a place to retrieve things, like plants, soil, or stones, to acquire those inherent magical energies. She can just absorb them through her body or capture them with the aid of magical tools. These are the places of empowerment that a Witch would visit to seek and obtain certain magical energies. Any Witch wise in the ways of magical energies would seek out such places of power and retain knowledge of them as a part of her secret ways for habitually and periodically collecting magical energies.

This also means that certain plants, minerals, metals, gemstones, crystals, and a host of other materials either found in such locations or innately by themselves can contain latent energies that can be released through the production of charged herbs, oils, lotions, unguents, powders, food, drink, medicines, elixirs, and crafted items such as cache bags, specialized tools, constructs, or religious amulets. All of these can be used as magically embodied products to absorb, direct, and dispense magical energies when needed or required.

Peculiar and Intrinsic Nature of Magic

Finally, we need to look at magic and our role as practitioners within it to truly understand that such a practice represents an important interrelationship. Because magic is not an inanimate process or force and is instead sentient, conscious, and at times seeming to have an independent will of its own, we need to realize this fact when engaging with it. Magic is made of the stuff of consciousness, and that imbues it with its own consciousness.

What I have discovered working magic for many decades is that sometimes magical workings turn out to produce unexpected or even startling effects. It is never a simple process of doing a set of steps and then gaining some expected results. Even the practice of Hoodoo or other forms of simple but very effective folk magic make the point of addressing the internal mindset, empowering faith and using practical exercises that can make a formula successful. Magic is never derivative.

Magic, if I were to personify it, is a being that acts like the mythical trickster. It is a true statement to say that working magic doesn't necessary get you what you desire, but more often than not, it will get you what you need or deserve. I know that some magical practitioners will hate the analogy that I am stating here about magic because they feel that it is more like a scientific process than engaging and dealing with an invisible, cunning entity. However, I believe that ignoring the sentient nature of magic produces its own troubles.

A competent Witch should consider that the magic she is wielding is like a two-edged weapon—it can and does produce unexpected outcomes. When approached with respect, magic becomes an important ally for the Witch, often helping her to discover more about herself and what she really needs to grow, thrive, and evolve. However, magic can also deceive and delude, cause minor catastrophes, or even refuse to work altogether when approached with cynicism or callousness. Working magic won't make you crazy, but it could trigger internal issues and difficulties if approached in a manner that disregards caution or clarity. We will also spend some time talking about this particular phenomenon and how a Witch can avoid working magic to her own detriment in chapter 14, on practical magic.

Magical Energy—Recap of Chapters 1 and 2

To recap the definition of magical power or energies and of magic itself, I present the following list of qualities and characteristics that were described in the first two chapters.

- Magical energy is a metaphor
- Magical energy is both an individual and a universal phenomenon
- Magical energy is produced by the joining of opposites.
- Magical energy is not a mindless energy
- Sigil magic is a component of the energy model of magic
- Magical energy can be found in places of power and in other material things
- Working magic alters the person who is practicing it in subtle ways
- The pentagram is used to generate magical energy as the four elements

These are the various topics I will be covering in greater detail in this work. My objective is to help you progress from using a form of basic energy magic and spell work to adopting a more complex ritual system that can be added to the lore you already possess and thus dramatically extend the kind and quality of magic you can perform. This ritual system incorporates the use of the four elements as they occur in the sixteen elementals and the forty qualified powers, giving the practitioner a very specific set of tools to magically alter and change for the better any area of their life that needs it. This magical methodology will also allow for a greater level of success and accomplishment, since it uses a combination sigils and magical powers in such a way that is both compelling and complete.

If you wish to be more proficient magically and to have a greater effect when using magic both materially and psychically, adopting this magical technology will help you achieve that end. Additionally, *Spirit Conjuring for Witches* is meant to be a companion to this work; used together, they will assist you in mastering the spirit model of magic and the energy and information models of magic too.

Someone who has added both of these ritual systems to their basic Witchcraft lore will undoubtably become the most complete Witch, since it will mean that she has mastered all of the worlds of magic that combine magical powers, deities, spirits, and a universally pervading consciousness into a single magical discipline.

Not since Alex Sanders formulated his multi-tiered approach to Witchcraft, magic, and occultism could one achieve the unification of these different systems of magic and thereby become a Pagan magus. For those who might be unfamiliar with Alex Sanders, he sought to incorporate a full system of magic and occultism into his brand of Witchcraft although with very mixed results

Along with the spirit model, mastering the magical arts of the energy and information models of magic will deliver to the Witchcraft community the long sought-for methodology to fully practice a Pagan based system of ritual magic. In the next chapter, we look at this as a problem and a challenge that those who are interested in having a fully capable system of Witchcraft magic may approach.

Chapter Three

TALES OF MAGICAL POWERS PRESENT AND PAST

> Seek the wisdom of the ages, but look at the world through the eyes of a child.
>
> —Ron Wild

In the previous chapters, I touched briefly on the evolution of the concept and use of magical powers in ancient and modern Witchcraft. I would like to discuss this topic a bit more because I believe it is relevant to my case for a ritual magical system to conjure, generate, and project various magical energies that appear to be both spirits and powers.

The hybrid system of ritual magic that I developed years ago did not occur in a vacuum; there was precedence for pursuing this kind of path where ceremonial magic and Witchcraft magic intersected in the Alexandrian tradition. I used this system to harness and project magical powers, yet it is the same system I used to conjure spirits into some kind of manifestation.

These rituals of magical evocation were covered in *Spirit Conjuring for Witches;* what I intend to do here is to outline my path and history along with the history of Witchcraft magic and the use of magical powers, since I am a small part of that history and current methodology.

Witchcraft Magic Today

Today, Traditional Witchcraft is a combination of a religion and the practice of magic. If the Gardnerian Book of Shadows is any guide (and these can vary considerably from group to group, or even for individuals), we can see basically five components operating within the modern practice of Witchcraft. These consist of personal practices for self-control (such as meditation), basic free-form energy workings using the cone of power, liturgical operations (godhead assumption, communion, and consecration), and basic mystery ceremonies (seasonal and lunar mysteries and initiation). Added to that are various folk magic spells, herbal recipes, and the creation and use of power objects and discovering and using geographic places of power. The lineage of Alexandrian Witchcraft that I was initiated into also used a simple system of celestial or planetary magic (Book of Planets) and the practices taken from Spiritualism.

If we examine these five components, we can see that most of these practices are not part of the antiquity of Witchcraft but are modern borrowings from other sources. Very little of ancient Witchcraft survives today except as the magical practices of the cunning men and women that have come to light through the work of historians. Let me list these five components, and we can examine each one and see whether it has or could have had an ancient provenance.

Meditation and Trance: The art of meditation, including asana, concentration, mantra, and pranayama of course come from India. While there was a system in the West that taught some of these techniques, it became part of the Christian monastic system and didn't emerge into Protestant forms and practices and was thus basically lost to modern Witches. These practices are the foundation of energy work, so we might conclude that energy work is also from the East. The one exception is trance, which was taken from techniques and practices from the Spiritualist movement, although it started with forms of self-hypnosis that has its own history.

Energy Work: The cone of power generated by the Witches' dance is the basic staple for energy work. While some of the methods appear to come from the East, e.g., as breath control, repetitious movement, and the circulation of bodily energy (prana), other aspects might considered part of folk-magic traditions (such as the apocryphal childhood nursery rhyme and dance

"Ring around the Rosie"). The idea that energy can be projected from the body would appear to have an eastern source, such as kundalini yoga and pranayama yoga.

Liturgical Operations: Godhead assumption, communion, and consecration are very old themes that have their sources in Catholic rituals. The assumption of godhead is something that is supposed to happen to the priest when he assumes the role of Christ to transubstantiate the sacraments. It was also something that was developed in the Golden Dawn, but it has antecedents in Hermetic and Neoplatonic practices in antiquity. Communion and consecration are taken from Catholic beliefs and practices, but once again those ideas were also current in the Pagan religions of antiquity.

Basic Mystery Ceremonies: The eight Sabbats and the lunar Esbats represent the solar and lunar mysteries. The sabbats are based on a combination of recent folklore and the old Catholic calendar more so than some ancient underlying Pagan provenance. The basic rituals in the BoS (Book of Shadows) are so simple and rudimentary that nearly everyone has filled them out and added many folk practices and beliefs to them. The full moon esbats are a part of the traditional Witchcraft lore, at least that which was publicized by the Church during the Witch trials, and it does appear to have an ancient provenance. However, what was supposedly practiced according to those same trials is not what modern Witches would do today. This is true at least as far as I am acquainted with what goes on in covens and with individual practitioners. There are no Black Mass, orgies, or devil worship going on, at least as far as I am aware.

The traditional initiation rites penned by Gardner have been shown to have been loosely based on the first two degrees of Masonry: Entered Apprentice and Fellow Craft. The third-degree Great Rite is also loosely based on Crowley's Gnostic Mass. The circle consecration rite was cobbled together from the Golden Dawn Watchtower rite with elements from the Key of Solomon for consecrating the water and salt. Many ritual elements of modern Witchcraft were taken from modern sources because there was so little available that could be used to forge a modern system of Witchcraft. Despite knowing this to be true, we still find these rituals powerful and compelling, and they have been made wholly our own rites. We have also liberally added to this practice from many different sources, and this too is expected and acceptable today.

Folk Magic: These types of magical workings vary considerably within different traditions and groups, but they represent different folk traditions. These are spells such as making and blessing a poppet or fith-fath; binding rites; making herbal caches and medicine pouches; recipes for different kinds of remedies, food and drink, oils and perfumes, potions, stones, simple amulets, and a host of other techniques and methods that have come down to modern times through various means, whether traditional, historical scholarship, or through a more modern contrivance. All of these methodologies are a valuable resource and system of magic that Witches have acquired and continue to build.

Examining these five basic components, we can see some kind of ancient provenance operating to pull all of these sources together to forge a modern practice. It also reveals the most obvious missing component, which is the conjuration of spirits through the use of a familiar spirit. I have provided a modern methodology for the conjuration of spirits within a Witchcraft base. Yet there are still a couple of other components that I believe should be included in a full practice of modern Witchcraft. These would consist of an advanced system of energy workings and celestial and talismanic magic. This book seeks to provide the advanced energy workings and another planned book will complete the practice of Witchcraft magic with a book on celestial magic. Curiously, there would then be a total of eight components to the full modern practice of Witchcraft magic, becoming the actual eight-fold path that would be part of the basic teachings of the BoS.

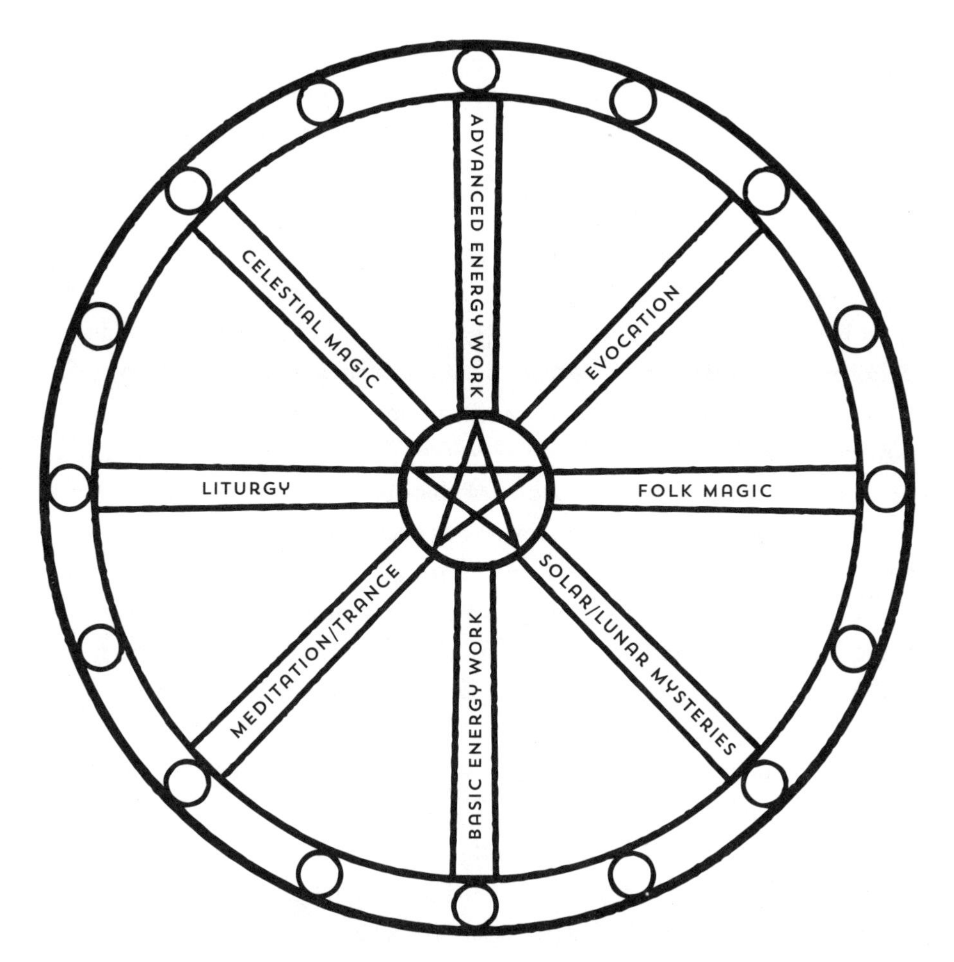

Diagram of Witchcraft Magical Eightfold Path

History and Provenance: Three Threads

Over the years, I have become aware that there were basically three threads of lore and practice that wended their way through the ages from antiquity to the modern age to become included in Witchcraft magic. Some of these threads were lost or diverted, but the need for them to be restored was operating behind the scenes. These three threads were the practices and beliefs of ancient Witchcraft conjuration and folk magic, Neoplatonic philosophy and Theurgic practices, and ancient celestial magic based on Chaldean astrology. Included in the Neoplatonic practices were the disciplines of meditation, breath control, physical exercises, concentration, trance, voice, and all of the regimen we are familiar with that is now associated with eastern Yogic practices.

What I see when I examine the history of Witchcraft and look at my own comparatively short history are the three basic threads that wend their way from antiquity to end of the twentieth century. I would like to briefly elucidate those three threads since they are interesting, and to some extent, illuminating.

As previously stated, the practice of Witchcraft in antiquity required a spirit helper or familiar that would give to the Witch the power and ability to perform supernatural feats. Witches were feared and believed to be powerful, but that power came from divine sources in one way or another. The magical power wielded by such individuals was supernatural, and therefore it had no real limitations other than the nature of that source of power. If a Witch was the daughter of a deity then her power was nearly unlimited and only checked by other deities; but if her power came through a familiar spirit then her abilities, although seemingly miraculous, were limited. It was a difference between being a demigod or being a mortal human being. The basic accepted belief in antiquity was that human nature was weak and powerless without the intervention of powerful deities or spirits.

Because most Witches and Wizards were mere mortals, they had to rely on supernatural helpers in order to achieve their works. Much of ancient Witchcraft relied on the art of evocation for the achievement of great works through intermediaries, but also engaged in herbal lore, potions and medicines, and folk magic to round out their repertoire. This was the first historical thread.

At the same time, there was a second historical thread consisting of the teachings and practices of the philosophers. Now the study of philosophy in antiquity was not the same as it is today. Students were taught and practiced meditation, concentration, and performed various physical exercises as part of their discipline. They strictly controlled their diets and moderated their activities—it was a strenuous regimen that was difficult to master and certainly not for everyone. Some of the traditions, most notably the Pythagoreans (but likely also Plato and his academy), believed that men could be trained to harness unusual powers and abilities. One such early philosopher was Empedocles, who put forth the whole notion of the four elements and their use in a kind of magical power as a major part of his teachings. (We will be focusing more on his teachings in chapter 5.)

Neoplatonists took these vigorous practices and added rituals to them, producing the first system of what would later become Ceremonial Magic. Those who developed theurgy took liturgical rites and rewrote them to mediate the powers of the gods and their intermediaries, the daimons. They used rituals to perform godhead assumptions, project the spirits of deities into statues, or wield their powers to help people or whole communities overcome difficulties, such as droughts, floods, and other calamities. Theurgy was basically defined as "God Work."

These various philosophers believed that there was more to human nature than was commonly supposed, and that the disciplined and trained mind and body could perform minor miracles and achieve astonishing insights into the nature of the human condition and the material world. Sadly, much of their inner teachings did not survive, although some of it found its way into the Christian church and was incorporated into the monastic tradition.

Ancient philosophers and their practices were actually quite similar to the practices and teachings of yogis and rishis in India. While India still has its vibrant class of philosopher mendicants practicing their austerities, these disciplines disappeared in the West. They were replaced by Christian monks working in monasteries; over time, they became less appealing with the general populace. This is why there was such a transformative cultural event when yoga and Indian philosophy were introduced to the West in the late nineteenth century. Westerners were recovering something that they had lost over the centuries.

Mystery traditions could have been the third historical thread: they were grounded in both the mythopoetic world of the old Pagan deities and their engagement and association with human beings. They almost always had something to do with the mortal weakness of the human condition, and whether it was to demonstrate the immortality of the soul (Eleusinian Mystery, Mystery of Isis and Osiris), give an oracle (Delphi), heal the sick (Apollo, Hygeia, and Asclepius) or reveal the mystical secrets of the spiritual military brotherhood (Mithraicism), it embodied a relationship between human and deity and imparted something of the divine to the initiates. Unfortunately, the mystery traditions of antiquity died out without passing on its wisdom.

Celestial magic was the actual third thread, and it continued on through the ages, from antiquity and into the Renaissance. It was probably the primary driver for most of the magic that was worked since it was so well represented in the various grimoires, from the *Picatrix* and the *Key of Solomon* to the planetary ceremonial magic of Ficino and Agrippa, and the Enochian magic of Dr. John Dee. Although celestial magic was tightly connected to the various practices of astrology, it became disconnected from those practices in the advent of the modern age, likely due to the pressures of the Inquisition and later, empirical science.

These three threads were still operating in Europe during the Renaissance. Added to it was the rediscovery of the writings of Plato, Neoplatonism, and the Hermetic corpus. There were also the alchemical writings and magical practices of the secret society of the Rosicrucians that appeared. Supposedly, magical practitioners would use the monastic discipline, routines, and calendar to round out their workings, since that part of the regimen of the mind and body once practiced by the philosophers could only be found within that tradition.

At this time, Witchcraft conjuration was being coopted into a more literary goetic grimoire tradition, but it was generally more common for these practices to be kept completely secret due to the renewed legal zeal of the Protestant Reformation and the counterreformation of the Inquisition. Once merely frowned upon, these books and their practices were now sources of prosecution; even legitimate scholars such as Galileo were having to recant some of their work to escape the deadly consequences of their words. Still, this was a golden age for occultism, with published works in a variety of fields. These works would leave behind a kind of highbrow legacy that would be later examined and picked over.

By the middle of the nineteenth century, two of these threads had for the most part disappeared or gone underground. What little of the Neoplatonic philosophers and the Hermetic studies that had been reestablished in the Renaissance were by now merely the avocation of scholars and academics. Spirit conjuring and forms of goetic magic still had a few adherents here and there in Europe among the cunning folk, but it too was dying out. There were a few grimoires that were popular amongst the collectors of the obscure that maintained this tradition, but only those who lived in the Portuguese diaspora in the New World were keeping this tradition alive; in the Old World, not so much.

Celestial magic was being touted as a practice distinct from Astrology by this time and was packaged in grimoires distributed to the same obscure collectors of goetic grimoires, but empirical science had pretty much diminished the belief in the magic of the planets and the use of talismans for good fortune. Since the scientific community had rejected astrology as a science and western religion had previously restricted its use to benign (harmless) purposes, the third thread was slowly becoming irrelevant. Like the Catholic church itself, religious beliefs were becoming less magical and more rational and secular over time. This caused the overall diminishment of practical magic in the West, since such beliefs and practices were considered superstitious and the purview of the eccentric or the delusional.

When these three threads died out in Europe, they made the later occult revival in the late nineteenth century much more challenging. What was left of these practices were to be found in rare and obscure books and manuscripts from the Renaissance or somewhat later. Parts of these threads were no longer represented by the remains of the fragmentary lore, such as the disciplines of meditation, concentration, bodily exercises, bodily energy work, and the methods and rites of practical theurgy. There were many fragments of these threads to be found, but there were also large holes where there was nothing to be found whatsoever.

Rediscovery and Magical Revitalization

We've now covered how the once-continuous three threads of magic seemed to disappear, but thankfully, it is not the end of our story. Nothing ever seems to really disappear permanently in the world of ideas, and things can reappear by emerging from other disciplines when some idea or belief has faded away. This endurance is especially true regarding the philosophical practices of the second thread—the mind and body—as we shall see.

Bodily and mental disciplines reemerged and became part of what I call a kind of human potential movement, not to be confused with the Esalen institute's movement of the 1960s. Starting with the late eighteenth-century Franz Mesmer, who discovered what he thought was an energy phenomenon he called "animal magnetism," it later became known as hypnosis and autosuggestion, eventually becoming one of the tools of modern psychology and later brought into Spiritism as techniques of trance. Hypnosis was seen as a way to explore the unconscious mind, and it was theorized by Freud and others that the unconscious mind held certain powers and abilities that were not part of normal consciousness. What closely followed was the Spiritualism movement of the middle nineteenth century that proposed that the living might communicate and learn from those loved ones who were dead.

When Blavatsky, Vivekananda, and others began to make Indian metaphysical practices and teachings available to the West in the late nineteenth and early twentieth centuries, it had quite an impact on the fertile imagination of the Western mind. It seemed that previous beliefs in the weakness and mortality of the human condition were challenged and thoroughly revised. What wasn't known at the time is that similar techniques had been a part of the second thread of magic and were the provenance of the philosophers and their discipline. It changed the popular conception in the West that human beings were capable of seemingly miraculous powers, and that perhaps many occurrences that had been thought to be supernatural were actually natural but unknown abilities.

All of these beliefs in the possibility of a greater human potential gathered momentum during the twentieth century and greatly affected the minds of those who rejected the empiricism of science for a more amendable and romantic conception of human abilities. Eastern philosophy and its practices inundated the West and they became a part of the western culture. People talked about prana, karma, or nirvana without really knowing what they were. This movement impacted the practice of magic as well starting in the late nineteenth century, and it was the base for magical workings in modern Witchcraft and Paganism in the 1950s and '60s. Later on, in my time, all my Wiccan and Pagan peers were told to study yoga for at least a couple of years and pick up breathing techniques (pranayama), sitting meditation, mantra yoga, kundalini yoga, and many other subjects. We performed sitting meditation before *and* after working magic.

It is therefore no surprise that the focus of magical energy was the body and that there was a belief in a universal energy that under certain conditions, could be engaged and passed through one's body. This was a marriage of Eastern mysticism and practices with Western magic, and it made a profound difference to the method and techniques of working magic. After this event, magic was never quite perceived or understood in the same manner. I tend to see this marriage as the rediscovery of part of the lost second historical thread of philosophy through the practices and teachings of the East. The question then would be: where is the other part of the second thread?

The other part of the second thread was to be found in the rituals and teachings of the Golden Dawn, oddly enough. Those who wrote the lore of the Golden Dawn were steeped in the writings of Renaissance sages such as Ficino, Pico della Mirandola, Agrippa, and Dee, in addition to the translated works of Neoplatonism and Hermeticism. Included would be practices and studies of Masonry and Rosicrucianism, and the newly translated magical grimoires. Additionally, there were the published writings of the Theosophical Society that were also great sources of practical lore.

It was from these sources that Westcott, Mathers, and later Crowley created the lore of Ceremonial Magic based on elemental and celestial magic, with the inclusion of Eastern teachings and practices. This amalgamation of East and West created a revitalized tradition of Ceremonial Magic that included the practices of nearly all three threads of the magical tradition from antiquity. The weakest representation was in the area of the first thread, evocation, but even then, they had started a process that has continued until today. We now have all three threads fully active and functional in the Western magical tradition.

I see the Golden Dawn as reconstituting part of the lost thread of the philosophical traditions of antiquity. Because I borrowed parts of the magical rituals from the Golden Dawn to forge my own tradition, I was unwittingly pulling together the threads of both old and newly revised formulations into a magical practice made for modern Witchcraft. Everything I did merely expanded on the five points of Witchcraft magic; the shameless borrowing from the Golden Dawn rituals was part of the Witchcraft magic tradition started by old Gerald Gardner himself. Other initiates in the Alexandrian tradition continued this practical expansion, and it produced quite a variety of traditions and even a few separate magical orders.

What I have produced by following this methodology is to reconstitute the advanced energy magic as the seventh component for a full system of Witchcraft magic. I have worked with this system of magic for decades and have taught others to use it as well. It follows the basic premise of Witchcraft magic and is based on structures both old and new. What I have produced has both an ancient provenance and a modern utility. It is the best of both worlds, and it has the added advantage of working quite well.

Chapter Four

ENERGY MODEL OF MAGIC

The world is full of magic things, patiently waiting for our senses to grow sharper.

—W. B. Yeats

The energy model of magic represents a particular perspective when it comes to working magic, and that is the single-minded focus on some kind of energy as the sole operator behind and within all magical phenomena. Of course, magic is much more complex than that and it accommodates many different points of view simultaneously. I have mentioned the basic three, such as the spirit, energy, and information models; there is also the psychological model, the metaphysical model, the stochastic or chaos model, a time-based celestial model, and many others. Every system or method of magic could have its own model and perspective on the practice of magic.

All of these points of view, of course, are by themselves inaccurate and completely misleading if they are not joined to together to create a more holistic perspective. However, by viewing magic in a singular fashion we may be able to deduct and reason out a rich variety of ideas and practices. We can use a simple and slightly inaccurate model and build an entire magical system based on it. As long as we do not mislead ourselves into believing that our construct is the one and only truth and that it is in fact one perspective out of many then we can profit greatly by taking this approach.

This is exactly what I did many years ago and it helped me to develop a very useful and unique approach to working magic. Luckily, I was never deluded enough to believe that the energy model approach to magic was the one and only approach to building a magical system. There were always the inescapable phenomena of spirits to consider.

Basic Energy Magic: Cone of Power

How did I come upon this perspective in the first place? Well, I made an assumption that was quite erroneous and inaccurate, at least at first. Because I was a fledgling Witch with a dearth of written materials and only a few books to guide me, I thought that the starting point for working magic was generating some kind of energy. My Book of Shadows taught me that Witches generated magical power through the use of the Witches' Dance that created a magical energy structure called the cone of power.

Since modern Witchcraft didn't have a specific discipline to evoke spirits, we were left with invoking our goddess and god, the dread lords of the watchtowers that warded the circle that we worked in, and used the environment of the full moon esbat to do our energy work. Based on that knowledge as provided to Alexandrians and Gardnerians, my approach to magic was to figure out how to generate that energy.

Most everyone now knows about the method used in modern Witchcraft to generate magical energy since it is so widely publicized. It was less popularly known back when I was a Witchling, so it was something of a revelation to me. I will briefly go over it here because it is very pertinent to our study of the energy model of magic.

The Witches' Dance resembles a traditional folk dance: the Witches form a ring alternating woman and man (as much as possible) around the magic circle, after which they proceed to move together in a ring, starting slowly in a sun-wise or deosil direction. One of the dance's features is its creative to receptive energy polarity that allows for the stimulation of magical energies with an assist from the presumed sexual polarity of the dancers. It is performed in two basic parts: generating the cone of power and then sending it out into the world.

The High Priestess stands in the center of the circle to direct the energy as it is generated. The Witches circle around the High Priestess starting slowly and increasing in velocity until they are running as fast as they can while chanting the "Eko, Eko" chant. When this circle dance reaches a crescendo, usually determined by the High Priestess who yells out at the key moment, "Harrahyah!" the Witches drop to the floor and project their bodily energies to the High Priestess who directs it up to the nadir of the circle. This is the first step to generating the magical energy. It will produce the cone of power.

The next step is imprinting the cone of power, where the coven members project their intentions into it. Imprinting is done by each Witch making a wish or a desire and pushing or projecting it into the energy field with their hands. Once they have imprinted the energy of the cone of power, then they stand and begin the dance one last time for a short burst of effort to exteriorize the cone. When they collapse to the ground for this last time, the High Priestess projects the energy out beyond the magic circle so that it is released and the intentions placed into it can become realized.

As noted, the High Priestess directs and shapes the energy field with her hands or with a sword. It takes on a cone shape because the Witches in the circle have stopped moving and have quickly laid down on the ground while the energy continues to spin and move to the center of the circle where the High Priestess collects it. She is also visualizing the energy as she shapes it.

The basic features of this exercise are movement, rapid breathing, and bodily excitement. There is visualizing, shaping, directing, and imprinting the energy field. All of these are important factors when working with magical energy. The energy is brought first to a kind of plateau; then, after the energy is imprinted, it is brought to a climax and exteriorized.

This simple pattern has obvious sexual connotations and can be compared it to the male sexual cycle of arousal: stimulus to a plateau and the final excitement and effort that brings on an orgasmic ejaculation. The climax will send out what some might see as a bolt of energy or even a flash of light as the cone of power is sent out of the circle and into the world. What remains is a residual energy that needs to be grounded.

There is a reason why grounding afterwards is necessary. If this ritual did nothing more than combine the bodily energies of the participants then there would be little need to ground the excess. The reason is that this ritual not only combines the energy of those participating, it also resonates, triggering the manifestation of a more universal energy source that greatly amplifies what would have been generated.

The intentions and visualizations of the coven members and the fact that the work is done in sacred space makes this a very special kind of exertion. Otherwise, you could expect to find the same kind of energy generation in a gymnasium or a dance club. You can experience energy within a group of people being physically active together, but it isn't a collective effort with a special intent and a guided visualization. Performed in a gym or a dance club, energy raising and dispersing of this type certainly could become a magical event that would produce external phenomena if it were also correctly imprinted and released.

For those who are sensitive enough to see it, magical energy has a faint blurry bluish color, and this bluish energy field takes the shape of a spinning cone when a group of Witches perform the circle dance. A consecrated magic circle before the dance assumes the basic shape of a ring of energy with a vague accompanying shape of a hemisphere. This is because a magic circle actually produces a field shaped like a sphere, but the floor or ground is the central plane that bisects it. What is visible is a hemisphere.

If you could see the energy field or aura around a standing human being under certain shadowy visual conditions it would look like an egg-shaped sphere, so that is the analogy of the ring and sphere shape of a consecrated magic circle—the human aura. The shapes consist of what I call *prismatic energy fields* that can be shaped and structured into many forms; often, they assume the shape determined by circle structures, such as the four watchtowers or other established circle points.

Once an energy field is generated in a magic circle, it must be imprinted with a purpose and then brought to a climax of activity that exteriorizes and directs it outside the circle. Without a purpose, the cone of power will simply dissipate upon release and the magical potential will be lost. The imprinting is typically nothing more than the coven focusing into the energy field a wish, need, or desire; the more emotions backing it up, the stronger the imprint. The best kind of imprinting is when the group imprints a single purpose or need into the energy so that when it is released, all the energy will be used to affect a single occurrence in the material world.

Not only is imprinting an important action once the energy is generated, it can also be qualified or specifically defined through visualization, words of power, or through the power of a symbolic device or magical tool to inscribe it. The imprinting device is a tool called the link. A customized sigil drawn on parchment can be used, or nearly anything that has significance or meaning to the practitioners, such as a doll or fith-fath, herbal cache, metal amulet, or a gemstone. All of these are links that qualify the magical energy and set to it the intention, medium, and target of the working—the basic three components of a magical energy working.

Magical energy has two basic uses within a magical working. It can be used to empower a desire or an objective, or it can be used to empower oneself directly through the body. The magical process is an empowerment of some kind, the energy and the instruments used to qualify and direct it is a part of the energy working.

Using magical energy in this very direct and simple method incorporates a number of important facts about using energy in magical workings. Let me list them here.

1. Iterative and repetitive movement, physical exertion, breath control (rapid breathing), and visualization are used to generate magical energy.
2. Polarity and attraction, resistance and desire, intensity of breath and action, and using the template of arousal with extreme stimuli to achieve an emotional plateau, and a final burst of effort to bring about an energy climax is the basic pattern of energy generation and exteriorization.
3. Magical energy can be shaped and directed through direct interaction; the use of tools or hands, and the use of the structure of the magic circle produces an effective, intensified and empowered field of energy.
4. Resonance occurs when the intensity of magical energy achieves a certain level and triggers a connection to a universal source of energy, thereby greatly amplifying the volume of the collected energy.
5. Magical energy can be imprinted with goals and desires, and it can be qualified through the use of symbols, sacred words or words of power, and more directly, by visualization.

6. Magical energy can be absorbed into the body (for personal empowerment), projected out into the world, or focused into a tool or a consecrated object.
7. The cone of power using the archetypal male sexual cycle is not the only structure or ritual pattern available in the use of magical energy—in fact, the possibilities are unlimited.

Polarity Considerations

Polarity is an important consideration that assists us in conceptualizing magical energy, and often it can receive a gender such as the polarity of masculine and feminine, as it is defined within a classical psychological perspective. This kind of binary approach may work appropriately when considering the polarity of magical energy; but it is not to be confused with physical gender in human beings (or any complex animal), which is not at all binary. When I classify energy in this manner, I am actually looking at what would be considered the archetypal masculine and feminine, such as Shiva and Shakti in Hindu metaphysics.

As a Witch, I can also agree with the concept of the archetypal feminine as a generic goddess and the archetypal masculine as a generic god, but when approaching traditional deities that have a history and a well-defined character, this approach cannot apply. While the archetypal Goddess might be considered to be completely feminine, a named goddess, such as Artemis, would be much more complex and incapable of being reduced to a feminine archetype. Neither would Dionysus be considered archetypically masculine simply because he is quasi-gendered as a male. We can generally classify things to make them more efficient and simplistic to conceptualize and discuss, but we must always remember that this is just a mental artifice.

The consensus of occult writers in our current time is moving away from a binary gendered perspective to one that is more descriptive and less loaded with the political issues of gender that are roiling our body politic. Therefore, I will use other terms such as receptive (passive) or creative (active) like the Chinese yin or yang instead of feminine and masculine wherever appropriate. What I am talking about is purely on an archetypal level, with the caveat that complex gendered humans have many qualities that would represent both energies operating within them. This is also true of the cycle and pattern of energies that I use in my magical workings. I describe everything on an archetypal level when considering polarity, even though things in the physical world are much more complex. Having made that clarification, let us continue with our discussion on magical powers.

Discovering the Magic Vortex

Early in my studies, I had thought that the ritual pattern for the cone of power appeared biased toward the masculine viewpoint of magical energy. In the Witches' circle, this was the only method used to generate magical power directly and send it out with a specific purpose. I played with an idea that I found intriguing, wondering whether there was a magical energy that could be modeled on a woman's sexual cycle. How would it be done and what would it be like? Since I am a man, you might even wonder if I knew what that was. Could I use the tools I already had at my disposal? I decided that maybe I would invert the features of the cone of power to come up with something that would be feminine instead of masculine, or so I thought. So let's try this approach as I did so many years ago and see what we can derive together. Here are the qualities as I saw them:

A cone of power travels in a sun-wise or deosil spiral, so the opposite would be anti-sun-wise, or a widdershins spiral. A cone of power has its polarity arrayed along the periphery of the magic circle. The dancers are in woman to man order, and although they are holding hands, the dancers' bodies never actually meet or touch. The opposite would be a meeting or a joining. The dancers keep the basic magic circle erect by dancing in a ring around the center, thereby polarizing it; so, the opposite would be to build a crossroads where the four directions are pulled into the center. The cone energy is projected to the heavens, and the opposite approach would project the energy into the underworld.

To put together a ritual pattern to generate this new kind of energy, I came up with the following steps.

1. Draw each of the four watchtowers together to the center of the circle with a sword—this creates a *cross-roads* structure.
2. Walk quickly around the magic circle widdershins three times from the outside to the center of the circle, starting and ending in the north.
3. In the center of the circle, project the force down and below the floor or ground level.

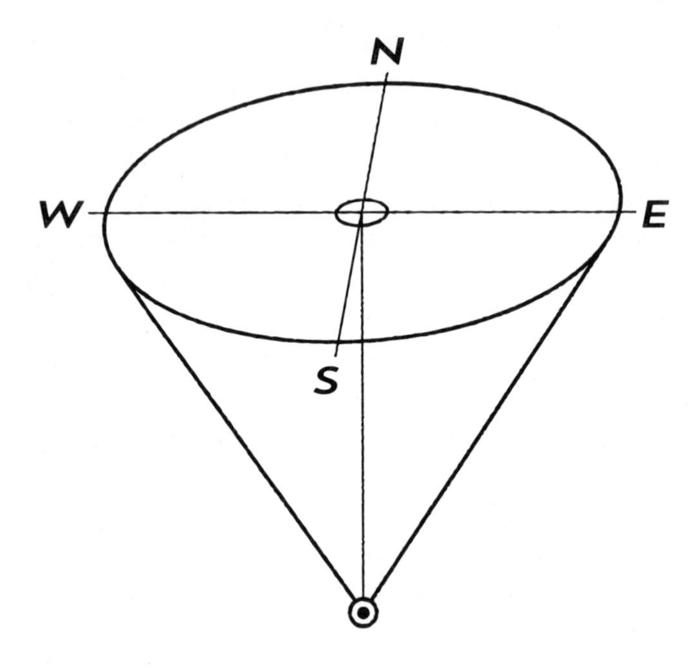

Diagram of a vortex

The widdershins direction and drawing the watchtowers together in the same working was not something that was done anywhere. First, it would cause the magical circle to implode and then it would snatch away all the energy in the magic circle—or so my teachers told me. However, the circle, having been cast as a boundary was strong enough to allow the new energy field to remain in place. Instead of draining the circle of energy, it generated a whole new kind of energy.

Where the cone of power was decidedly electric, expansive, and even explosive, this new power was magnetic, subtly penetrating, and contractive. Like the cone of power, it could be brought to a climax where it resonated with waves of energy. Unlike a cone of power, it could *not* be banished—it remained in place even after the watchtowers were dismissed. I called this new energy field a vortex and discovered that it had some amazing qualities.

A vortex energy field functions like a container and holds together whatever ritual patterns are performed within it, allowing them to merge and accumulate, because it cannot be banished. Instead, a practitioner would use what is called a sealing spiral to seal it and an unsealing spiral to make it available again. These spirals are different from the ones used to create a cone or vortex.

Another feature is that a vortex can be used to store the energies from a number of workings, allowing the energy to become more intense and powerful after each layer is applied. The combined energy can then be brought to a climax to cause a series of waves to emit from it, like a pebble dropped into a pool of water, creating ever-widening waves of energy. These rippling waves of energy are in fact much more conducive to making changes in the material world than a cone of power. A vortex has a central singularity that allows it to function as a gateway to other dimensions. I liken it to a kind of magical black hole, where energy is drawn into it and also radiated outward.

Including a vortex and the cone of power in a witch's arsenal can add many possibilities to a singular magical working, since a vortex can contain any number of cones of power and keep them intact and active until she wants to tap that power for a given objective. Once a vortex becomes a common working tool for the Witch, she has stepped outside of the modern definition of the energy model of magic and *extended* it to include new possibilities. This is because there are, indeed, many additional energy fields to be used than just these two.

The cone and vortex have two things in common. They use magical spirals to wind up the energy into a cone or fuse it and wind it down into a vortex singularity. They also represent the inherent polarity of magical energy, the creative and receptive fields.

The Magic Pylon

Drawing a line with a magic dagger will produce, in a consecrated circle, a line of force that will look like a light blue line for those who can see this energy. This is also true with the wand, sword, staff, and the naked hand. If a line is drawn between two objects, then those two objects are joined together within that line of force. A Witch can trace a magical device, such as a pentagram, in the air above her head, trace another one at her feet, and then join them together with a line of force. This creates another energy field called a pylon.

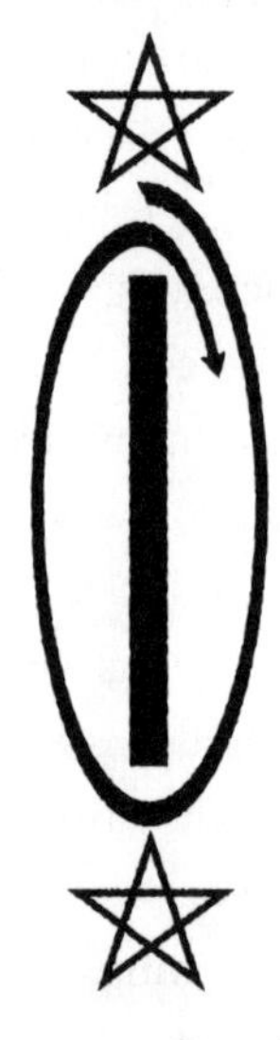

Diagram of a pylon

Pyramid of Power

When a pylon is drawn in the center of the circle and the four watchtowers are drawn in lines of force to the top of that pylon and to each other (forming a square base), a new energy field shaped like a pyramid is generated. This is called the pyramid of power, where the linear structure of the pylon and the four watchtowers join together to form a square base and an apex that shapes the prismatic energy into a geometric shape—a pyramid. The base of the pyramid, which contains the square in a magic circle, represents the symbolic joining of the creative and receptive energy fields, which produces an energy field that empowers the pyramid. In my own workings, I have found that the pyramid of power is much more effective than the cone of power in sending out a creative energy field. I use this ritual energy pattern to generate forty different types of energy that I call the qualified powers, described in chapter 8.

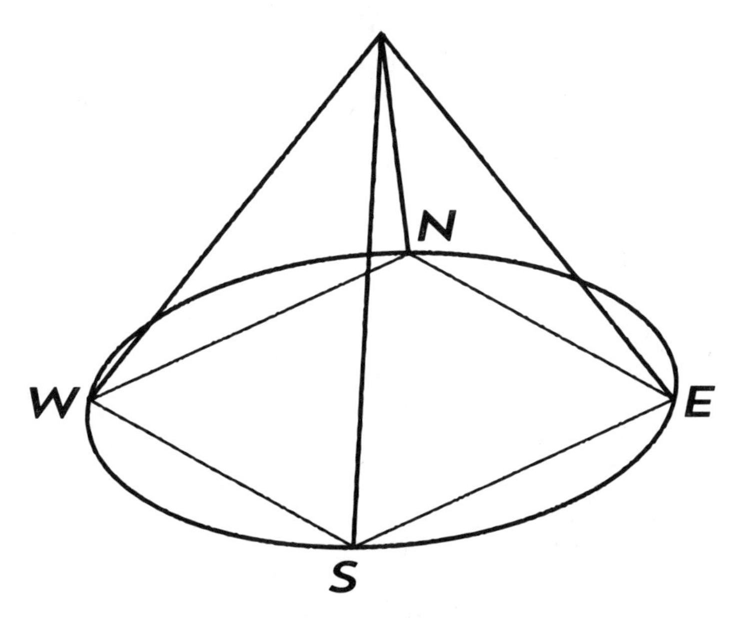

Diagram of the pyramid

Eight-Node Magic Circle

A magic circle has four cardinal directions within its structure but can be expanded to have eight directions or nodes where magical energy fields can be formed. The four cardinal directions also have four in-between directions, which I call angles. This is where the cardinal direction of the west joins with the north and south to produce the northwest and southwest angles, and the east joins with the north and south to produce the northeast and the southeast angles. These compass directions work well with the basic notions of wind directions. However, we could expand the number of nodes in a magic circle to be twelve or even sixteen. I usually use just eight, but some of the more advanced workings I have developed use expanded magical circle structures. There are also three points in the center of the circle as well, which makes for a total of eleven.

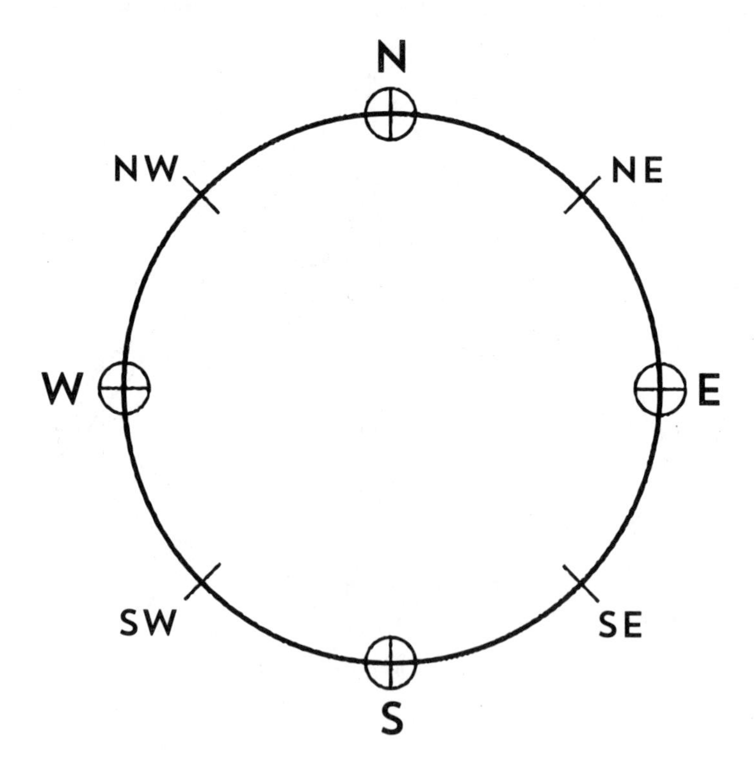

Diagram of the eight-node magic circle

Magic Octagon

Using an eight-node magic circle allows for the definition of two squares drawn in a magic circle, creating an octagon. If we use the central point that is above (the zenith) and the central point below (the nadir), then draw the watchtowers to the zenith and the angles to the nadir, and at a climactic moment, draw the two points together in the center of the circle to create a pylon line of force, an octagon energy field is produced. This magical action will join the energy of the watchtowers and angles together into a fusion of potent magical energy in the central pylon. I use this ritual energy pattern to generate sixteen types of energy I call the elementals, which will be covered in chapter 7.

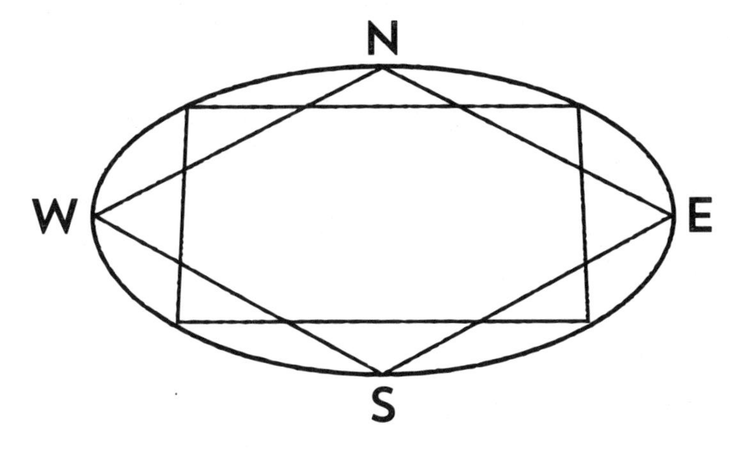

Diagram of the octagon

Western and Eastern Gateways

Finally, another energy field that I use extensively has the shape of the triangle and is used to establish a magical gateway. Typically, I use one watchtower and two angles that are opposed to it to form a triangle shape in an eight-point magic circle. I use the western watchtower and the southeast and northeast angles to define a triangle gateway that when opened, descends into a deeper level below the plane of the magic circle. I use the eastern watchtower and the southwest and northwest angles to define a triangle gateway that ascends into a higher level above the plane of the magic circle. The western gate is the gate of night and darkness and the eastern gate is the gate of day and light. These two gates, when used together within a working become the double gates of transformative initiation.

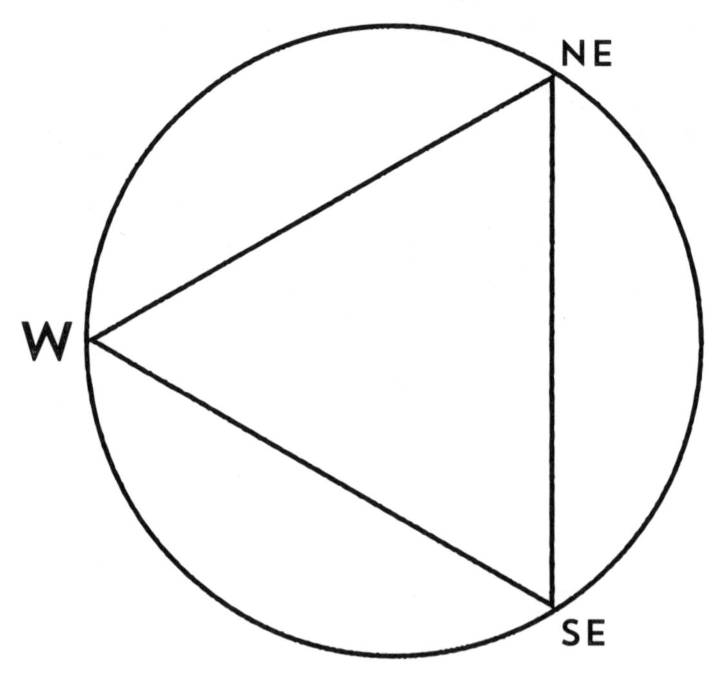

Diagram of the western gateway

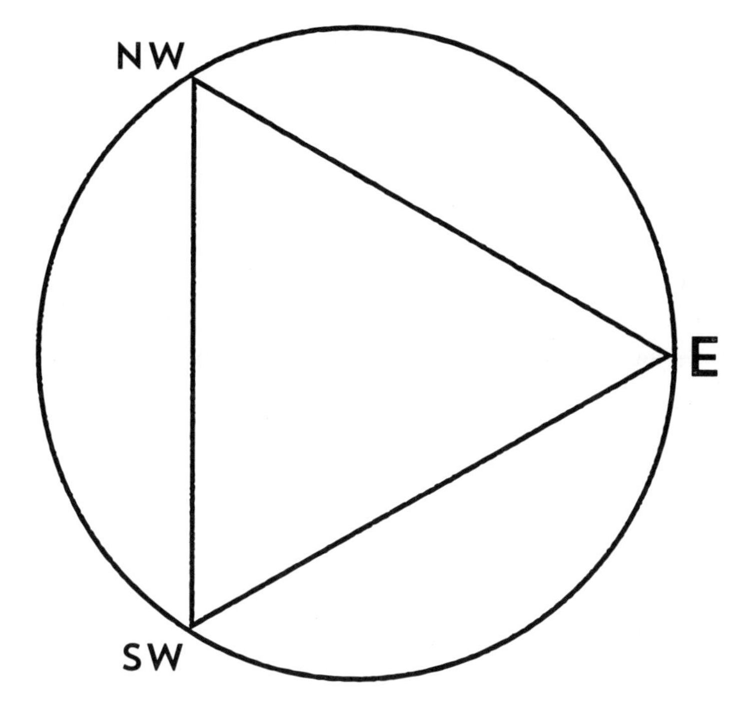

Diagram of the eastern gateway

Qualifying Magical Power

I spoke previously about qualifying the energy generated in a magic circle, and there can be no better method of qualification than the whole of the correspondences of the four elements and spirit. As said previously, the vital energy of an individual can be used to trigger a more potent universe-based energy to manifest itself in a magical working. However, that energy is much more easily accessible if it is qualified through the symbolism and visualization of the four elements. Because this is an ancient tradition that has been used through the ages and is some kind of ingrained mechanism that is a part of our collective consciousness going back to antiquity, using these symbols and correspondences transforms our magical energy into a much more efficient and powerful force. It triggers an automatic resonance that amplifies the raised bodily energy of the magician. So, it should be an important feature in the energy model of magic—and in this work, it is.

To complete this discussion of the energy model of magic, let us now discuss the four elements and spirit. We will look at the classical definition of the elements and we will also compare them to the more modern occult definitions. It is important that we understand that the four elements are not just different categories of magical energy. They are much more than that, as we shall see in the next chapter. The four elements are forms of energy, but they are also universal formulations that function as a cosmogony, a cosmology, an eschatology, separate geographic domains, cosmic deities, and even four elemental creatures and four elemental kings. They are an array of gods, goddesses, demigods, heroes, ancestors, demons, angels, and elemental spirits, all located and joined together within their own mythic worlds.

Chapter Five

MAGICAL FOUR ELEMENTS AND SPIRIT

> Nature that framed us of four elements, warring with our breasts for regiment, doth teach us all to have aspiring minds.
>
> —Niccolo Michiavelli

From the previous discussions, you can see that the foundation of the energy model of magic is the four elements. The occult system of the four elements goes back to the fifth century BCE with the philosophical writings of Empedocles. While we could spend a lot of time going over what we have from fragments of his writings and annotations of his ideas from later writers in antiquity, I thought that we should just cover some of the basic concepts that we know from his teachings. These will be relevant when we look at the more modern occult perspectives and help us to understand how these ideas evolved over time, and how some of it has not changed much since it was first declared centuries ago.

Empedocles and the Four Elements

Empedocles lived during the fifth century and was part of a philosophical tradition that had already started a century or more earlier, notably the famous presocratic philosophers from Miletus in Ionia (modern Turkey). However, Empedocles was something of a throwback because unlike the philosophers of his time, he still wrote his philosophical works in a poetic form while the rest had already adapted to prose. He also acted the grandiose part of the magus when philosophers had already toned down their involvement in magic and prophecy.

Before his time, Greek philosophy had already established that the soul of humanity was immortal. They taught that the cosmos was not created out of nothing, but had proceeded over time to be developed and evolved in a rational and natural manner. Greek philosophy had also determined that the principals of that creation were eternal and unchanging. While the earlier philosophers had discussed whether the nature of those principals consisted of a single element such as water, fire or air, Empedocles had declared that the principals were the four elements of air, earth, water and fire. These four elements were pure, incorruptible substances that had emerged from the singular unity known to philosophers as the One. Because Empedocles had been initiated into the Pythagorean mysteries, it is likely that his theories were based either wholly or in part on the teachings of that mystery tradition.

Empedocles taught that the four elements, as the mediator of the One and the Many, are as unchanging as the One. They combine and re-combine to undergo many formulations and transformations to account for the great variety of material things, but that they maintain their integrity and never really change. Therefore, the singularity and integrity of the One is preserved while the material reality with its surface illusions has within its core components that are real and true.[4]

The four elements represent the ultimate roots of material reality, replacing an Iron Age family of deities who represented the constituents of the world, both spiritual and material, with four principals that mediate a nameless underlying unity. The four elements act as an organizing template or model that

4. Thomas McEvilley, *The Shape of Ancient Thought: Comparative Studies in Greek and Indian Philosophies* (New York: Allworth Press, 2002), 307.

gives order and structure (as a quaternary) to the material world. This is so it can be resolved with the One that underlies it. So, Empedocles compared the four elements to four Greek Deities who act as cosmic representatives of the One that is not named. To Zeus he ascribed the air; Hera, earth; Hades, fire; and Nestis (or Poseidon) to water.[5]

The first element is air, called by Empedocles by the Greek *aer*. In the time of Empedocles, the air was considered the celestial domain, but later the meaning of the word *aer* changed to "mist," so it was thus relegated to a lower level element and replaced with the Greek word aether.[6] The element air according to Empedocles was tied to the air that living things breath, and so it also was synonymous with the word *pneuma*, or spirit. That air/aether was the primal element had already been explored previously, but from it emerged the other three elements. Later on, Aristotle distinguished the word aether from aer in his writings, and proposed a fifth element of spirit, both on a cosmic and individual level.[7]

Earth and water separated out from air to form the world of continents and seas, and fire was the infernal fire of the underworld enfolded within the earth. Because Empedocles spent much of his life on the island of Sicily, it is not surprising that fire would be seen as an infernal element since the hot springs and active vulcanism was (and still is) a common feature.[8] What that meant is that the sun was born of that infernal fire within the core of the earth and circled the sky from horizon to horizon to enter and return to the infernal underworld, which was its abode. It was not considered a sphere born of the celestial domain of air.

The four elements of Empedocles consisted of many different layers interwoven together, to include premiere creative forces in nature, four specific geologic domains ruled by cosmic deities, a cosmic and cosmogonic cycle of creation and dissolution, an eschatology, an endless cycle of life, death and rebirth, and ultimately a means of enlightenment and spiritual emancipation. The philosophic concept of the four elements had these many layers and meanings

5. Peter Kingsley, *Ancient Philosophy Mystery, and Magic: Empedocles and Pythagorean Tradition* (Oxford, UK: Clarendon Press, 1995), 13–14.

6. Ibid., 20.

7. Ibid., 27.

8. Ibid., 53.

applied to it, and it was never considered to be just one thing as it is today in some forms of occultism.

Spirit as pneuma or aether, has a specific quality in this system that we should also discuss. It is analogous to other terms that are defined as an energy or vital force and is a hallmark for what would pass as the energy associated with the energy model of magic. It is connected to the element aer (air) or aether, since it is by and large associated with the breathing cycle of all living things. It has become, over time, a kind of fifth element, and it is believed to be the force that gives form to substance, and into which form dissolves back into the formless One. It is like the glue that holds and binds all material things together so that they have form as well as substance.[9]

The pentagram would become a perfect emblem for the four elements drawn together into a fifth. For this reason, the pentagram is a perfect symbol of this process of union and creation, making it the perfect magical tool for its expression. It is used for the generation of each of these five element qualities.

There is a fragment from Empedocles's writings that seems to crucially state the purpose of his teachings and how they were to be used. Many later philosophers and historical scholars have either chosen to ignore this important fragment or to even attest that it is a forgery. What he states in this fragment seems to be the real purpose and rationale for acquiring and gaining this knowledge, and that is to transform the world through the artful and magical manipulation of the four elements:

> And you'll stop the force of the tireless winds that chase over the earth
> And destroy the fields with their gusts and blasts;
> But then again, if you so wish, you'll stir up winds as requital.
> Out of a black rainstorm you'll create a timely drought
> For men, and out of a summer drought you'll create
> Tree-nurturing floods that will stream through the ether.
> And you will fetch back from Hades the life-force of a man who has died.[10]

9. McEvilley, *Ancient Thought*, 545.

10. Kingsley, *Ancient Philosophy*, 218.

This is the magician side of Empedocles speaking, and perhaps it is the primary foundation of his teachings. To master the four elements requires you to first master yourself, and then to take that mastery as a keystone and use it as a fulcrum and lever against the four elements, thereby moving them into action. We will take this approach in our own practices and magical workings, and we will be indebted in a manner to Empedocles, who lived and died in the fifth century BCE, and who set his teachings in wondrous poetry, only some of which survived to this day.

Classical Four Elements

Based on what we have covered about Empedocles and his theories about the four elements, it is important to understand that the four elements are not just one thing. They are not a kind of mindless energy and they are not restricted to just those who wield them as bodily based energies. There are both individual and universal qualities to the four elements and much more.

We will focus on these qualities and try to understand that the correspondences that we will build from them are analogues of what these elements truly represent in the field of consciousness. Each element is greater than the sum of the correspondences that are used to qualify it.

Spirit, as the fifth element, emulates the quality of the One that we have already discussed. It links the individual with a cosmic and overriding unity so that all things are connected. It is the nature of this state of connectiveness through which magic is able to function. It is also a state of mind that is only apparent to the practitioner while under the most profound transcendental states of consciousness.

To begin our analysis, we should reexamine the qualities and substances of four elements as they were understood in late antiquity, well after Empedocles and his teachings had been canonized.[11]

The four qualities are hot, cold, dry, and wet. Each element substance takes its nature from two of the qualities. Fire is both hot and dry, earth is cold and dry, water is cold and wet, and air is hot and wet. Air and fire share the quality of hot, earth and water share cold; fire and earth share dry, and water and air

---

11. Aristotle, *On Generation and Corruption*, translated by Harold H. Joachim, book 2, chapter 3 of eBook (n.l., 2002).

share wet. Hot is active, cold is inert, dry is semi-volatile and wet is fluidic. From this we can rationalize the following correspondences:

Fire: The qualities of fire are ambition, movement, activity, and achievement—it is archetypically masculine. Fire is represented by the season of summer where the first fruits, vegetables, and grains are harvested. Fire is symbolized by the choleric humor, also known as yellow bile.

Earth: The qualities of earth are maturity, balance, wisdom, and caution—it is archetypically feminine. Earth is represented by the season of autumn, where the final fruits and tubers are harvested and earth becomes dormant as the growing season ends. Earth is symbolized by the melancholic humor, also known as black bile.

Water: The qualities of water are death, dissolution, purification, and simplicity—it is archetypically feminine. Water is represented by the season of winter, where the earth is in hibernation, frozen and silent. Water is symbolized by the phlegmatic humor, also known as phlegm.

Air: The qualities of air are birth, growth, awakening, youthful optimism, and the vital force—it is archetypically masculine. Air is represented by the season of spring, where the earth is reborn and reactivated with renewed life. Air is symbolized by the sanguine humor, also known as blood.

Modern Occult Four Elements

We can now examine the four elements as they are defined in modern occultism. The definitions have not changed a great deal over time, except where more modern analogies have been applied, such as comparisons to electricity and magnetism that were recently added by such occultists as Franz Bardon.

I have combined the definitions of the four elements found in modern occultism with some of my own insights to produce definitions that I feel are more useful specifically to magic. Here are my definitions of the four elements, and you can see that what I have derived is not entirely dissimilar to what are traditional definitions. I have added what I think are some clarifications, which would justify my different approach. Yet I also need to explain why I have different perspectives from what is traditionally accepted.

Fire: Action guided by wisdom, insight, illumination, inspiration, aspiration, abstract ideation, and philosophy. I added knowledge to the qualities of fire because I have compared it to light and a focused awareness that produces an ontology about the thing focused on. Franz Bardon, in his book *Initiation into Hermetics,* has added electric to the qualities and declares fire to be the first element.[12] Tarot attributions: Wands, Ace of Wands. Element creature: Salamanders. Color: Red.

Water: Emotions, feelings, sentiment, intimacy, connections, engagements, relationships, immersion, love and fear, placid or tempestuous. I believe that feelings best represent water. Bardon adds the quality magnetic. Tarot attributions: Cups, Ace of Cups. Element creature: Undines. Color: Blue.

Air: Will and volition, movement, restless, impulsive, pure action, knowledge gained without wisdom (opinion or conjecture), poly-sexuality, and mercurial. All of these states are, of course, stimulated by the mind. I also compare air to the qualities of the wind, which is highly volatile and always moving. Activity suggests a direction and an ultimate goal, so I have also added the quality of the will, because the will is often quite changeable like the wind. Bardon adds the quality mediator of the polarity of fire and water, creative and receptive. Tarot attributions: Swords, Ace of Swords. Element creature: Sylphs. Color: Yellow. While Sylphs are depicted as winged aerial creatures, they were originally believed to be tree spirits, hence their name is derived from the same root as sylvan.

Earth: A synthesis of all three elements into one, inert but active, the biosphere, vital spark, slow changes through adaption and evolution, health, wealth, material happiness, fortune (rise and fall), fruitful, sedentary, ephemeral, and impermanent. Bardon adds the quality of electromagnetic and tetra-polar (combines all three elements into one that is four-fold). Tarot attributions: Discs/Pentacles, Ace of Discs/Pentacles. Element creature: Gnomes. Color: Green.

---

12. See Franz Bardon, *Initiation into Hermetics,* ed. Ken Johnson, trans. Gerhard Hanswille and Franca Gallo (Salt Lake City: Merkur Publishing, 2014. Originally published 1956, Verlag Hermann), 19–22, for all of Bardon's definitions of the four elements.

While the traditional definition of the four elements are typically based on the Qabalistic Tetragrammaton (Yod, He, Vau, He), where fire is defined as action and air as intellect, I have felt that these distinctions are too simplistic and don't match up with an actual observation of these elements in nature. Because fire and air are attributed to archetypal masculine qualities, they both represent a kind of materialized power, nature as a force, which can be beneficial but also highly destructive. However, when examining these elements from the standpoint of the four magical tools, things become a bit more complicated.

The wand is more refined and represents action performed in accordance with authority, therefore it is appropriate to summon a deity with a wand. The dagger or athame is less refined, aggressive, and actionable: it cuts, divides, severs, coerces, and protects. The wand unites, draws together, convinces, and heals. Both represent an action and a kind of knowledge, but they approach these qualities in a very different manner. You would never summon a deity with a dagger unless you were also seeking conflict with it.

In the tarot cards themselves, the wands cards are more idealistic and socially-based whereas the swords are more about conflict and action. The polarity of the four elements would also support my definition. Active outward knowledge (fire) polarizes against internalized and deep emotions (water), and the volatile restless mind (air) polarizes against the placid and ossified state of nature (earth).

What I have proposed with my definitions for the four elements is more like a synthesis of the triplicity of the three zodiacal signs for each element. When we look at fire as a combination of Ares, Leo, and Sagittarius, it would seem to me that blending them would soften the Aries with the thoughtfulness of Sagittarius and the sunny genius of Leo. Similarly, the combination of Libra, Aquarius, and Gemini would stimulate Libra's stoic intellect with the restlessness of Gemini and the social consciousness of Aquarius. Whatever way we define these four elements, the differences between how I define fire and air and what is traditional are quite minor, if we understand that both are a form of knowledge and action approached from different angles.

The four cardinal directions associated with the four elements can vary depending on the source of this information. One perspective a number of Witches employ explains that the elements and the directions should represent your actual geographic location. If there is an ocean, lake, or sea to your eastern direction, then east would be water. Many others use this methodology as well.

If we choose the elements based on the four classical winds, then air (Eurius)–east; fire (Notus)–south; water (Zephyrus)–west; earth (Boreas)–north. This is the correspondence used in many Witchcraft traditions, including my own. This is the basic structure that I learned from my tradition of Witchcraft and is accepted in many situations. There are many different methods for associating the elements to the directions, and some use the elements of the signs of the zodiac to determine this association.

Of course, the color scheme for the four elements is just as variable as the cardinal direction attribution. I am using my own color scheme; there are many others that can be used instead. What I chose seemed obvious to me, but that may or may not work for you.

Having established a solid definition of the four elements will help us when we start looking at the derivations for the elementals (element combined with an element) and the qualified powers (element combined with one of ten number attributes). However, we must examine each of the four roots of the four elements, and these will assist us in developing a base for generating and conjuring each of them.

The root is, of course, the spirit or deity associated with each element. We can and should approach the four elements with both an eye to the energy model as well as the spirit model of magic. By giving each element a deity or spirit attribute, we can summon them as we would any spirit but can also generate the energy and qualities of each in a more direct and comprehensive manner. The key is that these spirits are also powerful energies, so summoning them is a lot easier than performing a classical evocation because they are far less complex, closer to the earth, and rooted in the four elements.

Four Element Kings and Emperors

As previously stated, Empedocles saw each element function as four deities and he gave the names of the four greater deities of the Greek pantheon, and that is Zeus (air/sky), Hera (earth), Poseidon/Nestis (water), and Hades (fire/underworld). We can substitute these deities with any from any pantheon, be it Egyptian, Sumerian, Roman, Norse/Germanic, or Celtic. However, in the magical tradition these four deities became the four element kings with potential infernal or even demonic qualities.[13] This is because they are close to our world and immersed in the element with which they are associated. Unless the Deities that you are working with are also chthonic and engaged with the earth sphere, it is better to work with an intermediary to the gods to preserve that earth-based connection.

Let me explain that traditional elemental magic does have both a chthonic and a demonic character to it. You will discover this fact the first time that you examine other sources for this lore. The element kings appear to have the names of demons in some magical traditions and in others they are the kings of the element creatures, such as the salamanders, sylphs, undines, and gnomes. As Witches, we should not be dismayed when we encounter Christian diabolism in various magical grimoires and sources, nor should we find ourselves drawn into the polarity of angel and demon, and the Christianized moral implications that they appear to have.

We can selectively choose how to perceive and characterize the spirits that we engage, and at least accept that they might be called by other names that are notoriously demonic. The reason these associations exist in the first place is due to the fact that these spirits are associated with the earth and have their roots in the core of the underworld.

However, to avoid using demonic names for the four kings, we can use instead the elemental kings of the four classes of elemental creatures whose names are Djin (fire, salamanders, east), Ghob (earth, gnomes, south), Paralda (air, sylphs, west), and Nickasa (water, undines, north). We can also use the four emperors. We need to classify these four kings or emperors as the mediators for the elemental spirits with whom we wish to engage.

Here are the correspondences of the four emperors.[14] You will note that the element to cardinal direction is different than the kings, matching with the four wind deities that I mentioned earlier. We will be using the four emperors in this work because the *Theurgia-Goetia* also has a list of spirits (grand dukes) for the sixteen elementals, but we will get more into that in chapter 7. One other point is that there are variances in the spelling of the spirit names, depending on the

13. Jake Stratton-Kent, *The Testament of Cyprian the Mage* (London: Scarlet Imprint, 2014), 32.

14. Stephen Skinner and David Rankine, *The Goetia of Dr Rudd: The Angels and Demons of Liber Malorum Spirituum Seu Goetia Lemegeton Clavicula Salomonis* (Singapore: Golden Hoard Press), 215–222.

source, whether it is the *Lemegeton* or its precursor, the *Steganographia*, a book written by Trithemius. These names are taken from the version of the *Theurgia-Goetia* in the possession of Dr. Thomas Rudd.

Element	Emperor Name	Direction
Air	Carmasiel	Eastern quadrant
Fire	Caspiel	Southern quadrant
Water	Ameradiel	Western quadrant
Earth	Demoriel	Northern quadrant

In order to access the spirit and energies of the sixteen elementals and the forty qualified powers the Witch will need to access the appropriate chthonic deity, element king, or emperor. When we examine these spirits and their relative hierarchy and the qualities that they represent, we will get deeper into the mechanism for deploying them in a ritual that will also generate a charged field to accompany it (chapter 12).

Having both a spirit name and a specific hierarchy and quality along with various correspondences, will greatly assist the Witch in visualizing, generating, and charging a very specific energy field to perform a very specific task. As we will see, fine tuning the energy in a magical working will make it more likely to be successful, and here we are using both energy correspondences and spirit names to aid in that task.

Magic Pentagram

This brings us to discussing the magical mechanism for generating an element energy field. When a Witch draws an invoking pentagram for a specific element then that element will be generated. There are five points to a pentagram and the top most point is assigned to spirit. The other four points are attributed to the four elements; where the left upper point is air, and the bottom left foot is earth. The right upper point is water, and the right foot is fire. The polarized elements are on the same side of the pentagram, such as fire and water, and air and earth. This makes the pentagram intrinsically charged and even more so when activated.

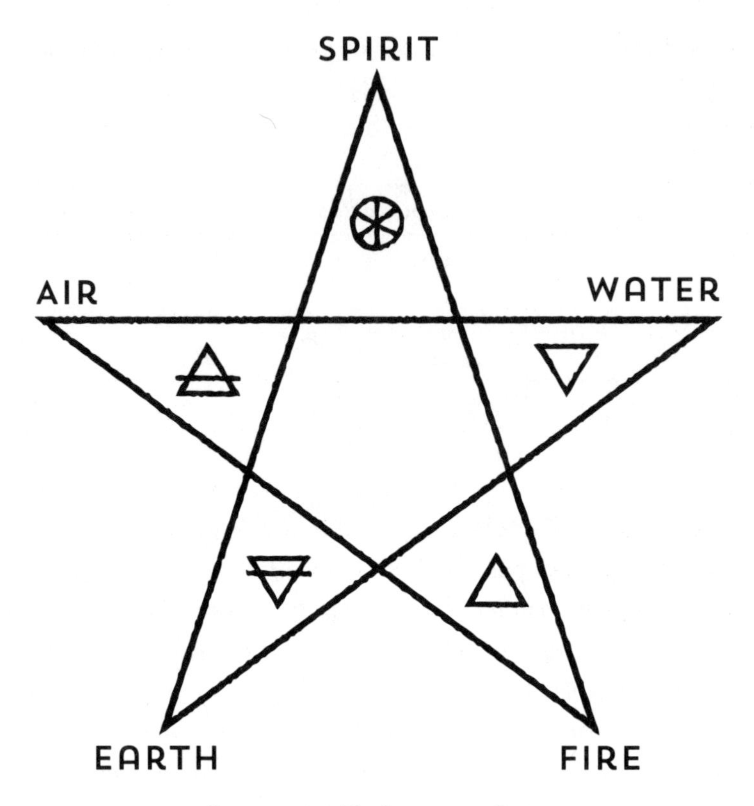

Pentagram with element attributes

Drawing a pentagram device in the air with a magical tool has basically two steps: first, drawing either toward or away from the element point (invoking or banishing) and following the line of the pentagram to draw six strokes, and second, drawing an invoking spiral (sunwise from outer to inner) or a banishing spiral (anti-sun-wise from inner to outer) over the completed pentagram drawing. This is somewhat different than traditional Witchcraft where the Witch points her athame at the center of the drawn pentagram to complete it. The addition of a spiral comes from the Alexandrian tradition of Witchcraft I was taught and it was added for a reason: this added component helps to differentiate between whether a pentagram is an invoking or a banishing one, since there can be some ambiguity.

The invoking or banishing spirals either project energy into the pentagram to empower it or to disperse the energies of the pentagram already invoked.

Drawing the invoking lines on the pentagram actually charges it and causes it to spin. The basic common exercise to all traditions, however, is that you always draw towards the element point to invoke that element and away from it to banish—that is the basic rule for drawing a pentagram. Another important rule is that when drawing the pentagram, you should avoid using the lateral lines running diagonally under the two arms; that way, there will always be only one point opposite the point that you wish to invoke or banish. I have found that drawing an invoking pentagram of an element always involves the simultaneous drawing of the opposite element banishing pentagram. The invoking pentagram of air is the banishing pentagram of water, and vice versa. The invoking or banishing spiral drawn in the center determines which one is to be employed.

For an invoking pattern that generates an element energy, the Witch starts at the point of the pentagram opposite of the element point to be invoked and draws a line toward and then past that point, following the lines of the pentagram until reaching the starting point and then moving toward the target point one last time, drawing six continuous lines in all. To banish or disperse the element energy, the Witch starts at the target point of the element to be banished, then drawing a line toward its opposite point, continuing on until reaching the starting point and then moving to the point opposite. This is done while the Witch visualizes the element and its associated qualities and color, while calling the associated deity or spirit in her mind. An invoking spiral or banishing spiral is drawn over the completed pentagram to charge/drain and activate/deactivate the device.

The top point of the pentagram is attributed to spirit, so it too can be invoked by starting at either the left or right leg of the pentagram then drawing a line up to the top point and following the line of the pentagram until reaching the starting point, then moving beyond it to the top point again. The banishing pattern would start at the top point and drawing a line down on either side of the pentagram to follow the lines until the starting top point is achieved, then further drawing a line to either of the legs. The right leg of the pentagram to the top point of spirit is the arc of creative spirit and the left leg of the pentagram to the top point is the arc of receptive spirit. This is different from other traditions, but it uses the rule stated previously about drawing pentagrams.

I have called these the pentagrams of creative and receptive spirit because such a representation makes sense in a Witchcraft circle where the archetypal Goddess and God are the chief deities. While this is different than what is done in ceremonial magic rituals, I think that they are appropriate in a Witchcraft or Pagan setting. This is just one other area where my Witchcraft teachings slightly differ from what is found in the Golden Dawn tradition.

While there is an invoking and banishing quality to drawing a pentagram device in the air, we will only be using the invoking pentagram for the rituals in this work. This is because we will be using vortex ritual structures in all of the rituals, and a vortex energy field cannot be banished. It can only be sealed with a sealing spiral. We will discuss more about that distinction later in this book (chapter 12).

Additionally, there are two more lines to be found on the pentagram device that we haven't yet covered. These are the lateral lines running diagonally under the two arms that we avoided using when drawing invoking or banishing pentagrams. There is one starting at the right foot and then drawing a line to the left upper arm point then proceeding to follow the line of the pentagram until the starting point is reached, then proceeding beyond it to end at the upper left arm point. That is the general banishing pentagram arc, also known as the lesser banishing pentagram.

There is another one that starts at the left foot, draws a line to the right upper arm point, and then proceeds to follow the line of the pentagram until the starting point is reached, where it then proceeds beyond it to end at the upper right arm point.

That is the general invoking pentagram arc, also known as the lesser invoking pentagram. These pentagrams have also been labeled as the spirit inferior and spirit superior pentagrams, but they don't involve the point of the pentagram that is attributed to spirit, so I have found this to be inconsistent with the basic rules for drawing a pentagram as I was taught them. Also, in the system of magic that I am presenting in this book there is no need for either the lesser invoking or banishing pentagrams.

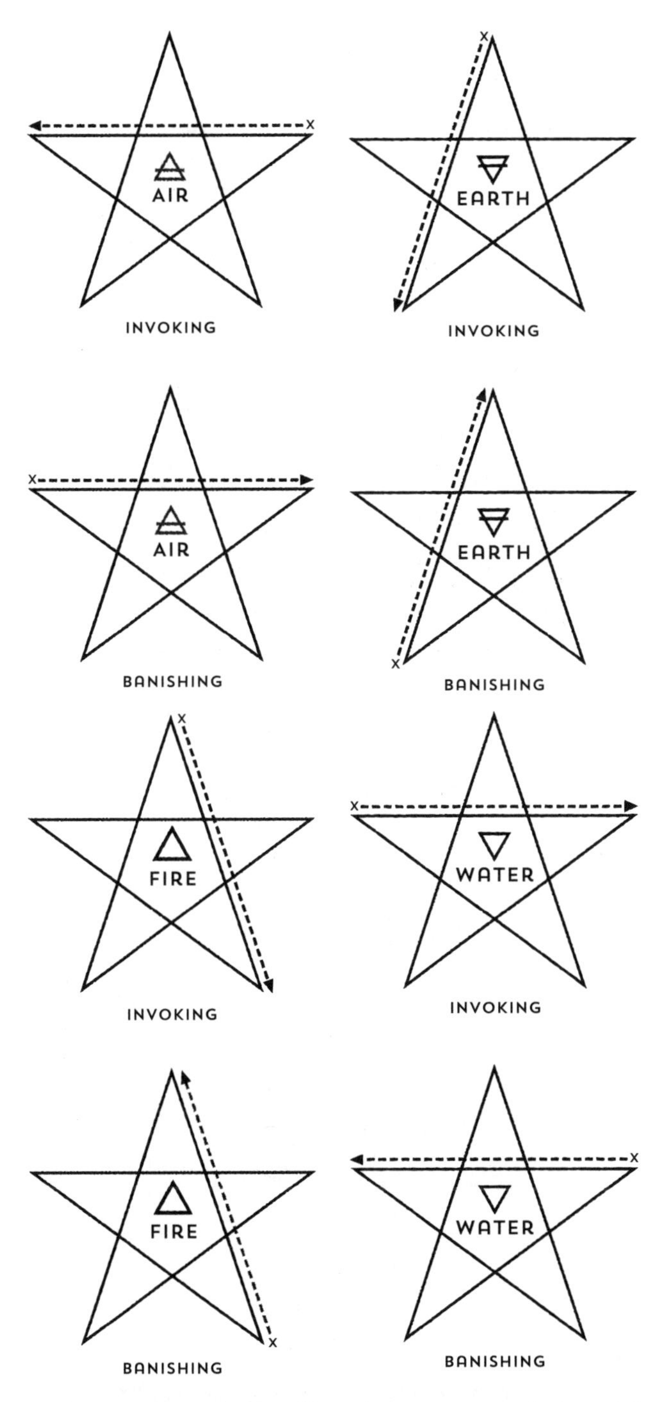

Diagrams showing the invoking and banishing pentagram devices with arrows

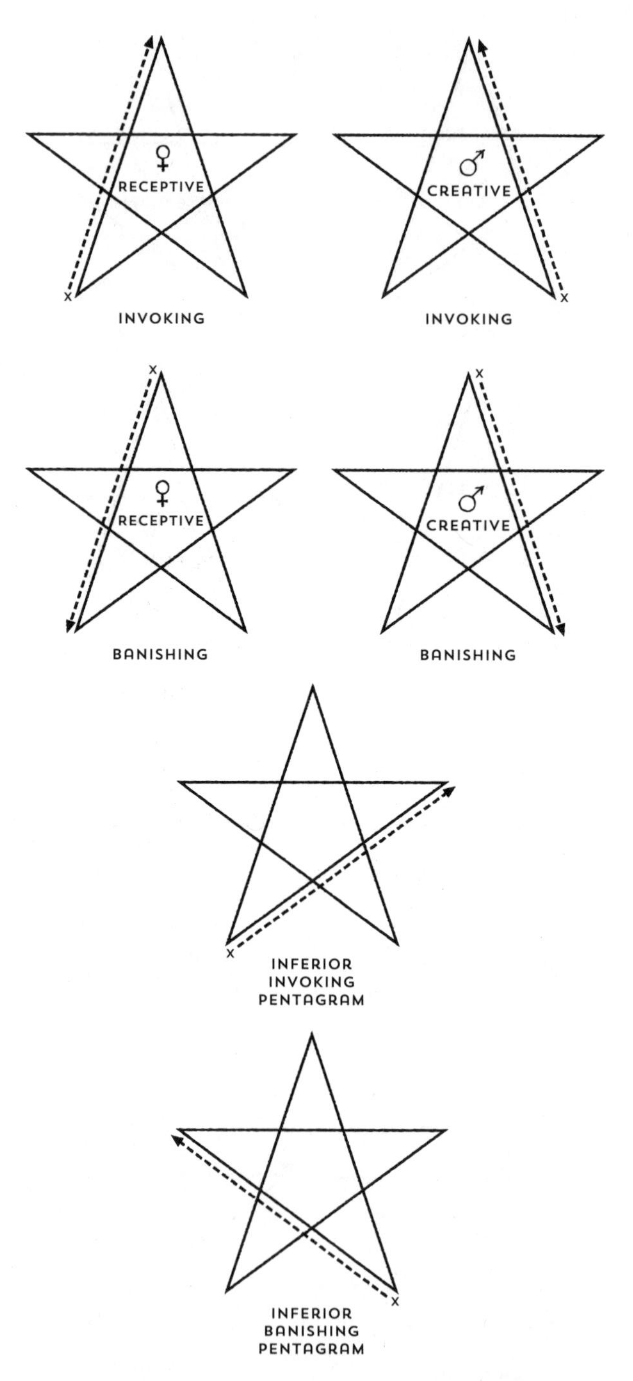

Diagrams showing the invoking and banishing pentagram devices with arrows countinued

While the methods that I have demonstrated differ from the device drawing directions as found in the Golden Dawn or other books on Witchcraft, I was taught these simple consistent rules in my Alexandrian coven for drawing the pentagram device and I have found that it works well for me. I don't believe that my way is the only way or that the Golden Dawn method is incorrect. I do believe that what is important is to use one specific method consistently. Doing that will basically achieve the same results regardless of the method used. You can choose to ignore what I am presenting here or consider it and possibly add it to your repertoire.

Inverted Pentagrams: An inverted pentagram, as opposed to the obverse pentagram that we are working with here, has a different meaning, but it is not what you might think it is. Conventionally, the inverted pentagram is a symbol of diabolism or the face of the Satanic goat and it is typically avoided by some Witches and Pagans. This is because it is defined as the dominance of the four elements over spirit, which is contrary to Christian doctrine. Since we are putting an invoking spiral around the pentagram after drawing it then that would make the pentagram device spin, so it would be both obverse and inverted as it spins, switching back and forth after it is drawn.

However, the inverted pentagram does not indicate diabolism. As the obverse pentagram symbolizes the ascent of matter into the One, the inverted pentagram is the opposite, which is the manifestation of the One within the four elements. It is a symbol of the materialization of spirit, so it would be defined as a kind of holy sacrament rather than a symbol of diabolism. To a Witch, this is the wine and cakes blessed by the Goddess and God. The inverted pentagram can be freely used without any guilt, and is used where needed in my own workings; but the supposed stigma is based on a nineteenth century superstition. If this were not true, then the Masonic Order of the Eastern Star would be diabolic, and so would a number of Islamic traditions and national flags, where the inverted pentagram along with the crescent moon is proudly displayed.

Rose Cross Device

Another important symbol that is used in element energy work is the rose cross. The cross used in this device is the five-part cross, consisting of four equal arms and an attached base. It is particular to Christianity as a symbol of that faith. Yet in a purely practical and magical expression it is an emblem of the five parts of the four elements and spirit joined together. When an invoking spiral is drawn in the center of it (clockwise, outer to inner), it represents the passion and love of the One for the many. It is a sign of creation representing the ascent of matter into spirit; it is similar in that respect to the pentagram.

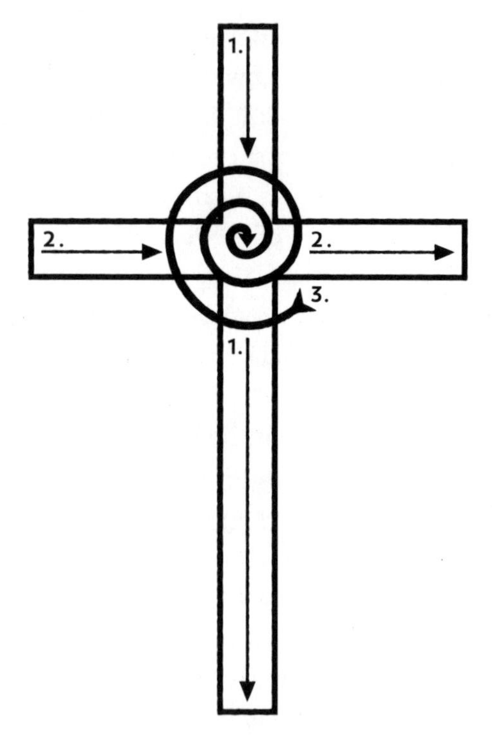

Diagram showing the drawing of the rose cross

We will use the rose cross to generate a powerful, solar-based, and aspiring energy field to work along with the element energy generated through the pentagram device. The rose cross is drawn with three strokes; the first from top to bottom for the body, then left to right for the cross piece, and finally, the invoking spiral in the center.

Organizing Principle for Elemental Magic

Now that we have covered the energy model of magic, the four elements and their correspondences, along with the magical symbol and device of the pentagram and the rose cross, we must now explore the organizing principle behind all of these components. The four elements, and their hybrid offshoots, the sixteen elementals and the forty qualified powers, are part of an overarching hierarchy, and they are all interrelated.

Typically, spirit lists and their associated qualities are to be found in some kind of grimoire or an extended Book of Shadows along with the rituals, regalia, and barbarous words of power to conjure them. Luckily for us, there is an amazingly powerful storehouse of symbols, archetypes, and analogies all linked together and beautifully illustrated in the modern tarot deck. Everything that you need except the rituals, regalia, and words of power are supplied by these seventy-eight illustrated cards. I will supply the rituals and describe the tools later in this work to complete the system of energy magic; for now, let us explore the images contained in the tarot, which are extremely useful.

Simple note: For the other elements of magic that you could use to fill out this system, I can tell you where to find the barbarous words of power that will greatly affect your work—if you want to use them. You can find them in books that I will reference later on in chapter 7. I didn't want to either infringe on copyrights or have to ask permission to reprint them in this work. This is also true for any of the magical seals for these spirits. You can use or skip them; the magic will still work. It is wholly a matter of magical esthetics.

The tarot succinctly ties all of the components of the four elements tightly together into an elegant and visually stunning occult system. In fact, the tarot functions as the most important and powerful grimoire that a Witch can possess, and nearly everyone at some point or another will own and use a deck for divination. Yet the Tarot also functions as an illustrated table of correspondences and as a repository of magical images that the Witch can use when she accesses the powers behind them—the various hosts of the element system.

Before we get into a more detailed discussion of each of the spirits associated with the four elements and their hierarchy and qualities as well the rituals and techniques to access them, we should understand the organizing principle behind it all. Therefore, we should examine the tarot with new eyes and a different approach that will show us how magical it is, and how integral it is to a mastery of the four elements.

Chapter Six

USING THE TAROT AS A BOOK OF SHADOWS

> It's said that the shuffling of the cards is the earth, and the pattering of the cards is the rain, and the beating of the cards is the wind, and the pointing of the cards is the fire. That's of the four suits. But the Greater Trumps, it's said, are the meaning of all process and the measure of the everlasting dance.
>
> —Charles Williams

In our present time of the post-modern era, the fad of using and incorporating grimoires from the Middle Ages and the Renaissance is supremely popular. It is probably one of the hottest topics around and numerous newly translated versions of these manuscripts are being published at a rapid pace. This fad is revealing previously obscure and unknown arcane grimoires to the adoring eyes of occult afficionados. Where grimoires are the exciting new thing in ceremonial magic, variations and additions to the Book of Shadows is a hot topic for Witches. It would seem that magicians and Witches have this fad in common with each other.

Yet this fad has overlooked probably one of the greatest grimoires or Book of Shadows of all time, a stupendous collection of occult lore and a powerful system of symbology all in one concise work, which I might add, is still very relevant today. What book is that, you might ask? Is it some new version of *The Greater Key of Solomon*, the *Lemegeton*, the *Grimoirium Verum*, Agrippa's *Four Books of Occult Philosophy*, a previously unknown Book of Shadows predating Gardner, or perhaps a book that no one has even heard of yet? No, it is the tarot, known in its time as the *Devil's Picture Book*.

In fact, I truly believe that the tarot is the greatest of all grimoires because it contains a veritable arsenal of magical knowledge, symbology, analogies, spiritual hierarchies, and the mechanism of transformation itself. Like other grimoires, it doesn't have everything that is needed to practice ritual or ceremonial magic, but it has all of the source material needed to formulate and build all of the other components. The tarot is the container of active symbolism for Western occultism as well as the master-key of those correspondences. In this chapter, I will cover both what the tarot is lacking as well as what is greatly abundant in it.

I can already hear your thoughts about this seemingly lame revelation: "The tarot is a divination tool, not a grimoire!" I have my reasons for making this statement and know a couple occultists—such as Lon Milo DuQuette and Aleister Crowley (the Beast himself)—would agree with my assessment.

If two of the notables in the field of magic and occultism agree with my declaration, then perhaps you may find that I am not in fact pulling your leg. I am quite serious about my hypothesis, and I think that you will agree (maybe) once I am done explaining myself.

First from Crowley:

> The Tarot is, thus, intimately bound up with the purely magical Arts of Invocation and Evocation.[15]

15. Aleister Crowley, *Book of Thoth: A Short Essay on the Tarot of the Egyptians, Being the Equinox Volume III No. V* (York Beach, ME: Weiser, 1969), 84.

Then from DuQuette:

> The Hebrew Qabalah forms the foundation upon which the Western Hermetic arts (astrology, tarot, geomancy, and the various branches of ceremonial magick) are constructed. The tarot is a visual representation of qabalistic fundamentals and is the common denominator between the various Hermetic arts. One could even say the tarot is the DNA of the Qabbalah. Properly decoded it reveals not only the mysteries of the Qabalah, but also that of all other Qabalah-based systems"[16]

Aleister Crowley and Lon Milo DuQuette respectively appear to perceive the tarot as not only a contiguous source of the Qabalah (as it is practiced and understood today by Western occultists), but that it's also a system of magic in and of itself. DuQuette even titled his book *Tarot of Ceremonial Magick,* and there have been others who have linked the two subjects in a very intimate way.

DuQuette wrote his book to show a very ceremonial magical perspective on the tarot, even putting together a hybrid of the two systems. However, I would go even further and state that they are already intimately related to each other, because the tarot contains everything that a decent grimoire should contain.

As for DuQuette's references to the Qabalah, I have found that the relationship of the tarot and the Qabalah symbologies are useful (if not somewhat contrived) to occultists and ceremonial magicians, but that the Jewish Kabbalistic tradition, both the antique and modern versions, omit the Tarot from their writings altogether. The merging of the two systems is something that occurred in the middle nineteenth century pushed by French Christian occultists (such as Éliphas Lévi and Papus) who had a fondness for the Marseille tarot deck. I believe that the ten pip cards in the Tarot deck more properly align to the Pythagorean symbolic meanings for the numbers 1 through 10 than the Qabalah.

So, what does a grimoire typically have within its pages? What would you expect to find if you went to all of the trouble and expense to buy one of the rarer, leather covered, coveted, and collectible grimoires that are being sold

16. Lon Milo DuQuette, *Tarot of Ceremonial Magick: A Pictorial Synthesis of Three Great Pillars of Magick*, (York Beach, ME: Red Wheel/Weiser, 1995), xxiv.

these days? Well, let's make a list. In fact, let's imagine the ideal grimoire, the very one that we would like to own but doesn't exist in the real world.

An ideal grimoire would contain rituals and ceremonies, words of barbarous evocation (the infamous *verba ignota* or unknown words), lists of tools, magic circle designs, and various other sorcerous regalia. It would also contain lists of spirits and the sigils, characters, and devices for conjuring them. It might contain some talismans and amulets for various uses as well as special prayers and rites for performing the necessary preparations of atonement and purification. For Witches, the book would be rumored to be a personal grimoire of Andrew D. Chumbley acquired from some unknown yet authentic antique source.

The book itself would be printed on nice heavy acid-free paper, housing all sorts of cool, colorful illustrations, a readable but archaic type face with lots of medieval looking graphics, a blood red leather or a snake skin cover, topped off with a metal frame with locking clasps. Maybe there would be the leering face of a demon embossed on the cover or some wicked looking arcane sigil, along with gold leaf sparingly applied to the title. A typical geek sorcerer would pay a week's IT salary for such a book, maybe even more. Just opening the book would be a cause for concern, and there would be lurid tales about its misuse or careless handling.

Now that I have listed what an ideal grimoire would look like and contain, I understand that someone might say, "None of that stuff is found in any tarot deck; how can it be considered a grimoire?" I agree somewhat—the tarot doesn't contain any specific spells, incantations, talismans, sigils, characters, barbarous words of evocation, or anything like that.

What the tarot *does* contain are other things that are just as important, such as all of the symbology and associated spiritual hierarchies for most of the systems of magic in the Western Mystery tradition. It contains an active methodology for personal transformation, and it is protected by a powerful angelic or demigod guiding intelligence who can be accessed to answer any question or pierce any mystery.

The tarot is a living system of magic and mysticism, so it could also function like any other magical book or manuscript. It may not have everything needed to practice ritual or ceremonial magic, but then quite a number of grimoires appear to be incomplete as well, even though in the end, the determined magician or Witch will have assiduously filled in all the omissions and blanks. For this work, I will supply all of the missing ingredients needed to perform the energy workings.

So, my point is that the tarot is a grimoire, plain and simple. Now let's get down to showing how that is a fact and not some obscure idea that I have pulled out of my ear to obfuscate or amuse you.

Some Tarot History

The origins of the tarot date to the late fifteenth century, and it has evolved, been copied, changed, and revised over time into the form that we know and take for granted today. However, something happened to it in the late seventeenth or early eighteenth century in France. The artist who crafted the Marseille tarot deck changed the tarot from a fancy and expensive card game deck to something magical, philosophic, and occultic. No one knows the identity of the artist who made this substantive change, but it was at this time that the tarot deck was greatly embellished with occultic and magical symbols and themes, especially the trumps. Coincidentally, that period of time was also when most of the more famous grimoires were penned or published.

As said earlier, this put into place the eventual adaption of the tarot into the Qabalah and thence into the workings of modern Ceremonial Magic. While Lévi and Papus started this process, it was completed by Mathers, Westcott, and Crowley. However, you don't need to know the Qabalah in order to use the tarot as a magical source or vice versa, and we shall not be going in that direction in this work.

I have said that the Tarot is a magician's arsenal, and this is what it contains in a pictorial form with lots of symbols, images, analogies, and designs giving it a power and animation that other occult manuscripts or books might lack. Let us look at the five structures within the Tarot to view all that it contains.

Five Functional Groupings of the Tarot

There are five major groupings within the tarot, and each represents a powerful system of magic all by itself.

1. The four aces represent the divine tetrad of the four elements; from these, all manifestation proceeds. They can also be seen to represent

the four cardinal directions that define the domain or world of the Witch, functioning as watchtowers in some systems of magic (such as my own). Associated with them are a plethora of symbolic attributes, probably representing the first key of correspondences that any budding occultist or magician attempts to master. We have already covered the four elements, but I might also add that the four aces are the four domains of the four elements, and reigning over those four domains are the four kings or emperors. In order to access the elemental powers of the tarot we must first contact and engage these four principals.

2. The sixteen court cards or dignitaries, as they are sometimes called because they depict a feudal power structure associated with the four elements and have an entire hierarchy of powers, spirits, and domains within the inner planes associated with them. The court cards represent the forces that the Witch will wield to acquire that which she desires to manifest in the material plane. Implicit in this system is the lunation cycle that consists of eight phases and directs the temporal waxing and waning of psychic forces, both collectively and individually. This is an entire system of magic all by itself. One could even tie in the sixteen Enochian calls or keys to add even more intensity to a magical system devoted to the elementals, and I encourage the practitioner to examine these barbarous words of power and possibly add them to the Elemental Octagram rite (chapter 12).
3. The thirty-six pip cards of the lesser arcana are associated with the astrological decan, and the Pythagorean mystical numbers 2 through 10 as projected through the four elements. The thirty-six pip cards are also said to contain within them gateways into yet another matrix of the inner planes. The decans consist of ten-degree facets of the 360-degree wheel of the zodiac, and they contain a planetary intelligence (the ruler), a zodiacal quality, and a powerful elemental energy.
4. If the four aces are added back to the thirty-six pip cards to produce an array of forty cards in all then a new structure is revealed, the forty qualified powers. These forty qualified powers represent a matrix of both magical powers and spiritual intelligences, being therefore a

combination of mystical number attributes and the four powers of the elements. The ritual of the Pyramid of Power rite generates this kind of power, and I have found it to be highly adaptable and useful in many magical applications (chapter 12).

5. Finally, the twenty-two trumps of the major arcana represent two concurrent cycles of transformation—the transcendental initiation of the individual spiritual seeker (in seventeen steps), and the transformation of the world and the universe at large (in five steps)—the cosmogonic cycle.

The seventeen stages of individual transformation are modeled on the stages of the mythic Hero's Journey that represents the cycle of psychic regeneration, where the self undergoes internal dissolution and reconstitution. It is a form of psychological death and rebirth that is typical of a transformative initiation. Each of these seventeen stages can be matched to seventeen of the trumps in the major arcana of the tarot, making it a powerful illustrative representation of the greater mysteries of personal transcendence. Human nature, as it is understood, must undergo many cathartic and profound changes to ultimately become prepared for the ultimate mystery, union with the One.

Added to the seventeen stages of the Hero's Journey is the greater cosmogonic cycle—the mythic and never-ending cycle of birth and death of the whole world as it passes through the four stages or epochs of the elements. The fifth element in this cycle is, of course, the indivisible union that is eternal, immortal, changeless, and perfect. The cosmogonic cycle merges with the Hero's Journey as the vision or boon that the hero receives upon achieving his ultimate apotheosis. He is given the vision of the cosmogonic cycle and his destiny or place within it.

These two mysteries, one individual and the other cosmic, join together to forge the twenty-two steps of the initiation cycle. The Witch may use it to not only ascertain her own current spiritual disposition, but may deliberately use this archetypal cycle to foster a state of transformation. In this manner, the twenty-two keys of the major arcana represent the Witch's mastery of her own personal transformation and spiritual evolution. There are few if any grimoires that can give the individual Witch such a powerful tool to be used in whatever manner imagined—its use is nearly unlimited and its effects, most profound.

Over this great array of archetypal symbols, analogies, hierarchy of spirits, magical powers, and domains of the inner spiritual planes is the presiding genius of the tarot, called Hru by members of the Golden Dawn and Aleister Crowley, the great angel set over the living and secret wisdom of the greater and lesser arcana.[17]

This entity is a very powerful spirit residing in the tarot—it is also the guide, guardian, and secret initiator of the Hermetic path of magic and mysticism. It is to this great spirit one is directed to seek out all knowledge that is yet unknown, obscure, or omitted from that which one knows.

Whatever is missing or omitted from the "great grimoire" of the tarot will be discovered through meditation, divination, and an active spiritual and magical research. We can be certain that all questions will ultimately be answered and all mysteries revealed through the power and majesty of this being. One need only consult with it in a regular, periodic, and consistent fashion. Few grimoires can boast of an active spiritual guide and superior entity who will come to the aid of anyone who takes the book (as the tarot cards) and simply summons its presence. The only exception that comes to mind is the spirit Scirlan, who presides over the True Grimoire.

So, now we can see that everything that is essential and necessary to the profitable work of magic is to be found in the tarot. If one were bereft of all books, tools, and even a place to work magic, having possession of a tarot deck would suffice to mastering all of the rest of the occult arts.

To recap, the tarot contains the following symbolic systems:

10 mystical symbolic numbers of Pythagoras

22 stages of transformative initiation

12 signs of the zodiac

7 planets

4 elements

16 elementals

36 decans

40 qualified powers

---

17. Crowley, *Book of Thoth*, 250.

All that a Witch needs in addition to the tarot are the rituals, techniques, words of power, barbarous words of evocation, sigils, spirit characters, and tools to practice basic energy workings. All of these topics will be reviewed later in this book; for the moment, I give you the gift of seeing the tarot with all of the imagery, mystery, and wisdom as the greater tool of magic to be used not only for divination but also for conjuring spirits and projecting magical powers into the world. May you use it with great good fortune.

Chapter Seven

SIXTEEN ELEMENTALS

> The appearance of things change according to the emotions, and thus we see magic and beauty in them, while the magic and beauty are really in ourselves.
>
> —Kahlil Gibran

> Watson: "Holmes, who could have done this deed?"
> Holmes: "Elementals, my dear Watson, Elementals!"

In the energy model of magic, the elementals are hybrid elements consisting of paired groupings of single elements to create a more articulated expression of magical power. It must be remembered that magical energy is defined as the agency that causes the transformation of consciousness and aids in the overall expansion of self-awareness, spiritual growth, and also the successful deployment of powers in the material world. Magical energy, of course, is used for self-empowerment or for the empowerment of a goal. So, it can be plainly stated that the more precise the definition of that quality of magical energy is then the more optimal will be its outcome in a magical working.

For example, water is the element generally associated with feelings and emotions. If you were to work a love spell that would assist you in attracting a mate, then just using the element of water might not do the job because it is too general. However, qualifying water with, say, earth (earth of water) to express love and sexual attraction would certainly be more helpful. A more qualified and specific energy raised in a magical working will greatly assist the outcome. Keep in mind that the message is the desired magical outcome, but the energy raised is what embodies the magical link. A precise energy is very advantageous to a successful magical working.

The elemental spirits affect consciousness through a person's emotions, so the quality of the elementals is expressed in terms of human emotional experiences. This is because the elemental spirits operate close to the earth plane, giving form to feeling and substance to psychic activity. Because many human motives are based on emotions and the day to day activities are colored by emotions, we are subject to the elementals and their dynamic interaction at all times. Deliberately deploying them for a magical working gives the Witch the ability to manipulate her own feelings and emotions, influencing those who are around her. An elemental spirit is also an energy field, and in fact, the two are synonymous; summoning one always brings about an emotional charge of energy through a spirit interface.

Through the application and use of an elemental spirit, a Witch can either empower herself or a focused objective with an emotional based energy. It bestows a kind of confidence (control) and insight (penetration) into oneself or upon a goal that is greatly enhanced, allowing for a more successful outcome. Since there are sixteen emotional-based energies that a Witch might call upon for any given operation, the utility is nearly endless. Magical energy helps to bend probabilities so that desired outcomes occur, and they also empower, enhance, and build up the practitioner who uses them. Working with elementals always has a double benefit to those who use them, including benefits such as self-empowerment and material success.

Elemental Spirits of the *Theurgia-Goetia*

As we have seen, the sixteen elementals are associated with the tarot's sixteen court cards, representing a kind of feudal hierarchy. Yet there is another hierarchy that we can associate with the elemental spirits, one that comes from the early Renaissance grimoire, the *Theurgia-Goetia*. I have incorporated this lore in order to provide a spirit name for a focus and as a way of bringing all the elemental correspondences together. An alternative would be to focus and repeat the key word if you want to forgo using these spirits, but I think that this approach lacks the depth of using a spirit name for the elemental. (In my time, I have tried it both ways.)

The spirits of the *Theurgia-Goetia* which appear in the second book of the *Lemegeton* (Lesser Key of Solomon), are reputed to be wind demons arrayed in a hierarchical structure.[18] That hierarchical structure consists of three stations: emperor, prince, and duke. Dukes and princes serve one or more of the four emperors. The princes are considered outliers, since they are not part of the tight relationship between emperor and duke. The four emperors and the sixteen grand dukes reside within the structure of the four elements and the sixteen elementals.

The *Lemegeton* has a curious history in that it was invented in the mid-seventeenth century with the assembling of various manuscripts from older magical traditions. For instance, the *Goetia*, the first book in that collection, was cobbled together from a manuscript that was originally penned by Johan Weyer, a student of Agrippa, and a grimoire named the *Heptameron*. The *Theurgia-Goetia* was taken from a manuscript written by the sage and teacher of Agrippa named Trithemius. That source manuscript was the *Steganographia* (circa early sixteenth century), which contained the system of spirits we are using for the four elements and the sixteen elementals.

Some of the artifacts found in the *Steganographia* were not present in the *Theurgia-Goetia*, such as the magical seals and the barbarous words of evocation. The *Steganographia* has not yet been translated and published in the English language. Therefore, my source book for these spirits comes from a manuscript version of the *Lemegeton* in the possession of Dr. Thomas Rudd, in the early eighteenth century, published by Stephen Skinner and David Rankine. Skinner and Rankine have pulled together elements from both the *Lemegeton* and its earlier precursor, the *Steganographia*, into their book.

According to the lore as stated in the grimoire, the spirits of the *Theurgia-Goetia* were believed to consist of both good and evil entities. Since they were aerial and associated with the turbulent winds, some were even considered to be dangerous. However, it would seem that there was no indication as to why

---

18. Skinner and Rankine, *Dr Rudd*, 34–37.

some were considered good and others inherently evil due to the meager information supplied with the original manuscript. It does not distinguish between good and evils spirits.

Since these spirits are associated with the four winds and the sixteen directions in which the wind might travel, it must be assumed that such a power is actually neutral since it could be used for good or ill depending on the velocity and the turbulence that sets such a spirit in motion. Like the weather itself, some storms are beneficial, helping to clear the air and give life to all of nature, while others are destructive and terrible when they are unleashed to their full negative potential.

I would assume that since the Witch is the one *stirring* and setting into motion one of these spirits, the quality of the spirit and the outcome of its use will be solely determined by her intent. Passions, anger, hatred, violence, or the desire for ill would certainly stir the invoked spirit to do evil (as is the manner of actual storms in nature), while conversely self-control and a desire to aid, heal, or give life motivates the invoked spirit to do good. Thus, it is entirely up to the Witch who unleashes this spirit whether it will do good or evil. This is, of course, the nature of Witchcraft at its core—the intention can often be the sole motivator in a spell.

Therefore, in examining the qualities of the sixteen elemental spirits, we will merge the lore of the Spirits of the *Theurgia-Goetia* with that of the sixteen court cards and the sixteen elemental energy fields.

If you want to use these spirits as the names for your sixteen elementals, here are some considerations that you might find useful.

- The spirits are invoked to either project or receive their associated energetic qualities. What this means is that you may absorb the quality of the spirit into your being and receive the benefit that it offers directly onto your person. You may also project that quality into another person, thing (talisman), or a group to cause a specific outcome to occur. You can also seek to acquire or fetch something that is associated with the spirit's purview, but usually this is automatically accomplished with one of the servitor spirits. You don't have to either know or summon the servitor for the fetch to be successful.

- These spirits cannot help you to acquire or gain undeserved merits, riches, or achievements. It must be understood that anything that you might target using one of these spirits must also be achievable by your own hand or be within the realm of possibility. These spirits will help you bend probabilities so that you can achieve something that you desire to happen, but they cannot cause outright miracles or highly unlikely outcomes.
- Offerings to these spirits are suggested if you are approaching them in a more traditional grimoire-based manner, both for the target spirit and the four emperors. I would recommend that the token seals of the emperors be regularly charged with incense offerings whenever a circle is cast, and the target spirit should be offered a specific incense associated with one of the four elements when it is needed in a working. Incense is the proper offering to an aerial spirit. This is, of course, an esthetic embellishment that is typically not required.

Now that we have derived as much structure and meaning as is possible from this antique system of magic, let us examine an appropriate and useful list of spirits and their associated functions.

Elemental Magical Spirits—4 Emperors and 16 Grand Dukes

The four Emperors are ritually invoked and set to the four directions using their seals. You could also add the supplemental invocations as supplied from the *Steganographia*, which can be found in the book *The Goetia of Dr. Rudd*,[19] but they are not required for this work. You also don't need the seals either. Another approach that you could do is to make a simple angular sigil using the English Alphabet wheel, if you want the esthetics for invoking a spirit. *However, just saying the name of the spirit repeatedly in the magical working will summon that spirit because spirits of the elements are close to the earth.*

Therefore, to work this system of magic using these spirits you should always invoke the four Emperors as part of the ritual structure and then the established spiritual hierarchy below them. I can quickly describe their nature and function

19. For the qualities of the four Emperors and the supplemental conjurations, see Skinner and Rankine, *Dr Rudd*, 215–222.

here. They are directly related to the four Elements (and the four winds and their associated lesser Greek gods). What we will be more interested in examining are the functions and characteristics of the sixteen grand dukes.

Four Elemental Emperors and Their Invoking Seals[20]

Air: Carmasiel (Carnesiel)—ruler of the eastern quadrant—air—color: yellow—wind god: Eurus—incense offering: galbanum, mastic, anise. (Volition, activity).

Fire: Caspiel—ruler of the southern quadrant—fire—color: red—wind god: Notus—incense offering: dragon's blood, red sandalwood, olibanum. (Wisdom, knowledge).

Water: Ameradiel—ruler of the western quadrant—water—color: blue—wind god: Zephyrus—incense offering: lotus, myrrh, onycha, lavender. (Internal perceptions, feelings).

Earth: Demoriel—ruler of the northern quadrant—earth—color: green—wind god: Boreas—incense offering: storax, musk, copal, patchouli. (Growth, acquisition, life force).

Elemental Grand Dukes

Base Element: Fire—wisdom, knowledge—southern quadrant

Air of Fire: Godiel—pursuit of knowledge, desire to know, thirst for knowledge, act of seeking, sensing and detecting subtle phenomenon.

Earth of Fire: Maseriel—application of knowledge, past experiences, pragmatic outlook or perspective, structural understanding, organization.

Fire of Fire: Barmiel—inspiration, insight, ideals, ethics, moral guidance, breakthrough, reformation of past opinions and beliefs.

Water of Fire: Asyriel—intuition, inner subjective perception of truth, gnosis, spiritual knowledge, introspection, affirmation of faith.

20. For the magical seals of the four emperors, see Skinner and Rankine, *Dr Rudd,* 215–221. Alternately, the seals are available online at Joseph H. Peterson's Esoteric Archives website (accessed December 2, 2020): http://www.esotericarchives.com/solomon/theurgia.htm.

Base Element: Water—internal perceptions, feelings—western quadrant

Air of Water: Cabariel—restlessness, inner stirring, seeking through feeling, emotional regeneration, revitalization of interests and pursuits.

Earth of Water: Dorochiel—lust, sexual desire, manifestation of wishes and desires, fantasy, crystallization of one's intuitive needs, possible obsession upon fulfillment of desires.

Fire of Water: Usiel—the desire to give love selflessly, compassion and understanding, the quest for spiritual union, emotional purification.

Water of Water: Malgaras—sensitivity, emotional empathy, psychic and supernatural phenomena, emotional healing and restoration, deep insight into other individuals.

Base Element: Air—volition, activity—eastern quadrant

Air of Air: Pamersiel—action, extreme decisiveness, pursuit of activity, communication, clarity of perception, dispeller of illusion and falsehood.

Earth of Air: Camuel—discipline, structured or planned action, purposeful activity, goal pursuit, expression of one's personal self or identity, self-discovery, self-control.

Fire of Air: Padiel—self direction, self-motivation, realization of one's purpose in life or in any given situation, understanding one's inner motivations.

Water of Air: Aschiel (Aseliel)—fantasy, pursuit of illusion for artistic expression, tapping the well-spring of the imagination, the strong desire to express one's inner perceptions.

Base Element: Earth—growth, acquisition, the life force—northern quadrant

Air of Earth: Armadiel—work, building, growth of ambitions, realization of goals through a step by step methodical process, perceiving the method of achieving of one's goals.

Earth of Earth: Rasiel—physical regeneration, healing, self-grounding, medium of physical manifestation of psychic phenomenon, the desire to procreate or heal (medical restoration).

Fire of Earth: Baruchas—responsibility, understanding the meaning of life in simplistic and basic terms, stewardship of the land, farming, giving of beneficial (monetary) assistance.

Water of Earth: Symiel—fertility, physical growth, fruitfulness, intuitive understanding of individual physical needs, feeding, nurturing, giving of life (birth or rebirth).

Working with the Elementals

To work with the sixteen elementals, you will first need to use the Elemental Octagon rite described in chapter 12. There are some additional components that you can use, but there is one obligatory item required for performing this rite.

You will need a consecrated parchment for the sigil that represents your intention to use along with invoking the elemental. You can make a consecrated parchment talisman bearing the seal for the emperor and grand duke drawn on it purely for enhanced esthetics.[21] If you opt for the embellishments you can put the sigil for the intention and the seals for the emperor and grand duke all on a single consecrated parchment to be used one time. (We will briefly discuss how to consecrate a talisman or a sigil in chapter 9.)

The sixteen grand dukes also have their own specific invocation consisting of barbarous words of evocation to summon them. While each one of these invocations is short in duration, you might find pronouncing the unfamiliar words to be challenging at first, and of course, practicing them is important before attempting to use one of them. Using this kind of invocation adds some extra intensity when summoning one of these entities, but it is not necessary since it is an esthetic affectation that is not critical to the success of the actual working. All you need to do is to say the spirit's name repeatedly in the magical working.

Another alternative, you can use one of the sixteen Enochian keys to invoke the elemental energies and you can use one of the sixteen court cards in the

---

21. For the seals of the 16 Grand Dukes and their servitors, in addition to supplemental conjurations to summon them, see Skinner and Rankine, *Dr Rudd*, 223–277.

tarot to represent the grand duke you are summoning.[22] Using the tarot card would be helpful, but intoning the Enochian key would be an esthetic choice. Incidentally, if Enochian magic is something that you would like to integrate into your elemental workings, there are also the divine name pairs that rule over sub-elements that could be used instead of the spirit names of the grand dukes. The qualities of the sixteen elementals would not change, only the spirit names would be different. I have also used these Enochian divine name pairs for the names of the elemental spirits and have seen good results.

Here is a table showing the correspondences between elemental key word, tarot card, Enochian divine name pairs ruling the sub-elements, and Enochian key or call.

Elemental	Grand Duke	Keyword	Tarot Card	Enochian Divine Name Pairs	Enochian Key
Fire of Fire	Barmiel	Insight	King of Wands	Rzionr Nrzfm	6
Water of Fire	Asyriel	Intuition	Queen of Wands	Vadali Obava	17
Air of Fire	Godiel	Learning	Knight of Wands	Noalmr Oloag	16
Earth of Fire	Maserial	Organization	Page of Wands	Volxdo Sioda	18
Fire of Water	Usiel	Compassion	King of Cups	Iaaasd Atapa	12
Water of Water	Malgaras	Empathy	Queen of Cups	Nelapr Omebb	4
Air of Water	Cabariel	Regeneration	Knight of Cups	Obgota Aabco	10
Earth of Water	Dorochiel	Lust	Page of Cups	Maladi Olaad	11

22. Aleister Crowley, *Gems from the Equinox*, ed. Israel Regardie, (York Beach, ME: Weiser, 1975), 412–427.

Elemental	Grand Duke	Keyword	Tarot Card	Enochian Divine Name Pairs	Enochian Key
Fire of Air	Padiel	Realization	King of Swords	Aourrz Aloai	9
Water of Air	Aschiel	Imagination	Queen of Swords	Llacza Palam	7
Air of Air	Pamersiel	Decisive	Knight of Swords	Idoigo Ardza	3
Earth of Air	Camuel	Discipline	Page of Swords	Aiaoai Oiiit	8
Fire of Earth	Barushas	Responsible	King of Discs	Spmnir Llpiz	15
Water of Earth	Symiel	Fertility	Queen of Discs	Anaeem Sondn	14
Air of Earth	Armadiel	Work	Knight of Discs	Angpoi Unnax	13
Earth of Earth	Rasiel	Healing	Page of Discs	Cbalpt Arbiz	5

Chapter Eight

FORTY QUALIFIED POWERS

> Logic only gives man what he needs ... Magic gives him what he wants.
>
> —Tom Robbins

The forty qualified powers are the energies behind the forty pip cards in the lesser arcana of the tarot. We can break these forty into a set of four aces and thirty-six numbered cards. These correspond to two different number-based structures: the four base-elements and the thirty-six astrological decans. Each decan represents a ten-degree arc in its respective zodiac sign, and they have been used in both Egyptian and Assyrian-Babylonian astronomy. There are three decans to each sign of the zodiac, and there are nine decans for each of the four elements.

Another way of dividing up this number is to examine the Pythagorean number mysticism for the numbers from one to ten and then qualify each with one of the four elements, thereby producing forty qualified powers. We will use both methods to determine the quality of each magical energy. Yet the forty tarot cards perhaps best represent the symbolic quality evident in each. The Waite-Smith deck actually features vignettes on each card that help convey the mythic background associated with it. I have found that using all of these qualifications help to define each of the qualified powers. Since we are dealing with forty qualities instead of just sixteen, there is a greater variety of archetypical human circumstances to apply these energies to.

Where the sixteen elementals are energies that affect the emotions, the qualified powers affect the mind and material circumstances of the practitioner, making it a very effective energy to harness. The spirits associated with these forty qualified powers are the four emperors (associated with the elemental spirit hierarchy), and the angels of the thirty-six decans. However, there are a lot of different spirits associated with each decan, a sum that includes the thirty-six decan gods and goddesses of the Egyptian underworld pantheon. There are ruling planets for each decan, which would represent a kind of planetary intelligence, and there is the quality of the ten-degree segment of the zodiacal sign to which the decan is associated. However, we are concerned with just the energies associated with each of these qualified powers even though the planetary ruler and the astrological sign cannot be eliminated or ignored for deeper insights into the qualified powers.

What we should focus on first are the ten sacred numbers used as the qualifiers of the four elements. We have already covered the four elements in great detail, so we should just examine the symbolic qualities of the ten numbers since this kind of symbology can also be found in other systems, such as the Qabalah.

Pythagorean System of Ten Numbers

While only fragments exist of the teachings of the mystery school of the Pythagoreans, one of the areas of knowledge that has come down to us over two millennia was a system of numerology still in use today. It was likely embellished and extended considerably over time to become an occult discipline unto itself. How this system looked in antiquity when it was practiced by the Pythagoreans is not actually known, but we can imagine that it was extensive just based on what we have today.

Writing in depth on numerology is not something I will attempt to do in this work, but we can at least examine the symbolic qualities of the ten numbers and that should be sufficient. To that end, I will consult with three books on numerology in order to get a precise idea of what the ten numbers mean and also how they were used in defining the four aces and the numbered cards in the lesser arcana of the tarot.[23]

I will also consult with Aleister Crowley on his *Book of Thoth* entries for each of the numbered cards, since he appears to be the only one in all of the tarot books that I possess who actually looks at each of the numbers distinct from the specific cards.[24] Like many occultists, Crowley was wedded to the idea that the numbered cards represent the ten sephiroth in the Qabalistic Tree of Life. I believe that it is better to use definitions that we have from numerology and then add to them some of the definitions that Crowley described for the numbered cards.

The Pythagoreans believed that numbers were the most basic elements of the material world and that everything could be reduced to mathematics. They were astonishingly more correct in their presumption than even they might have imagined back then. With the advances in hard sciences during our present era, nearly everything that is physical is reducible to mathematical models, laws, and theorems, including the stochastic phenomena outlined by chaos theory.

Still, the Pythagoreans would have been dismayed by our approach to the universe as a thing of material substance with no life or soul beyond complex biological beings. To the Pythagoreans, the universe itself was a living and breathing being, both in a material and a spiritual sense. Numbers were not dry facts to them; they were inspirational quanta that expressed a deeper spiritual meaning about everything.

Let us now examine each of these ten mystical numbers to see how they can be directly applied as the qualifiers to the forty qualified powers. I would like to make some comments about the structure that I am proposing for these numbers.

First, I see these ten numbers as three triads of spirit, mind, and soul with an additional number (ten) representing the material world as the body. Some

---

23. David A. Phillips, *The Complete Book of Numerology: Discovering the Self* (Carlsbad, CA: Hay House, 1992), 6–8; Hans Decoz, *Numerology: Key to Your Inner Self* (New York: Perigree, 1994), 13–14; and Manoj Kumar, *Principles of Pythagorean Numerology* (New Delhi: Educreation Publishing, 2018), eBook, chapter 2.

24. Crowley, *Book of Thoth*, 178–189.

numerology sources also conceptualize such a division.[25] Most texts, however, don't have any entries for the number ten, but I think that we can use some common occult knowledge available today to derive definitions for that number.

Secondly, while the modern numerologists see the nine numbers as being represented by either an archetypically masculine (creative) or a feminine (receptive) gender, I would like to propose that we consider three of these nine numbers to be neutral or consisting of both genders, starting with the number one. The tenth number would also be neutral since it combines both the archetypal masculine and feminine. The basic rule of thumb laid down by Pythagoras is that even numbers are archetypically feminine and odd numbers are masculine. Still, I believe that the ten numbers transition from archetypically neutral, to feminine, and then to masculine, which is similar to what is written about the ten sephiroth in the Qabalah (except it goes from neutral to masculine and then feminine).

While my methodology might be a bit different than what numerologists and Qabalists propose, I think it works best with the levels of spirit, mind, soul, and finally, body. In taking this position, I am actually integrating both the Qabalistic and Pythagorean perspectives into a system that I believe works best for the numbered tarot cards. My reason for doing this is that I feel that merely applying the Qabalah to the tarot is ad hoc and not particularly neat and satisfying. I find that marriage of systems to be more derivative than descriptive.

Finally, the specific symbolic correspondences that I am attributing to the ten numbers are drawn from my own work and research. Each number has some basic qualities distilled from the four different sources cited above, but the symbol image and the Greek deity are my own attributions. I am certain that you could use a different arrangement or even substitute out a different pantheon. I chose the classical Greek pantheon because most people are familiar with it.

Triad of Spirit—Highest Ideals

Number 1: root of the four elements, spirit, individualism, independence, beginning, source, innovation (neutral). Keyword: leadership. Symbol: circle. Concept: union. Greek deity: Zeus

25. Phillips, *Complete Book of Numerology*, 9.

Number 2: original harmonious state, sensitivity, intuitive, cooperation, diplomacy, advice, or prophecy (receptive). Keyword: diplomacy. Symbol: light. Concept: creation. Greek deity: Hera

Number 3: stability, foundation, understanding, mediation, agreement, inspiration (creative). Keyword: inspiration. Symbol: eye. Concept: mitigation. Greek deity: Poseidon

Triad of Mind—The Inner Self

Number 4: solidification and manifestation, beauty, order, precision, honesty, trust, conservation (receptive). Keyword: order. Symbol: cross. Concept: compassion. Greek deity: Aphrodite

Number 5: revolution, stresses of change, freedom, dynamic, versatile, adaptable, problem solving (creative). Keyword: adaptable. Symbol: staff. Concept: resolution. Greek deity: Ares

Number 6: Mind within harmony and balance, creativity, sympathetic, healing, serenity (neutral). Keyword: harmony. Symbol: mirror. Concept: identity. Greek deity: Apollo

Triad of Soul/Emotions—The Feeling Self

Number 7: knowledge and discipline gained through suffering, seeking inner truth, contemplation, meditation, the inner life, wisdom, introspection (creative). Keyword: truth. Symbol: heart. Concept: mystery. Greek deity: Hermes

Number 8: adjustment towards internal balance, intuitive wisdom, independence, ambitious, persevering, visionary (receptive). Keyword: perseverance. Symbol: scroll. Concept: sagacity. Greek Deity: Athena

Number 9: Crystallization of mind and matter, sacred number of "perfection," altruistic service, responsible, brilliance, synthesis (neutral). Keyword: genius. Symbol: star. Concept: dreams. Greek Deity: Artemis

Material Point of Manifestation—The Body and the World

Number 10: Materialization, impermanence, constant change, completion and totality, reflection of the One, the divine tetractys, sum of the numbers one through four, contains the tetrad as the four elements (neutral). Keyword: fullness. Symbol: flower. Concept: world. Greek Deity: Hades

I would recommend working out the qualities for the ten numbers so that they match your own tradition and spiritual approach. I have used Greek deities to qualify these numbers, but it would be good to select your own ten deities or god-like attributes to associate with the ten numbers. This is because we use the attributes of the deities to help define and determine the qualified powers. Keep in mind that deities can have contradicting qualities and characters, so the match between deity and number will likely never be perfect.

Explanation of the Qualified Powers

The qualified powers represent a matrix of the ten mystical numbers (an aspect of the deity) and the four elements (the scale of manifested reality). This matrix is then organized into a table of forty correspondences that list all of the spiritual qualities of life, representing the archetypal and dynamic processes that link these forty powers with the symbology of the tarot. Each of these forty qualified powers are magically expressed by one of the pip cards in the lesser arcana. Each of these three components represent different qualities, but the qualified power is a synthesis of all three.

These numbered cards in the tarot represent the archetypal qualities of life in its various states using symbolic vignettes. They qualify each of the forty powers and they are the key to these powers. It is through the ritual pattern of the Pyramid of Power (found in chapter 12) that one of these qualified powers is actualized and manifested into the Witch's dynamic field of consciousness; but the cards of the lesser arcana also provide the symbolism and colorful images.

Qualified powers are defined as the cross correspondences of the ten mystic numbers and the four elements, as previously stated. The numbers are also grouped into three triads and the body, and this adds a hierarchical level to each group of numbers and how they relate to the individual and the cosmos. Therefore, there is spirit, mind, soul, and body.

Each number has the additional qualities of being creative, receptive, or neutral, acquired from its element and the number itself. The archetypal qualities of gender also cross into the combination of number and element to engender each of the forty powers. The exception is, of course, with the mystic number one, which has no creative or receptive quality and expresses the pure genderless quality of the element.

The four aces are considered without this polarity, being both creative and receptive and yet neither at the same time. The number six, although it is an even number making it receptive, has the qualities of assuming the multifold Self (Ego), which can assume either creative or receptive characteristics. The nature of Identity (the outward mask) is essentially polysexual, since it can assume one or the other, neither, or both, as it does in an actual person. This is also true of the number nine, the dark reflection of number six. (Apollo and Artemis represent, in this case, the sun and moon respectively.)

Each qualified power takes on a specific magical quality organized into a table of correspondences where the concept and keyword of the number and the characteristic of the element combine to express a unique quality.

As an example, the creative component of the triad of mind (number five) is represented by the ability to be adaptable. When this quality is merged with the element of water (emotions, feelings), it represents the qualities of inner strength as produced through flexibility, versatility, and problem-solving. The qualified power would then consist of the characteristics of being able to change and re-evaluate a situation that would help one to overcome all obstacles and achieve any goal. This is a good *upbeat* definition for the 5 of Cups. In the matrix of definitions, the qualified power of the number five and the element of water is defined as a magical power (resolution of adversity) associated with the images and correspondences of the 5 of Cups and is harnessed through the performance of the Pyramid of Power ritual.

One thing that I want to state clearly here is that although there are pip cards in the tarot that represent negative experiences in life, I wanted to give an upbeat meaning to those cards so that they represent a challenge that can be overcome and identify the forces that can help one resolve that challenge.

My tarot card definitions are therefore positive and upbeat for what might be considered negative cards.

For instance, the 10 of Swords could represent a hopeless defeat with little potential for a good outcome, even though the pictorial vignette shows the dark sky clearing in the distance. The card's main feature is a victim resoundingly defeated with ten swords piercing his body. The qualified power, on the other hand, can aid in materializing a solution or a means to reversing this catastrophic loss and turning it into a personal victory using the socialized power of myth. It is how a loss can become a gain. That, I believe, is what the underlying qualified power would represent, since it would be otherwise strange to invoke something that would only qualify one's losses as a form of self-pity. I have used this approach in all of the tarot card definitions that are a part of the qualified powers. There is no point in invoking something that cannot powerfully help the practitioner to resolve life's challenges as depicted by some of the cards. I developed these modified definitions over a decade of experimentation.

The above methodology is applied to all of the forty powers in order to determine their qualities. To assist the process of ordering and defining these powers, there are concepts defining the result of the synthesis of both number and element. There are also ten basic symbols and four primary colors that can be used to form a simple system of symbolism that will assist the magician to cue the quality of magical power needed; but it is the tarot card that truly denotes the quality of the energy summoned.

Therefore, if one were interested in invoking the power of knowledge-based creativity through the Pyramid of Power ritual, the symbolic construct would consist of light (number 2) and the color red (symbol of wands, fire, and knowledge) producing a red light or ray symbol. This power can also be determined by the 2 of Wands.

The forty pip cards of the tarot can be studied and analyzed so that the forty powers may become further defined. However, we should recognize that there are variations between the many tarot decks. These differences may require you to adjust the magical qualities as defined by the forty powers to your own tarot deck and definitions. My definitions may not exactly match what you are accustomed to using for your deck, so I would recommend using your own. Still, each qualified power is a solution, resolution, or enhancement to a particular issue confronting the practitioner who seeks to use these powers in magic. Keep this in mind when reworking any definitions.

As a final note, each of these forty powers represent one of the forty worlds of the inner planes. Therefore, the use of these powers opens the magician to their associated inner plane influences. However, the ritual of the Pyramid of Power was not designed for the realization of this higher level of truth, but it does manifest the forces of the inner planes in an indirect fashion. To activate this capability, you would need to employ planetary and zodiacal magic. You can consider that each of the forty tarot cards represents a separate domain or a kind of inner world that the qualified power opens to the practitioner.

Performing the Pyramid of Power ritual (chapter 12) can produce many layers of magical effects simultaneously and these can be useful to a wide range of magical practitioners. It is the standard in ritual evaluation that if a ritual has many layers of significance acting at different levels of awareness simultaneously, it is deemed to be both elegant and artful. I believe that the Pyramid of Power ritual arises to that degree of usefulness.

The following is a cross-reference of the forty qualified powers, including the associated tarot card, the symbolic image, and a description of the qualities associated with each power.

Table of Correspondences for the Forty Qualified Powers

Base Element: Fire–Knowledge–Red

Fire of Union: Ace of Wands

Emperor: Caspiel

Symbol: Red circle. The power of gnosis is the ability to perceive the relatedness of everything and to experience everything as one. This power is a determinant of peace, goodwill, and illuminating wisdom. (Union of Spirit and Knowledge)

Fire of Creation: Two of Wands

Angelic Ruler: Zezar

Decan: Mars in Aries (0°–10°)

Symbol: Red light. The power of pure creativity is the ability to anticipate the patterns of probable manifestation before manifestation occurs. This power allows one to engage in unfettered visionary experiences and intuitive prophecy. (Receptive Spirit and Knowledge)

Fire of Mitigation: Three of Wands

Angelic Ruler: Behhemi

Decan: Sun in Aries (10°–20°)

Symbol: Red eye. The power of unbiased perception, the understanding of the world as it truly exists. The ability to see beyond one's personal perspective to realize the true value of all things. This power dissolves everything into a single truth, thus cutting through all irrelevancies. (Creative Spirit and Knowledge)

Fire of Compassion: Four of Wands

Angelic Ruler: Setneder

Decan: Venus in Aries (20°–30°)

Symbol: Red cross. The power of higher guidance that helps one realize the hidden patterns of one's personal destiny, relating the cosmos and its greater cycle to that of the individual. This power attunes the operator to various subtle and personal directives as manifested from higher spiritual realities. (Receptive Mind and Knowledge)

Fire of Resolution: Five of Wands

Angelic Ruler: Lusnahar

Decan: Saturn in Leo (0°–10°)

Symbol: Red staff. The power of equilibrium and balance establishes itself through an empowered disciplined mind that overcomes chaotic emotions or the circumstances of calamity. This type of forced balance restores order to disordered emotions or impassioned feelings through the use of rationalization and mental clarity. (Creative Mind and Knowledge)

Fire of Identity: Six of Wands

Angelic Ruler: Zacha'ai

Decan: Jupiter in Leo (10 °–20°)

Symbol: Red mirror. The power of illumination is revealed as the exaltation and transcendency of self-knowledge. It is the revelation of the spiritual dimension of the self and its collective and absolute truths. This power causes the ineffable secrets of one's soul to become revealed and known. (Androgyne of Mind and Knowledge)

Fire of Mystery: Seven of Wands

Angelic Ruler: Sahiber

Decan: Mars in Leo (20°–30°)

Symbol: Red heart. The power of love and charismatic glamor that causes the breakdown of differences and the establishment of love, peace, and conciliation amidst strife. This power is the embodiment of diplomacy and peacemaking, literally the knowledge of transforming love. (Creative Soul and Knowledge)

Fire of Sagacity: Eight of Wands

Angelic Ruler: Mesheret

Decan: Mercury in Sagittarius (0°–10°)

Symbol: Red scroll. The power of eloquence in speech and writing and the knowledge of how to communicate to anyone. This power transcends language and reveals the source of understanding and communication between sentient individuals. (Receptive Soul and Knowledge)

Fire of Dreams: Nine of Wands

Angelic Ruler: Vaharin

Decan: Moon in Sagittarius (10°–20°)

Symbol: Red star. The power of emotional exaltation of the self, the power of inspiration, ascendancy through the agency of the emotions, and the imagination overcomes obstacles. This power causes the reversal of misfortune and sorrow through the application of projecting fantasy in a creative "as if" manner. (Resolution of Soul and Knowledge)

Fire of World: Ten of Wands

Angelic Ruler: Abuha

Decan: Saturn in Sagittarius (20°–30°)

Symbol: Red flower. The power of deductive reasoning and the practical application of wisdom, divinely inspired, to the problems of everyday existence. This power is the great problem-solver. When applied to the internal problems of the individual, it assists in their resolution. (Materialization of Knowledge)

Base Element: Water—Emotions—Blue

Water of Union: Ace of Cups

Emperor: Ameradiel

Symbol: Blue circle. The power of spiritual love or devotion. This is the power that connects individuals in alignment to the Deity, however that Deity is perceived. This power directs the forces of harmony to still the lake of one's emotions so that it becomes like a mirror to reflect the wisdom of Spirit. (Union of Spirit and Emotions)

Water of Creation: Two of Cups

Angelic Ruler: Methraush

Decan: Venus in Cancer (0°–10°)

Symbol: Blue light. The power of emotional balance and equilibrium, the ability to cause emotions to find a greater depth of awareness. This power makes the operator experience a profound mind-state of tranquility that is very contagious. This power also fosters love between individuals—the high-minded kind of spiritual love associated with religious devotion. (Receptive Spirit and Emotions)

Water of Mitigation: Three of Cups

Angelic Ruler: Rahdax

Decan: Mercury in Cancer (10°–20°)

Symbol: Blue eye. The power of true love, that mysterious force that determines the destiny of one's life and the lives of others. It also determines whether one's love has a higher spiritual alignment or is based on illusion or deception. This power can also generate potent bonds of spiritual love between individuals if their destiny will allow it. (Creative Spirit and Emotions)

Water of Compassion: Four of Cups

Angelic Ruler: Alinkayer

Decan: Moon in Cancer (20°–30°)

Symbol: Blue cross. The power of divine compassion, love and its spiritual effect, charisma. This power represents the process of overall emotional healing through the benediction and intervention of the Spirit upon an issue. It may even correct inequalities through the power of inspiration, which through self-empowerment and positive thinking brings good fortune. (Receptive Mind and Emotions)

Water of Resolution: Five of Cups

Angelic Ruler: Kamox

Decan: Mars in Scorpio (0°–10°)

Symbol: Blue staff. The power of internal emotional adaptability overcoming adversity or loss. It is the force that fuels one's convictions and allows one to undergo and transform all adversity into gain. This power represents inner stability and the ability to heal one's troubled relationships in a very versatile manner. (Creative Mind and Emotions)

Water of Identity: Six of Cups

Angelic Ruler: Nindohar

Decan: Sun in Scorpio (10°–20°)

Symbol: Blue mirror. The power that reveals the mysteries of the hearts of others assists one to become emotionally opened and connected, encouraging the abolition of all barriers. This is the power that establishes a network of sympathy, the web of emotional connection, and the compassion of giving and receiving love. (Androgyne of Mind and Emotions)

Water of Mystery: Seven of Cups

Angelic Ruler: Vathrodiel

Decan: Venus in Scorpio (20°–30°)

Symbol: Blue heart. The power of passion and desire, the lighting of the fires of sexuality between individuals. Intensifying this power will cause heightened states of sexual stimulation that can result in ecstasy and the liberation of the soul, but it can also cause delirium or the loss of self if it is unwisely used. This is a difficult power to control because it fans the flames of irrational desires, so one should be cautious and careful in its use. (Creative Soul and Emotions)

Water of Sagacity: Eight of Cups

Angelic Ruler: Bahalmi

Decan: Saturn in Pisces (0°–10°)

Symbol: Blue scroll. The power that reveals the actual value and truth associated with social and emotional connections. It facilitates the ability to see the truth behind friendship and love, revealing whether it is real or based on deceit. This power also fosters peace and tranquility between people of different persuasions or backgrounds if their connections are tenuous and fraught with difficulties. (Receptive Soul and Emotions)

Water of Dreams: Nine of Cups

Angelic Ruler: Auron

Decan: Jupiter in Pisces (10°–20°)

Symbol: Blue star. The power of the imagination as it impacts one's feelings and fully opens one's soul. It produces an inner knowledge of the heart that is expressed through desires, imaginings, and fantasies. This power allows one's desires to be expressed freely and without inhibition even if they are hidden, buried deep, or kept secret. (Resolution of Soul and Emotions)

Water of World: Ten of Cups

Angelic Ruler: Sateriph

Decan: Mars in Pisces (20°–30°)

Symbol: Blue flower. The power of the theatrical expression of love as an archetypal romance that ends in happiness and fulfillment. This power not only expresses itself as a common and often-played theme, but also has many deeper levels. At its most fundamental level, this power is the ritual drama of the soul's ascendancy through the union of love. (Materialization of Emotions)

Base Element: Air–Action–Yellow

Air of Union: Ace of Swords

Emperor: Carmasiel

Symbol: Yellow circle. The true will is the power of the realization of one's principal destiny. This true will is forged through challenges and adversities and it is derived by much thought, design, and deliberate artifice. The method of gaining insight into one's motives is a potent technique for unleashing the power of personal direction. (Union of Spirit and Action)

Air of Creation: Two of Swords

Angelic Ruler: Taresni

Decan: Moon in Libra (0°–10°)

Symbol: Yellow light. The power of courage that assists one in successfully meeting challenges. This is the power of perseverance and the empowerment of self-belief that is instrumental in resolving difficulties and actualizing through adversity. This power is experienced through decisiveness, which facilitates the quick achievement of results, overcoming obstructions and stalemates. (Receptive Spirit and Action)

Air of Mitigation: Three of Swords

Angelic Ruler: Saharnax

Decan: Saturn in Libra (10°–20°)

Symbol: Yellow eye. The power of clarity of one's motivation that enables one to be decisive and confident. This power represents the faith in one's own internal process and the belief that all of one's choices are indeed deliberate and significant, and that they reflect the ultimate good of one's life process. This power of clarity also causes one to resolutely adhere to a specific direction and endure all its vicissitudes, including the pain of betrayal or secret conflict. (Creative Spirit and Action)

Air of Compassion: Four of Swords

Angelic Ruler: Shachdar

Decan: Jupiter in Libra (20°–30°)

Symbol: Yellow cross. The power rectifying legal inequalities and injustices. This power is very potent in that it causes justice to be wrought upon all wrongs associated with a specific issue, always weighing in favor of the absolute truth, regardless of who is rewarded or punished. Thus, this power must be used with care, since it shall neither aid nor hurt one, but only follow the path of truth. It unleashes judgment on all parties by the higher and inscrutable law of equality. (Receptive Mind and Action)

Air of Resolution: Five of Swords

Angelic Ruler: Saspham

Decan: Venus in Aquarius (0°–10°)

Symbol: Yellow staff. The power of dominance, the elimination of that which is irrelevant and incapable. This power is very intense and will cause a brief burst of disharmony in order to clear the atmosphere of disassociated and discordant beliefs. This power also causes one's mind to become consolidated and complete. It can also be used to rid oneself of false allies and deceptive friendships. (Creative Mind and Action)

Air of Identity: Six of Swords

Angelic Ruler: Abdaron

Decan: Mercury in Aquarius (10°–20°)

Symbol: Yellow mirror. The power of self-realization and the atonement of guilt. This entails the dual revelations of the spiritual self (higher principles) and one's destiny (future path based on past actions). This power of revelation is managed through the agency and inner knowledge of the higher self (self as Spirit) that is experienced directly through one's personal identity. It fosters an unflattering revelation of one's destiny based on one's past misdeeds that can be changed through atonement and penance. (Androgyne of Mind and Action)

Air of Mystery: Seven of Swords

Angelic Ruler: Garodiel

Decan: Moon in Aquarius (20°–30°)

Symbol: Yellow heart. The power of initiating or ending relationships with other individuals that have shown themselves to be false. The key to this power is understanding the importance of relationships in one's life and how to deal with them effectively. It can sever bonds that no longer serve any positive purpose, and it can also protect one from imprisonment or false claims. (Creative Soul and Action)

Air of Sagacity: Eight of Swords

Angelic Ruler: Sagaresh

Decan: Jupiter in Gemini (0°–10°)

Symbol: Yellow scroll. The power of maintaining one's direction and the integrity of one's purpose through discipline despite all adversity. This inner discipline causes one to undergo a continual process of self-purification and self-correction. It can also be used as an unbinding spell or an uncrossing spell if one is bound or crossed. Therefore, when this power elevates one out of adversity, it does so without a corresponding inflation of the petty ego. It becomes the wisdom of lessons learned. (Receptive Soul and Action)

Air of Dreams: Nine of Swords

Angelic Ruler: Shahdani

Decan: Mars in Gemini (10°–20°)

Symbol: Yellow star. The power of self-determination that is expressed through the actualizing of one's potential by the artifice of the imagination. It fosters a profound inspiration and boundless willpower. When one's true will is inspired in this manner then nothing can halt the process that ultimately brings success. This power should be called upon when all hope is lost and one is engulfed by despair. It will be like a great light in the darkness of one's suffering soul and allow for the possible resolution to problems where the darkness would obscure it. (Resolution of Soul and Action)

Air of World: Ten of Swords

Angelic Ruler: Bithon

Decan: Sun in Gemini (20°–30°)

Symbol: Yellow flower. The power of establishing ideas and beliefs as permanent features in the collective mind. This can be accomplished only if one projects an archetypal process (usually a myth) into the social collective, and through inspiration spreads it throughout the masses. Thus, the occult power of empowering beliefs is revealed and given to the practitioner to change his/her world, however minutely. This power counteracts the grave losses of defeat and misfortune. (Materialization of Action)

Base Element: Earth–Fortunes–Green

Earth of Union: Ace of Pentacles

Emperor: Demoriel

Symbol: Green circle. The power of growth, well-being and physical goodness. This power represents the source of all life in its purest manifestation, which is the egregore of existence and the spirit of life. This power causes fullness, wholeness, and material perfection in all that it touches. However, it is necessary for one to be able to mediate the spiritual essence of life in order to harness it. (Union of Spirit and Fortunes)

Earth of Creation: Two of Pentacles

Angelic Ruler: Masenin

Decan: Jupiter in Capricorn (0°–10°)

Symbol: Green light. The power of evolution, revolution, and transition. It is the power of the transformation of the physical world. This power causes all things physical to change, particularly within the sphere of the individual practitioner who works with these forces. All static situations are swept away and trapped psychic energies are released. Change causes all physical things to complete their cycles, and this power unleashes change, both good and ill. (Receptive Spirit and Fortunes)

Earth of Mitigation: Three of Pentacles

Angelic Ruler: Yasiseyah

Decan: Mars in Capricorn (10°–20°)

Symbol: Green eye. This power represents the organizing forces of nature that draw all individuals together to work and enjoy the fruits of their labors. This is the socializing power that assists the individual in manifesting his/her inner desires so that it is shared and realized by many. (Creative Spirit and Fortunes)

Earth of Compassion: Four of Pentacles

Angelic Ruler: Yasandiberodiel

Decan: Sun in Capricorn (20°–30°)

Symbol: Green cross. This power represents the use of laws and rules to ensure the security of one's person and one's belongings. This is the power that protects one against calamities and unforeseen misfortune by invoking the social symbols of the protective institutions and using their powers to protect one's interests. An image of this power is the fortress, wherein one is ensured protection. (Receptive Mind and Fortunes)

Earth of Resolution: Five of Pentacles

Angelic Ruler: Kedamadi

Decan: Mercury in Taurus (0°–10°)

Symbol: Green staff. This power represents the kind of steadfast commitment required to cause great changes or reforms that affect many people, particularly those who are bereft. This is the power of social destiny, the realization of self-direction and the successful conclusion of one's primary aspirations. Once unleashed, this power establishes a continuous wave of willpower to help fortify the pursuit of one's desires, but also to add material compassion to the world for the poor and the needy. If this power is summoned then the good that it does must be shared with all. (Creative Mind and Fortunes)

Earth of Identity: Six of Pentacles

Angelic Ruler: Manacherai

Decan: Moon in Taurus (10°–20°)

Symbol: Green mirror. This power represents the material knowledge for solving problems and achieving one's ultimate ends through equality. This power is the continual regeneration of life that inspires one through intuitive wisdom to achieve material success and physical accomplishment so long as it helps the greater good. Intuitive wisdom may also be used to creatively resolve issues and establish methods for the successful pursuit of one's material desires. This power is dedicated to long-term instead of short-term gain, and the benefits for all instead of just the lone individual. (Androgyne of Mind and Fortunes)

Earth of Mystery: Seven of Pentacles

Angelic Ruler: Yaksagnox

Decan: Saturn in Taurus (20°–30°)

Symbol: Green heart. This power is the force of mediation, the establishment of long-term partnerships (marriages or business partnerships) and the bestowing upon them a potent favorability for material realization. This power is known as the forger of life bonds that cause material well-being as well as spiritual bonds, resulting in harmonious partnerships. This is a material-based power for long-term growth and investment. (Creative Soul and Fortunes)

Earth of Sagacity: Eight of Pentacles

Angelic Ruler: Ananaurah

Decan: Sun in Virgo (0°–10°)

Symbol: Green Scroll. The power of seizing the initiative and collecting small-term gains. This is the power that assists the gambler or the seeker of fortune, because it gives to one the sense of timing that enables very fortuitous coincidences. However, this power also enables one to overcome small issues (selections or other random choice types) and to perceive the patterns of events in order to realize gain. This power is experienced as serendipity. (Receptive Soul and Fortunes)

Earth of Dreams: Nine of Pentacles

Angelic Ruler: Raidyah

Decan: Venus in Virgo (10°–20°)

Symbol: Green star. This power causes the manifestation of dreams and desires so that they may be acted out in a full realization. This power is the fruitful desire that causes dreams to become reality. It is also the power of pleasure and its associated feelings of fulfillment and satiety. (Resolution of Soul and Fortunes)

Earth of World: Ten of Pentacles

Angelic Ruler: Mashephar

Decan: Mercury in Virgo (20°–30°)

Symbol: Green flower. This power is represented by all forms of healing; the life force is poured upon the earth and all that it touches is potently revitalized and regenerated. This power could, if completely realized, provide the practitioner with eternal potency in life (eternal life). This power also represents the maximization of all that is in material potentiality, thus causing it to gain physical form. (Materialization of Fortunes)

Working with the Qualified Powers

Qualified powers are unique in that they combine an element with a number-based quality to address a specific life-based circumstance. While the correspondences and the spirit associated with them (keyword or angelic ruler) might give the impression that they are very complex and would therefore be less accessible than elementals, they are in fact just as localized to the earth-plane and accessible as elementals.

You need only to repeatedly call out the qualified power's name (either the keyword or angelic ruler) to summon that power when at that point in the ritual working. You can also visualize the corresponding symbols and the associated Tarot card. As with the elemental working, you should also include a specially devised sigil that represents your magical objective drawn on a piece of parchment and also charged and consecrated. The sigil will be used to imprint the pyramid energy structure when it is ready to be exteriorized.

If you want to embellish this working, then you can use the name of the angelic ruler and create a parchment talisman that has both the angular signature of the ruling angel (based on the English alphabet wheel) and the seal for the emperor of the element. This parchment talisman should be properly charged and consecrated.

I would advise using the tarot card itself as a visual aid in the working to help you distinctly identify the qualities of the qualified power being generated. I usually place the tarot card on the altar prior to performing the working. Because there are forty of these powers with which to work, I would tend to use the tarot card to identify each one through the use of images and/or vignettes, which is not really required for the sixteen elementals.

Chapter Nine

A BRIEF OVERVIEW OF SIGIL MAGIC

> Artistic symbols and myths speak out of the primordial, preconscious realm of the mind which is powerful and chaotic. Both symbol and myth are ways of bringing order and form into this chaos.
>
> —Rollo May, "My Quest for Beauty"

Sigil magic is defined as a magical system that makes use of occult characters, diagrams, condensed verbal intentions, geometric symbols, mystical alphabets, angular signatures of spirits, and other kinds of symbolic or hieroglyphic representations.[26] The word "sigil" comes from the Latin word *sigillum*, which means "seal." Of additional significance is the Hebrew word SGULH or *sagulah*, which means "some kind of word or action" that has a specific spiritual or magical effect. The use of sigils in magic has its roots in antiquity, possibly from Hebrew sources (although Greek magic also used them), since sigils often accompanied magical squares, which were used extensively in the Jewish tradition of ceremonial magic.

---

26. Sigil: pronounced like "sidjel."

Most often, sigils or specialized characters (seals) were incorporated into grimoires and had a traditional use that required the wielder to copy them exactly as depicted even though they had to have been invented by someone at some point in history. These kinds of sigils were carefully crafted using very specific techniques (and not derived from either one's imagination or revelation), but the methodology used for their creation is typically missing from those same works.[27]

Some believe that magical sigils or characters have a power and potency all to themselves. Others believe that a sigil has to be activated, at the very least, by the imagination and will of a trained and competent magician. Some grimoires are notorious for the sigils and characters they contain, lending weight to the belief that sigils have an independent power quite separate from whoever invented or used them. Most often, sigils are reputed to be the specialized symbolic names of angels, demons, or various spirits, and the sigil is used to summon and evoke them. This makes a sigil similar in some ways to the *vévé* as found in Haitian Vodoun. Still, sigils based on the symbolic name of a spirit assumes that the sigil is a more pure and direct representation of that spirit's true nature, and of course, whoever knows the *true* name or nature of a spirit has direct power over it.

The foundation of sigil magic and the reason why it is so efficacious is due to its incorporation of a powerful magical model known as the information model. The information model is based on the communication of information, which could include nearly everything that humans do to communicate. Everything in magic from the symbols, correspondences, and regalia to the ritual actions can be seen as a stream of information; things with an inherent quantum of information are the very *packets* or *kernels* of data that are pulled or woven together to fashion a special kind of media called magic.

Magic is therefore a linguistic event. What drives the whole process is the precision of the stated intention and weight of the other supporting communications that are grouped around it. This is basically how the Chaos magicians of the 1990s defined their model of magic. They also believed that it nullified all other models making it the one and only true model. Of course, the folly of such a belief is that the spirit, energy, and psychological models of magic still

27. A good example showing how these sigils were developed can be found in Donald Tyson's version of *Three Books of Occult Philosophy* (St. Paul, MN: Llewellyn Publications, 1997, originally written by Agrippa), particularly appendix V, on magic squares.

stand—there are spirits, there is energy, and there is the mind itself. However, the information model of magic is still quite useful and important.

Scott Stenwick has written an article that has refined the information model of magic and merged it with information theory, making it much more useful and easier to comprehend.[28] Basically, there are three components to information theory: the message, the carrier, and the transmission. Since magic is a kind of communication, he proposed that one could use the information theory to qualify it.

In a magical working, the message is the intention, or what you want the magic to do. The magical energy is the carrier used to push the message. The magical link between the source and the target is the transmission line upon which the message travels. Scott has stated that each of these three components must be clearly present in a magical working in order for the message to be accurately sent to the target.

For instance, the transmission can be subject to *noise* or interference, so it is important that the intention is clearly determined and succinctly stated. Likewise, the link must be clearly defined so that a proper transmission line is established between source and target. In fact, a kind of succinct and simple definition of the link will make the transmission less likely to be interrupted or miss its intended target. The reduction or compression of the message into a sigil is the most efficient and effective method for simultaneously establishing the line of transmission and simplifying the message. A sigil functions as both message and transmission line.

A sigil is a compressed and symbolized statement of desire that is used to imprint a magical energy field before it is released and transmitted to its objective. The sigil should identify the receiver of the message as well as the desired outcome, and in this manner determine the message and the transmission line to the receiver. This will allow an effective communication of information from subject to object, and that is what is intended. Additionally, the magical energy (and the desire driving it) will help to push the transmission and overcome any noise in the magical "circuit," or link.

Identifying the message and the transmission line with a sigil of some sort and the carrier with an energy field is a highly effective magical mechanism.

---

28. Scott Stenwick, "Regarding Magical Models—Part Ten," Augoeides: Spiritual Technology for a New Aeon (accessed May 17, 2020): http://ananael.blogspot.com/2016/11/regarding-magical-models-part-ten.html.

It requires the use of both the energy model of magic and the information model of magic joined together. As you can see, because we include spirits in these kinds of element-based workings and visualization, we also work with the spirit and the psychological models of magic. All four are integral to an effective working in the kind of energy magic discussed in this work, even though my emphasis is on the energy model. Now, back to sigils.

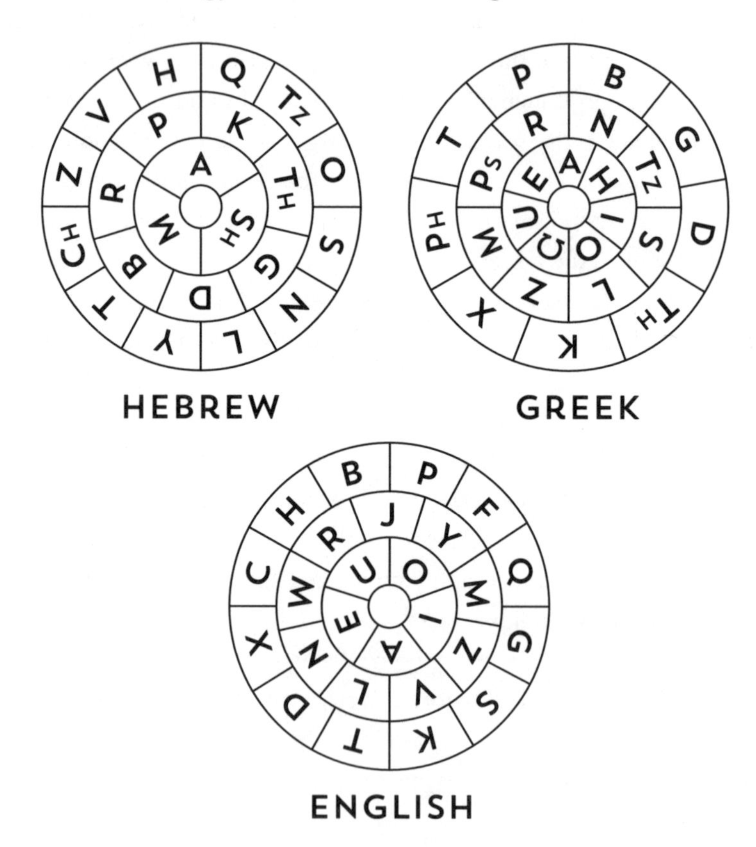

Example of the Hebrew Alphabet Wheel, Greek Alphabet Wheel, and the English Alphabet Wheel

When I perform an invocation or an evocation, I employ a sigil crafted from the name of the target spirit. That sigil can be derived from a number of sources, but I generally use the alphabet wheels based on Hebrew, Greek, or English/Latin. The Hebrew alphabet wheel features the Hebrew letters drawn on the three concentric circles, representing the triple division of those same letters (three mother letters, seven double letters, and twelve simple letters). This wheel can thus be used to create sigils based on a Hebrew word or name.[29]

One could derive a spirit sigil from one of the appropriate magical planetary squares, depending on the spirit's hierarchical association, since there are different squares for each of the seven planets. There is also the Aiq Bkr magical square that can be used to craft a sigil from a spirit's name. Still, alphabet wheels are used extensively for this kind of sigil drawing, and they are the simplest manner of crafting a name or word sigil.

A sigil is a graphical magical sign of some sort, whether it's taken from some traditional body of magical lore (grimoire or tradition) or created by the magician to represent the name of a spirit or to encapsulate a specific intention or desire. Manufacturing sigils on demand became the hallmark of the famous British witch and sorcerer, Austin Osman Spare, who proposed a system of creating sigils by condensing and extracting the forms of the letters from a phrase that stated the magician's intent.

Spare called this methodology "sigilization," and it was later adopted by Chaos magicians and others who use it as an independent system of magic. Sigilization is employed for casting spells, organizing and deploying an "alphabet of desire" for the same, or building up thought forms. However, it is probably one of the most direct and useful methods for creating a magical link that I ever seen or heard about.

We have briefly discussed the nature of a magical link while working with the information model of magic. A link is a symbolic image that establishes a connection (transmission line) between the magician, the desire, the magical power raised, and the intended target, whatever that happens to be. The magical link is employed whenever a magician seeks to make something happen in the material world. It is usually tangible in some manner and it should model or symbolize the magician's intention.

In folk magic, the link was usually something that was directly "linked" or attached at some point to the target, such as hair, fingernail clippings, blood, jewelry, or clothing, if the target was to be a person. This is based on the law of contagion as found in the definitions of sympathetic magic. If the target was more general, the link consisted of herbs, power objects (stones, crystals,

29. For a more in-depth presentation of the use of alphabet wheels, see Frater Barrabbas, *Spirit Conjuring for Witches* (Woodbury, MN: Llewellyn Publications, 2017), 116–119.

odd shaped pieces of wood), bird or animal parts (or even human parts), bits of metal (magnets, nails), or other curious odds and ends collected while on the hunt for internal occult connections. Using a table of correspondences would also help the Witch sort out and select analogous items consisting of colors, incense, herbs, gemstones, precious and semi-precious metals—the list is nearly endless.

These various objects would be put together in an artistic manner to symbolize the intent, such as piercing an apple with rusty nails, piercing dried organs or herbs with thorns, or creating a poppet or miniature human shape out of wax or some tuber, adorning it with bits of hair, fingernails or cloth, and then baptizing and naming it for the intended target. The objects would be blessed, charged, assembled, and the final product would be used in a spell to make something happen. The completed link-object could be put in a metal container or a bottle, or a leather or cloth pouch to be kept, buried, or burned. In some cases, words could be printed on the object, or perhaps even a scrap of cloth or paper could be used to contain drawings and words or names. In antiquity, curses were drawn and written out on lead sheets, and then folded and dropped into wells or stuck between the stones of the victim's home.

Organic or inorganic links are called "gross links" because they are made from organic or inorganic materials, where the actual physical form and structure determines its use and intended purpose. Writing something down on a parchment, paper, cloth, or a thin sheet of metal is a very different kind of link. A drawing or writing represents a transitional kind of magical object, becoming more of what I call a symbolic link due to its use of symbolic forms to depict and establish the link.

A symbolic link is more versatile than a gross link (which is normally used just once). A symbolic link often caries no trace of any previous spell on it, so it can be reused for other purposes. A link that could be fashioned to be used multiple times would require that the original intent was the same. For instance, you could fashion a symbolic link for acquiring money, use it for yourself, and then at another time use it for a friend. So long as there were no identifying factors or names, a general symbolic link can serve multiple purposes. A more effective link would clearly identify the intention and the receiver—so as long as those items establishing the link are the same for both magical workings, a sigil could be reusable.

In the energy model of magic, a link is used to imprint the raised energy before it's exteriorized to fulfill the Witch's intention. The raised energy can be highly qualified or not, but it still has to be imprinted with the Witch's desire. In the system of magic I use, a sigil is employed to function as a link. The act of imprinting the energy is where the Witch projects the link, in the form of a sigil, into the raised energy, creating a unified field. (This technique is covered in more detail later in chapter 11.)

Crafting a sigil to be used as a link doesn't usually trigger its inherent effect or cause the desire to become manifest by itself. This is because one needs to charge or consecrate the sigil after fashioning it, and then apply it as a link within a magical working where the energy is raised. Others may perform sigil magic as an independent magical mechanism, so in that situation it's possible that the act of crafting it might actually trigger the spell. Still, there has to be a carrier, and in sigil magic the carrier is the practitioner's desire and passion.

Since it is my habit to always craft a sigil just prior to performing a working (and I have never, to my knowledge, crafted one without it being used in a working), it would be difficult for me to judge whether the act of crafting the sigil prematurely triggered a working. I just know that in order for a ritual working to be successful, a link must be fashioned and used to imprint the energy. The two magical operations performed sequentially are being blended together, but it's possible to fulfill a working with just the internalized application of the link and one's desire to make it so. Now that I have explained how I use sigils in my magical workings, I should probably describe how to actually craft a sigil without using an alphabet wheel or a traditional source.

The general rule for crafting a sigil is to start out by writing a phrase that encapsulates the intention of the rite. I would recommend printing this phrase on paper using upper case letters to minimize the possible shapes. The next step is to take the phrase and reduce it to a simple pictographic diagram through a process of reduction and simplification, where the curves, lines, and intersected forms of those actual letters are reduced to a unique set in a given order and then reassembled into a kind of simple logo.

Instructions for Building a Sigil

Let's go through the steps that one would typically follow to produce a sigil, keeping in mind that there are many variations and methods used in this technique.

How I do it may not be exactly the same as how others do it, but each practitioner will ultimately find a technique that works for them.

1. Write out a phrase of your intention; make it as simple, clear and specific as possible. You can also eliminate words like "I" or "desire" or "will" from the phrase since that would be redundant. Just state what you intend or seek to make happen and also include the receiver or target of that intention.

   To make things easier, print this phrase out in all capital letters (although as an advanced user, I prefer to add the nuance of having larger and smaller letters in the mix). As mentioned, using all caps actually helps to reduce the number of linear forms in the sample of extracted letters.

   The act of succinctly stating one's intention also helps to simplify and refine the intention of a work. It's better to reduce the intention down to just one thing. If you are seeking to make more than one thing happen, employ more than one phrase and then build multiple sigils from them. (It might also be necessary to perform separate workings for each sigil link as well.)

2. Looking over the phrase, from left to right, eliminate all redundant letters—that is, letters which occur more than once. Now the phrase should just have all the unique letters in the order in which they first occur.

   SELL HOUSE MOVE AWAY ➡ SELHOUMVAWY

3. Next, eliminate letters that are variations of each other. For instance, M and W are similar to each other. Break out of the letters the various similar structures, like the cross bar in the E, R, F, A, H, or G, the curve in the B, C, D, G, J, P, R, S, or U, and the vertical, horizontal and diagonal lines that are found in the remaining letters, such as the N, the A, and the V. All of these forms are reduced down to a single form, or dual forms facing left or right. The O can become a small circle, or a dot or it can be fused with the rest of the curves, being reduced to a left and right curve joined together. What you have now are just single incidences of multiple structures (essential forms) arrayed in a line, like letters.

Sigil example 2

4. Assemble the line of essential structural forms together again to create a condensed linear form, which should look something like a pictographic representation or a logo of the original phrase. This last step may require several attempts to find a final structure that *looks* elegant and interesting to the eye. You can fashion a single sigil form or multiple sigils. Using multiple iterations to build a sigil makes for a less cluttered final sigil structure. If you are going to use a name in your sigil for an entity or a person, I would recommend making that a separate sigil form from the actual intention.

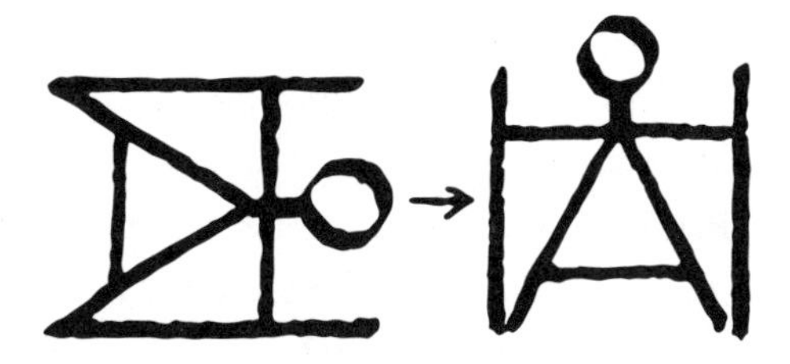

Sigil example 3

The point of this exercise is to produce a final structure that is simplistic, looks something like a pictograph of the intention, and the letters used in the original phrase can still be perceived in the final shape, although this last condition is not as important as creating a memorable pictograph.

I usually have to make three or four passes using this process before I am able to condense the form down to something that is esthetically pleasing and interesting to look at. Austin Spare was something of a graphic genius when it came to this kind representation. He could probably have done it automatically and in one pass. You don't have to measure your results by that very high standard.

While working out the sigil, I use a pencil on a scrap of paper, but the final form is rendered on parchment with a special waterproof ink. It could also be painted on a piece of board, cloth, etched on metal, or even drawn on the floor or wall of your temple. Whichever way it is finally done, it will become an important magical instrument. Therefore, the act itself should be executed as if it were a magical rite with the intention of the sigil and its associated desire strongly fixed in the mind of the magician.

Once the sigil is crafted, it will need to be consecrated if it's to be used in a magical working. This step is not typically followed by those who use sigil magic, but this is how I do it, and it keeps the sigil from being too active until its intended use. I will consecrate the sigil with just a spot of lustral water (saltwater carefully applied with a wand) and then I fumigate it over an incense burner just prior to performing the working. For the sigil of a spirit, I would use consecrated wine, leaving a small stain on the corner as a sign that the sigil parchment has been activated.

Although I don't actually work sigil magic without also performing a working of some kind, the basic idea behind it is to fill the mind with an emotional charge associated with the desire or intention so that no other thoughts or feelings are possible. This is a type of powerful obsession, often accompanied with a deep focused trance. This mind state is gradually built up through the process of crafting the sigil and then it's elevated once the sigil is committed to its final form, executed in ink on parchment or in whatever media is elected.

The Witch holds the sigil before his or her sight, focusing on the image of the design (not the words that were used to build it) while the emotional sentiments associated with the spell are worked to a climax. Then the sigil is either destroyed or set aside and promptly forgotten, allowing the image of the sigil to be transferred to the collective consciousness. The Witch can generate an intensely focused climax in a number of different ways, such as an orgasmic release through sex magic, masturbation, or even assuming Spare's death posture. Yet often just intensely focusing the mind for a period of time and then quickly releasing it, is sufficient to obtain a good result.

I should probably mention two other methods that are used to create a sigil device. These are the methods of fashioning a mantra or using condensed pictures. The mantra technique is similar to the word-based sigil, except the reduced set of letters and vowels are arranged to spell out a magical word or formula. It will most likely (though not always) be a nonsense word, but it will symbolize a specific intent. It will function as a barbarous magical word of power, which can be used in an incantation or as a mantra.

CAREER SUCCESS ➡ CARESU ➡ RESUCAR

A sigil derived from a picture or symbolic images (such as the symbols for the elements, planets, astrological signs, alchemical symbols, or even international traffic signs) uses the same methodology as stated in steps 3 and 4 for building a word sigil, where the forms are broken apart, condensed, and reassembled. However, it is manipulated into a kind of hieroglyphic structure that takes the form of the sigil beyond even the creation of an amalgamation logo of the first kind. This methodology can also be done just by using simple drawings (doodles) or crude pictograms instead of words and reducing them down to a series of symbols or a combined graphical logo. (Here is a pictogram of Sell House Move Away.)

A picture showing how to derive a magical picture image

That's briefly how to formulate and use sigils as links in the discipline of ritual magic. This is based completely on how I do it, so of course, there will be a lot of possible variations. I doubt that two Witches who use this technique do it exactly in the same manner, but I believe that I have revealed the basic steps that most would follow. A more thorough resource on the art of sigil magic is to be found in the book *Practical Sigil Magic* by Frater U.·.D.·. (Llewellyn, 1990), which I heartily recommend.

Chapter Ten

MAGICAL ENERGY WORKINGS AND SELF-EMPOWERMENT

> Everything is within your power, and your power is within you.
>
> —Janice Trachtman

Working with magical energy does not necessarily require you to use rituals or even define the four elements. In fact, being able to do this work without any rituals or qualifying the energy is an important step to mastering the more advanced energy workings as found in the extended energy model. So, we will be looking at all of the steps and techniques that you will need to do magical energy work. When we add the ritual component and qualifying the energy with a spirit to this kind of working in chapter 12, it will enhance this type of work to an even greater degree. However, let us look in detail at how this kind of magic works.

There are basically five components to performing energy workings in magic. We will examine each of these independently and also as a complete energy working form that will become your template for working with magical energy.

Here are the five components and some notes to make them clear:

1. Breath control: We use the breath to generate, intensify, accelerate, and express magical energy. Breath helps to circulate the energy through our bodies.
2. Movement: Moving the body from walking, dancing, turning in place, shaking the hands, and even stamping the feet help to activate the energy in our bodies—the movement can be repetitive and iterative or completely random and dynamic.
3. Visualization and sound: We use our visualization capabilities along with our imagination to help us see and feel the energy that we are generating and working. Seeing is important, but so is hearing. We use sound and music to drive the energy.
4. Emotions: Our passion and desire are the drivers for the generation of energy. Without them our actions are hesitant, awkward, and ineffective.
5. Intention: We are doing these exercises not for their own sake, but because we want to accomplish something. Our need or goal is behind what we do and unifies our actions.

Since magical energy is an aspect of consciousness it can be considered a phenomenon of the mind. We use the "as if" mechanism to sense, feel, generate, and visualize magical energy. A couple of phrases that I use when teaching people how to do magical energy work are: "visualize to realize" and "seek to feel and it will become real." You have to start out with a need to believe and then let your imagination inspire your visualization abilities to make it a real and physical experience. This is a kind of situation where you trust yourself and assume that if the five components above are being properly used that you will truly experience something amazing and profound—that magical energy does indeed exist.

Keep in mind that practicing these techniques will make the experience more tangible and physical. It might start out subtle and indistinct in the beginning of your experimental practice, or it might hit you over the head like a hammer the very first time you do it. Much of this depends on the power of your imagination; in truth, there is a phenomenon to experience. You just need to release your skepticism and doubt to make it work. (Of course, that is true for working any kind of magic.)

Component of Breath

Breath Control: There are four types of breathing techniques that are used in a magical energy working.

The first type of breath control is assuming an even, restful breathing cycle. You can slowly inhale, hold, then exhale, and hold the breath again. You can also initially use a mental counting technique during the inhale cycle, holding, then during the exhale cycle and holding, perhaps counting to five or ten for each of the four phases.

This is what you do when starting any kind of energy work and it is also where you end that work. You want to relax the body and mind and focus on just your breath and nothing else. You sit comfortably with your back straight and eyes partially closed, and hands in your lap. As a starting meditation asana, do this for several minutes to collect and relax the body and the mind. Do not think about the work that is about to begin. Just completely relax and empty your mind as much as possible. If thoughts intrude, just observe and don't engage them.

The second type is what I call cool breathing. This is where you close your mouth and allow for only a partial opening and then you suck in your breath—it will make hissing sound as you take either a full breath or a quick partial breath.

The third type is called the bellows breath, which is a rapid inhalation and exhalation with the mouth opened wide, allowing for no restrictions. It is similar to panting except that the mouth is open wide. You use this type of breathing technique for short periods of time to start the power generation phase of an energy working. I would recommend only six or seven rapid breaths in succession, followed by a slow and full breathing cycle. This will help the energy to form in the body, but it will keep you from becoming light-headed or dizzy.

The fourth type is a long slow exhalation that removes qualities from the body or projects it as energy into an object. The lips are made to form an O and the exhalation follows a very deep and thorough inhalation where the lungs are filled to capacity. Similarly, you can also perform a slow inhalation of breath in the same manner as the slow exhalation, following a very deep and thorough exhalation where the lungs are completely empty. With this technique of breathing, you can visualize a colored energy being either inhaled or exhaled slowly—in particular, the color associated with one of the four elements.

Component of Movement

Movement: There are any number of types of repetitive movement, but I would like to list a few and let you determine how you want to move about to help to generate energy.

The two simplest movements are walking fixedly or turning in place. Obviously, the starting point is standing still with a straight back and eyes straight ahead. Walking is a circumambulation around the periphery of a magic circle, and the directions can be deosil or widdershins. Turning in place can be clockwise or anti-clockwise. For just energy raising outside of a ritual context, the direction is not important as much as the movement itself. You can add other movements to these two basic movement techniques. You can stomp your feet, jump or leap, or perform a kind of contact impromptu dance with repetitive movements either around a circle or in place, depending on your ability or tastes.

The starting pace in energy movement is always slow and deliberate and gradually speeds up to a level that can be sustained for a few to several minutes without producing either excessive dizziness or excessive fatigue. This of course depends on a person's fitness. When you achieve a state that is exhilarating and exciting and you can feel the energy suddenly increase (pulse) to a much higher level than expected, you need to sustain that movement just a bit longer and then immediately stop and cease all movement.

You can drop to the floor or just stand erect and completely still, feeling the energy continuing to move around your body, directing and shaping it with your hands. While directing, let this energy stimulate your hands, causing them to shake and tremble. Let that kind of vibration and shaking be felt in your whole body, from your feet to your head. This is called feeling the vibrations of magical energy, and it helps to center it in the body and disperse it.

One kind of movement that is particularly helpful in the directing of the energy is what I call the descending and ascending waves. This movement is done while standing in place. You can visualize the effects of these movements as you do them.

For the ascending wave, imagine the energy collecting at your feet. Then lean down, exhale fully, and connect with that energy with your hands. Slowly draw it up your body as you inhale (slow breathing), moving from your feet all the way to your head. Then project the energy up and beyond your head with both hands pushing it beyond the ceiling and let out your breath as you release the energy.

The descending wave is the opposite from the ascending wave. Stand with your arms up to the ceiling, exhale your breath, then draw and collect the energy accumulating there and slowly draw it down to your head and into your body while you gently inhale the energy into your body, a kind of slow breathing. Do this while continuing to move the energy with your hands down across your body, pushing it down to your feet as you lean forward and exhale your breath.

The descending wave draws energy from the universal source down into your body, and the ascending wave pulls the energy from your core up to the universal source. This is an important and powerful method for centering and moving the energy through your body.

Component of Visualization

Visualization

This technique uses your active imagination along with a certain method of seeing subtle and indistinct energy phenomena. It will help you to realize and manipulate magical energy. This energy cannot be seen as ordinary light, so it requires some visual adjustment in order to actually see it.

In a dimly lit room, dim your eyesight further by partially closing your eyes. Use your imagination and look at your hands in this dim lighting and try to see something around your fingers. It would appear as a slight moving field with no distinct color, kind of like a shadow. Don't look sharply at your hands, but at the area around your hands to try and catch a glimpse of your own energy field.

Use breath control while you try to do this exercise. Try using the bellows breath for a short period of time (five seconds) then stop immediately and focus on the area around your hands. Do this exercise until you can see something shadowy around your fingers and hands. Try to feel yourself projecting energy through your fingertips while you are doing these exercises.

With practice, you will begin to see something. What you should do at that point is use your imagination to help define what you are seeing more distinctly and to give it a clarity and even a color. After a while, you will be able to sense and see energy around your hands and even sparks coming off of your fingertips.

What you will be seeing will be very indistinct and subtle, almost as if it is just beyond your visual ability; but with practice, it will become more obvious.

Try this same exercise while staring at your reflection in a mirror. Try to look around your head for the energy field that occultists call the aura, and see what it looks like when you are breathing and channeling energy through your body.

Another exercise is to take a lit stick of incense, one where the tip is a burning ember. In a dimly lit room with the eyes partially closed, draw magical diagrams with the ember tip. Draw a pentagram or a cross, watch the tracing as the ember tip is moved, but also try to keep the form that you draw in your mind as long as possible. Over time with practice, you will be able to do this without a lit stick of incense. Simply moving your magical tool or your hand will produce the same kind of light tracers along with the illuminated figure you drew floating in the air, only more subtle and less distinct.

You should get to a point where you can see the various energy patterns at night outside in the dim light of the moon or in a room with only a single candle lit. You will be able to see and then feel the energy that you generate with your movement and breath, and it will be as real as anything else is to your naked eye. You should be able to particularly see the magic circle when it is consecrated, see the watchtower wards when they are set, and see the lines of force that you draw with various tools. Practice and engaging your imagination will make this a very real sensory experience.

Component of Sound

Sound Vibration

Another thing that can help to enhance your senses regarding the generation and utilization of energy is sound. When I am engaged in energy work, I find myself intoning, humming, or making the *Aum* sound as I do my work. This is particularly important at the beginning of a working, when you are trying to establish the correct mind state and when you start the movement and breathing technique that sets the energy building in motion. Once the breathing becomes more intense and involved, the humming goes away completely. Yet when you stop all movement, the humming or intoning returns. This intoning is like a periodic *Aum* and is established by the breath, as it starts to slowly increase or during the moment of complete cessation of movement.

Another way that sound can help to generate magical energy is a specialized pre-recorded piece of music. The music should not be distracting, but instead, it should help the movement, where it slowly increases in speed and volume in a synchronized choreography with the accelerating movement of the body as it goes through a repetitive cycle, increasing speed until the plateau rhythm is achieved. The music must also quickly stop at some point to go with the cessation of all movement. Using drumming, either pre-recorded or performed as you move (holding and strumming a bodhran or shaking a rattle) or with assistants who supply live music is the most excellent kind of music, as long as the cadence mimics the acceleration and the final cessation.

Finding music that would match this kind of repetitive and ever-increasing speed might be challenging, but for the musically inclined, it could be produced using a certain digital sound sampling or recording talent. Imagine if you would, the tune "Around the Mulberry Bush," "Ring Around the Rosy," or the "Merry-Go-Round Broke Down" used to act as the iterative music that slowly increases to a crescendo and then suddenly stops. It would be whimsical, perhaps even silly, but effective.

Component of Emotions

Emotions

Energy work relies on desire and passion to drive, direct, and manifest it. Without passion, the actions used to generate magical energy will not have the necessary edge to them, nor will they be able to achieve the ultimate level of energy realization, which is ecstasy. It should be noted here that the full release of magical energy feels a lot like sex because when done correctly, it produces a similar kind of ecstasy. It is a powerful release brought to a climax by the passion and emotions pushing it to that point. Sexual visualization when done to stimulate the generation of energy uses the inherent powers of polarity in magical energy to dramatically enflame any working, helping one achieve ecstasy.

The ability to tap this power in the mind and to cause it to surface on demand is an important skill a Witch needs to develop. Whether you are very self-controlled or a real hot mess most of the time, being able to deliberately and in a disciplined manner release this emotional energy like a bomb within you is the key to energy work. There are a number of techniques to bring this out, but the best way is to know yourself well enough that you can be very emotional when called upon to do so by the necessity of this magical work.

Component of Intention

Intention

Probably the most important ingredient to passion is the intention behind it—the reason you are doing this work in the first place. If you are not nearly to the point of crazy and emotionally keyed to the outcome, then doing the work for whatever purpose is likely to fail to produce the level of energy needed to make a difference. That is probably the most important rule regarding any kind of magical energy work. You have to want it badly . . . but not desperately. Desperation typically leads to delusion, something to be avoided in energy workings.

Your intention must be therefore kept simple and clear. It must be something that you desire greatly and seemingly cannot do without. It needs to be just that one simple thing that you want and need to have in your life that will complete you forever, even though this would actually be a ruse to trick your mind and emotions to produce a powerful reaction. The next magical intention that you would work would have the same urgency and needy edge to it that the previous one had.

Energy Working—Putting It All Together

Assumption: Movement technique is a deosil circumambulation, use of a sigil to imprint the energy.

This is an example of an energy working without any ritual structures:

1. Perform around twenty minutes of sitting meditation to clear the mind and body as much as possible.
2. Stand erect and perform the ascending wave gesture to establish centering.
3. Walk around the circle area slowly in a sun-wise direction while engaging in occasional cool breathing—feel your emotions start to drive you as you engage in this activity and let your hands shake and your fingers twitch.

4. After having completed three rounds of the circle, engage in bellows breath for a short period of time, around three or four bursts of this activity. Also begin to release your pent-up emotions.
5. Starting to increase the pace, accelerate until you reach a comfortable but engaging speed. Let yourself fully connect with your emotions, pushing them toward a climax.
6. When you start to feel a kind of strange exhilaration, push yourself to a final burst of speed and let your emotions achieve a kind of ecstatic release.
7. Cease all movement suddenly—gently drop down to the floor and feel the energy continuing to circulate around you. Perform the bellows breath at least three times as you feel the energy flowing.
8. Stand erect and perform the descending wave gesture to center the energy into your body.
9. Bring out the sigil that you had on your person and project its image into the energy that is amplified all around you—say or intone your intention loudly, then drop the sigil to the floor before you.
10. Start walking around the circle a second time, except this time accelerate more quickly and seek to reach a second climax as before using the breath, emotions, and visualization—then ceasing all movement, dropping down to your knees and pulling the energy into your chest.
11. Stand erect and perform the ascending wave gesture with as much intensity as possible. As you project the energy up, send it out to either the left or right instead of directly above you, and visualize (as well as verbalize) that energy doing what you have directed it to do. This final energy projection should be done with all the emotions and passion that you can muster.
12. Sit down gently and perform around ten minutes of sitting mediation.
13. Finally, take your hands while sitting and lean forward to place them flat on the floor before you. Project any residual energy into the ground.

As you can see with this example, all of the components of energy work have been integrated to create a seamless practical method for energy generation.

Getting all of these elements to work together will take some time and practice. I recommend working on the components separately until you know how to do them without any thought or consideration, and then pull them together to build a full energy working. This kind of energy work is perhaps the simplest type that you can do, but it can also be embellished with other techniques as well. In fact, knowing how to do this kind of operation without ritual structures will greatly enhance the work when rituals are added.

Self-Empowerment

Probably the most important target for generating and projecting magical energy is yourself: your body, mind, and emotions. Magical workings are generally not very successful unless you believe in yourself and feel strong and confident. A weakened self-image or a lack of willpower will not only doom most magical workings but also ensure a lack of success in the mundane world.

If you take the above thirteen-step energy working outline and drop steps ten through twelve, and instead perform the slow inhalation breathing technique to inhale the magical energy deep into your body while sitting in the energy field, you will be performing a kind of self-empowerment. When the energy starts to dissipate, ground any excess energy into the floor (step 13).

Performing this variation of the energy work greatly helps self-empowerment. You can use a sigil and also affirmations and goals to imprint this energy before digesting it, but it will go a long way to energize yourself and help you feel more positive.

I would also add that this is not a palliative measure for any kind of chronic depression or other types of psychological afflictions. It is merely a way of building a foundation for a magically energized self-image and a buoyant emotional body.

In the next chapter, we will discuss some of the additional techniques that you can use in this kind of working that will embellish the simple but very effective energy working. All of these components will help build up the ultimate ritual workings presented in chapter 12.

Chapter Eleven

ADDITIONAL ENERGY WORKING TECHNIQUES

Energy of the mind is the essence of life.

—Aristotle

We have covered the basic energy working without any rituals or even qualifying the energy with one of the four elements in chapter 10, using the elemental spirit or the qualified power spirit. If the additional trappings don't inspire you then just using the basic energy working would add something to the kind of workings that you already do. This was an organized examination of looking at an energy working, so it will help to more clearly define how this kind of working functions.

However, there are certainly other topics to cover that completely fill out the basic energy working. These topics involve qualifying the energy using the pentagram; charging objects to endow them with power; working with polarities, grounding, and the proper flow of energy; magical links and energy circuits; practical use of magical energy; living in the world of magical powers; crystal magic; and using magical substances, i.e., drugs.

Using the Pentagram

The pentagram is used to qualify the energy raised to one of the four elements or spirit. You should practice drawing the invoking pentagrams until they become second nature. However, breath and visualization are used to make the drawing of the device an effective magical action. Since the magical rituals that are used in this work are vortices, there will be no need to employ the banishing pentagrams.

When drawing the pentagram, use your imagination to see the lines of force being revealed in the structure of the pentagram. Also, feel the energy you are raising. As you draw the lines of force of the pentagram, feel a kind of resistance as you move towards the final line drawn to the target. When you draw the invoking spiral around the device at the end, use your breath to project energy into the center of the device.

With practice, you can learn to sense and even see the energy that the invoking pentagram is generating, having a color specific to the element that is manifesting. Red is fire, blue is water, green is earth, and yellow is air. For the two attributes of the element of spirit, the creative spirit has a golden color and the receptive spirit has a purple color.

I would recommend performing a mini energy working in which you draw an invoking pentagram and then sit before it in a meditation state and use slow inhalation breathing to breathe in the energy while visualizing the element colored energy entering into your body to load and charge it. If you want to extend this working, try drawing the invoking pentagrams to the four quarters to create field of energy generating devices around you.

Charging Objects and Energy Storing

Using the method for self-empowerment as outlined in chapter 10, you can project the energy into an object instead of ingesting or absorbing it. Use the slow exhalation technique to focus the breath on the object that you wish to charge along with visualizing the energy impregnating the object and using the hands to compress and project the energy into it. You could also use the invoking pentagram exercise above to generate the energy and project it into an object in the same manner.

Charging and loading energy into an object is an age-old method for charging something that has been consecrated with lustral water (saltwater used to consecrate a magic circle) and incense smoke. Some objects will have a greater capacity to absorb energy and others will only be able to absorb a single charge. Metals are better than parchment or wood, stones are better than metals, and gemstones and crystals are the best. In fact, a multi-faceted crystal (natural or synthetic) can store seemly an endless number of energy charges.

A crystal can also be tapped for energy simply by touching it and performing the slow inhalation exercise. Crystals are therefore important components for energy work since they seem to be able to store energy and also make it available when it is needed.

Further Thoughts on Magical Polarity

As previously stated, magical energy relies on the dramatic occurrence of polarities that cause a kind of fission when they are realized. There are quite a number of subtle aspects of polarity that can be found in the various components of energy generation: motion and acceleration versus sudden cessation, curves versus straight lines (invoking/sealing spiral or pentagram), deosil versus widdershins, inward versus outward, ascending versus descending waves—the list is practically endless.

Yet the most explicit polarity to be found in magical energy is the archetypal male (active) and female (passive), and also deity and human. Human beings are polarized internally and externally, having both creative and receptive psychic attributes, and we also have that psychic element which causes us sexual desire. In whatever manner we engage our object of desire, we are all sexual beings. Sexual imagery used in magical workings helps to enhance the energy, and so does sexual stimulation and masturbation. I would recommend any and all of these techniques to help generate magical energy. That said, I leave the details of the "how" and the "what" to your experimentation and discovery.

Consensual sex between couples or groups is an obvious mechanism for generating magical energy, although the topic is better examined more fully from other sources than what I am prepared to do here. I will say this about sex magic, however: It is important to perfect your art with both magic and sexuality separately. You should be good at magic and at sex (with your partner or partners) before trying to combine them to successfully perform any kind of sex-based energy working.

Importance of Grounding

Magical energy work always seems to leave behind residual energy; depending on the intensity and the volume of energy generated, there can sometimes be quite a bit of leftover energy. It is important to know how to deal with this energy because it can cause you a lot of trouble if it is not properly drained. This draining is called grounding—in this process, you gather the leftover energy and place it into the earth.

In my many years of working magic with other people, I have seen firsthand what happens to folks who do not perform a proper grounding after doing energy work. It can make them intoxicated, irrational, irritable, and can even produce mild forms of hysteria. Even so-called sophisticated ceremonial magicians seem to forget either why grounding is important or even how to do it when it is a necessary operation. This simple act seems to be often omitted because it was never seriously learned in the first place or because it seems so rudimentary. However, it is important for all those who are practicing any kind of energy magic to perform a grounding exercise when the work is completed.

In the thirteen-step energy working in chapter 10, the last step performed is where the residual energy is grounded. From a restful sitting position, lean forward and place your hands flat on the floor or ground and slowly exhale all the magical energy left in your body into it. I would follow up that action by eating some food, drinking some water or wine, and—if you still feel too energized—go outside and put your fingers into the earth or hug a tree. This is a simple exercise to do and only takes a few minutes to accomplish. Yet it surprises me how many folks who work with magic don't seem to know that it is important or never learned to do it.

Magical Links and Energy Circuits

We have already covered the basic idea behind a magical link in the section on magical sigils (chapter 9), since they are, by definition, the magical link. What we haven't covered though is that magical energy also forms circuits, and that a free flow of magical energy requires a line to travel through to connect the subject's energized intention with its object.

Basically, a magical circuit is nothing more than a connection that gets established between the subject and object of a spell. A circuit can also be the lines of force seen in a magic circle or device hanging in the air after being drawn. Still, when I think about a circuit, I usually think about the magical link I have fashioned to make something in the outer world happen. It is important to understand that at certain points in a magical working, ensuring an effective circuit is important, while at other times the practitioner needs to know when to break a circuit or link after the working is completed.

If you wish to make something happen, such as getting a job, lover, or money where the target is not a specific person or thing, keeping a magical circuit open after performing the energy working is important. This is because you will want to keep the lines of force active to help draw the desired thing to you.

However, if you were to work magic to coerce an individual into doing something or (gods forbid) harm someone, then managing the circuit and the associated link would become much more important. To coerce someone requires the ability to establish the link and then to break it once the individual begins to make the desired moves. If you are working magic to harm someone, you would want to break the link as soon as the negative energy hits the target. Breaking a link is an easy task—you just need to destroy the sigil by burning it, do a simple closing rite, and then disconnect it in your mind. You can ritually do this by snuffing out a lit candle, closing your Book of Shadows, and ringing a bell (bell, book, and candle reversed).

The reason for this link and circuit breaking is that keeping the link open would subject the practitioner to what is called a rebound effect. This is where the magical intention would begin to reverse itself when the target person would either resist or take action against what was being done.

A rebound effect would cause the performer of a coercive love spell to become entangled in its energy and would exhibit obsessions about the person he or she attempted to charm. A rebounded love spell makes the Witch fall miserably in love with their target, leaving the target free of the magical energy sent to bewitch them. Similarly, a rebounded spell to work harm will cause that harm to the person who sent it, typically self-inflicted.

Even a skilled use of building and breaking links can go awry, so it is better to be ethical, not to mention it is frequently more successful. The object lessons of unethical magic going terribly wrong are too numerous to discount, so it would seem that any degree of guilt can cause an unethical spell to rebound.

Practical Considerations for Magical Circuits

Another topic that we have to examine is where a magical link or circuit is unsuccessful, so the magical energy raised has no place to go. Such a spell will fail harmlessly. Yet if there is something there in the psyche of the practitioner that the power can latch onto, the energy will activate something in the practitioner instead of doing what it was intended to do.

A failed spell can therefore empower something in the mind of the Witch that will respond with an unexpected result. It could even cause a reversal if the spell caster inwardly feels that achieving such a goal through magic is somehow either cheating or unethical in some way. In other words, the spell castor may have blockages within him or her that prevents the desired object from occurring. There could also be individuals or situations that interfere with the desired outcome. The only way to determine this is through the use of extensive divination.

Luckily, if it is an internal obstacle or blockage that is causing the problem, it can be magically resolved. This situation is called a crossing (named for cross-purposes), most of which are internal. What is required to resolve an internal crossing is a potent uncrossing ritual. I will provide a good uncrossing ritual in this work because such a rite is always required at some point in a Witch's magical workings.

Still, it is important to completely understand the nature of being at cross-purposes with oneself and how to fix it. It could be that we are internally conflicted, or that two or more starkly different or opposing objectives are entangled and need to be separated. Only divination will help you determine the cause and find a way to resolve it. I recommend engaging your favorite set of divination tools to any proposed magical energy working. You should perform divination before you do a working and afterward, to check on its efficacy. If there is a blockage, you may see it before you even do the working, or it will most certainly appear in post-working divination sessions.

A crossing caused by other individuals is another matter altogether. Such a situation could be caused by people who are in competition for the same given objective or who are just inclined to vindictiveness for the crossed practitioner. It is apparent that the way to resolve this issue is either to cast a wider net, have a more generalized object or to deal directly with the person or persons who are interfering. Resolving that kind of crossing is more difficult, but not outside of possibilities.

There is a way of using an uncrossing ritual to overturn the wills of those who are being obstructionist for no justifiable reason. It might also require some diplomacy or a direct willful facedown of a bully or gadfly (or maybe hiring a lawyer). Needless to say, magic may or may not be able to resolve these kinds of sticky situations. You will have to use your own good judgement to find a just resolution.

A World of Magical Powers

As mentioned before, there are magical powers within us and also a universal source of magical power that can be tapped under certain conditions involving resonance. What we haven't covered is the existence of places and things that seem to have a natural kind of magical energy.

Whether these naturally occurring places and things imbibe in the universal magical energy or somehow, as inanimate objects, have some kind of inherent quality is the larger question. It is my opinion that because magical energy is a part of our collective consciousness it would seem that this kind of magical energy is more a product of the eye of the beholder than whether it represents some kind of latent magical energy. That doesn't mean it is illusory or purely imaginary, because certainly there is a common agreement amongst magical practitioners that certain herbs, plants, minerals, metals, and gemstones have certain qualities. It also could be agreed that certain locations in the world have magical qualities associated with them. However, the manner in which these qualities are experienced and discovered represents a great area of subjectivity.

For instance, one of my power places was in the city of my birth, in a drainage valley that was part of the extensive sewer system in the city. Going there at night was an amazing magical event, and I had many powerful experiences in that same place for a few years while I lived there. No one except me would have found that place powerful except a couple of young friends who accompanied me when I went there to magically spelunk. While it is true that I was under the influence while there, my experiences were real to me and meaningful. Power places are important, but they are discovered as readily in a Witch's home locality as they are in some famous distant location in our world. The key is using the imagination to help locate them, since they are all around us if we could only see them.

As for magical substances, such as herbs, plants, minerals, metals, gemstones or crystals, we can group these within magical correspondences. We can organize them by comparing them to the four elements, seven planets, twelve signs of the zodiac, or the ten spheres and twenty-two paths of the Qabalah. These kinds of correspondences can help us understand the magical qualities of these substances, but the subjective part comes into play to determine what substance goes with what elemental, planetary, or zodiacal attribute.

Additionally, many raw substances are processed into herbal sachets, flower bouquets, unguents, oils, food, drink, jewelry, and magical tools. A knowledge of these things, including their qualities, use, and how to process them is important if the Witch has a proclivity for making things from magical sources. Since my gifts do not lie in that direction, I will simply say that I purchase already processed things that I need and then consecrate or charge them for magical use. However, there is enough information on herbs, minerals, metals, or gemstones, their use, and how to acquire and process them to comprise several books. I defer to the crafty individuals who have specialized in these areas to explain their lore.

Use of Magical Substances

This brings us to a topic that should be covered in any book on energy work—the use of naturally occurring or manufactured drugs. Are drugs an important part of energy work? That depends on the individual and also their age, probably. As for me, I do not imbibe in any substances to alter my perceptions when I work magic. Yet I would be lying if I said I *never* used substances in my work to enhance and intensify the experience and perception of magical energy.

Drugs, sex, and alcohol have always been a part of magical workings since the earliest time of humanity; in fact, it was probably the use of psychotropic substances that opened up the human mind to a world of transcendental consciousness. You could accurately say that I have done so many mind-altering substances in my day that it is no longer necessary, and that would be true. It is also true that in my old age, I can no longer handle using these kinds of substances without also doing physical harm to myself. However, I found that forms of meditation are sufficient for me to attain a similar state of mind necessary to work energy magic, and it has not lessened the degree or quality of the experience. I cannot either condone nor condemn the use of substances in magical workings. I can at least give some advice if you are planning on using drugs and then performing magical energy workings.

First of all, remember that you need to remain conscious while working magic and that you will need to be able to be fully present in your mind in order to aptly process what you are experiencing. So you probably should consider taking a bit less of the substance than you would if you were just going to party or "trip" without any magical work.

The type of drug is another important consideration. Powerful hallucinogens would probably not be a good substance to take when planning on working magic, nor would taking anything that would make you incapacitated.

Also keep in mind that the magic itself is the most important activity—anything that distracts from it would also degrade or interrupt the magical working. You can get high, but not as high as a kite. You can alter your mind, but not so much that you lose track of your work or what you are doing. You can use substances to augment and enhance your working but *not* to distract or halt it.

I knew some friends who took LSD and then tried to perform a complex magical working. It didn't go well, as you can imagine, but they thought it was cool in a disordered sort of way. They furiously wrote up a bunch of text and magical pictures as they were tripping, but later on when they returned to reality, what they wrote was useless. My comment to them at the time was that if you want to trip, then trip; if you want to work magic, then work magic. Trying to do both is a losing proposition. The same thing is true with alcohol: if you get drunk, you can forget about working any useful magic.

Therefore, it would seem that the lesson here is to use drugs or alcohol in a careful and measured fashion so that they enhance what is being done and not interfere with it. This is a sensible proposition, and it is the one that I recommend.

Crystal Magic

Crystal magic is an embellishment to working with the extended energy model, but I believe that using crystals in a limited and precise manner can greatly aid energy workings. This is particularly true when one considers that crystals can store magical energy like a battery over time. There are three basic tools used in crystal magic, and these are the base crystal, necklace emitter, and the transmuter wand.

When I talk about crystal magic and magical energy being used in crystals, what I am saying should not be confused with any energy based on the electromagnetic spectrum. I visualize magical energy as a form of colored light; when focusing on a charged crystal, I can see that the light is trapped in it, endlessly bouncing off of the internal reflective surfaces. I believe that this shows that the magical energy is absorbed or captured into the crystal, but it can be retrieved and externally projected when accessed through the use of another crystal. This is why crystal magic uses more than one crystal tool in the system that I developed.

Base Crystal: The base crystal is a large multi-terminated crystal placed at the foot of the altar, wherever that is in the magic temple. The base crystal is the main collector of magical energy and it acts like a battery. When performing rituals, the base crystal will collect and store a facsimile of all of the energy produced for every ritual that is performed in the magic circle.

Necklace Emitter: A necklace that has a large single crystal worn around the Witch's neck. It has a connection established between the base crystal and itself. This is done frequently, usually before a working and afterwards, where the Witch will take the necklace crystal and touch it to the base crystal, either selectively copying energy patterns from it or putting energy patterns into it, or both. The necklace emitter records the emotions and energy sensations the Witch is experiencing, so what it contains will be quite intimate to the working. Additionally, it can store energy patterns drawn from other workings as accessed and collected by the base crystal; the two can work together with their individual perspectives.

Transmuter Wand: A wand with a crystal tip, or one made of many crystals and metals to form a rod-like shape. Mine has such a combination of elements. The transmuter wand stores energy, draws it, and also projects it; it is a versatile tool. It works by itself quite well but actually has more heft if it is connected with the necklace emitter. This is done by physically touching the emitter with the wand and visualizing that they are both synchronized to each other. I would do this synchronization just prior to starting a magical working when I am fully garbed and prepared.

If you use a transmuter wand, you will find that you rarely need either the dagger or the wand, since it can easily act as both simultaneously. It also functions with a greater esthetic look and feel, so it would be considered to be more powerful than just a wand or dagger. You can anoint crystals with oil, clean them off with a moist cloth, and use them to dip and touch a sigil with wine or any sacrament (except saltwater, which may damage it).

Crystal magic relies heavily on visualization—you need to be able to see or sense the vibrating patterns of magical energy captured within them in order to properly realize their worth and utility. If you can learn to see the energy fields emitted by invoking pentagrams or the magical energy in a magic circle, I believe that with practice, you should be able to see or be able to feel the energy in a crystal. Once you see those energy patterns in the crystal, it will greatly help to creatively use them in your energy work. Their use in magic is as multifold as the many different types of crystals available to the average collector. How this is determined is through experimentation and an active and creative imagination.

There are many types and forms of crystals both natural and synthetic, and to this nearly endless list could be added semi-precious crystal gemstones.[30]

Now that we know most everything that we need to know about working with magical energy, we should examine the ritual structures and determine how to join the energy working with the energy-based ritual system in the next chapter. I would expect, though, that there is much to learn, practice, and master just by performing various types of energy working techniques and methods as outlined in this and the previous chapter. I have written what I know about this subject that will help you to extend the magical energy model, but it is up to you to make it work.

---

30. For a blog-catalogue with more information about crystals, see: "Quartz Crystal Properties and Metaphysical Formations" at Kacha Stones: Ethically Mined Crystals (accessed May 5, 2020): https://www.kacha-stones.com/quartz_crystals_properties.htm.

Chapter Twelve

THE TOOLSET AND RITUALS FOR ENERGY WORKINGS

> One of the greatest and simplest tools for learning more and growing is doing more.
>
> —Washington Irving

We will now discuss some of the tools that are used to perform the more elaborate energy ritual workings. There are some basic elements that you are already using in your Witchcraft magic, so we will only briefly touch on them here. The key components to this kind of magic will be highlighted here so when they are discussed while examining the rituals that we will use they will not seem strange or alien. All of these tools are based on the kind of tools used in modern Witchcraft magic, and are typically not part of the elaborate working toolset of the ceremonial or grimoire-based magician.

Revisiting the Magic Circle and Working Space

The basic foundation for a ritual energy working is the already set and established magic circle, the consecrated magic circle that Witches in many traditions use for working magic. While a component of Witchcraft magic, it is not a feature of Ceremonial Magic. I would like to review the elements of the basic circle consecration and the Witch's magic circle and compare it to what Ceremonial Magicians do. This distinction functions as a way to distinguish between the two methods.

In Ceremonial Magic, a magic circle is used almost exclusively for the evocation of demons. A Ceremonial Magician uses the magic circle to protect himself from the hostile or neutral spirits he might summon.

For a Witch, the magic circle is nothing more than a boundary between the sacred and the mundane, much like how the temple boundary was used in antiquity. It is not meant to keep spiritual or paranormal things outside of the circle but to hold things within it. It is also used to denote that everything that happens within it is part of the Witch's sacred religious and magical domain. While there are wards set to the four cardinal directions with watchtowers established at each, they are meant as the locations for the guardians that protect the sanctity of all that is within the circle proper. A consecrated circle encloses an activated temple of the God, Goddess and the four dread lord guardians of the outer spaces. This is what I was taught as an Alexandrian Witch.

If a Witch should conjure a spirit, it would have to be done in her sacred space, which is within the magic circle and not outside. So, as you can see, there is quite a bit of difference between a Witch's magic circle and one used by a Ceremonial Magician. There is also a difference in the type of magic that they would perform as well, especially when it comes down to ritualized energy workings and spirit conjurations.

In addition to having the space for a magic circle, there should also be some kind of table to act as an altar. The altar can be placed anywhere in the temple with the understanding that when a magic circle is set, it is within the perimeter of that circle. A Witch will normally embellish the altar, covering it with a decorative cloth and placing upon it other regalia, such as statues, et cetera. Often the room in which the temple resides also serves other purposes. It is typical for a practicing Witch to move around furniture to make room for the sacred space, but a small table is usually left somewhere in the area and functions as the altar. For energy workings, the altar is where the tools and any tarot cards and sigils are placed for convenience.

BASIC PATTERN FOR CIRCLE CONSECRATION

The basic ritual pattern for a consecrated magic circle might vary somewhat, but it is typically similar to all those working within the British Traditional Witchcraft regimen. What follow are four steps and ritual actions; you should check these steps against what you do to charge a magic circle. The important components are the consecrated sacred space, the four watchtowers, and the drawn magic circle.

1. Bless the salt, and charge and bless the water. Mix the two together to make the lustral water.
2. Bless the temple and circle area with the four elements as lustral water (water and earth), incense, and candle light. The movements around the circle are deosil, starting in the east, passing the north, and finishing at east again along the magic circle's edge.
3. Draw the outline of the magic circle with a sacred dagger or sword, starting in the east and proceeding deosil to end in the east.
4. Set the invoking pentagrams to the four cardinal directions, starting in the east (air—Eurius—sylphs), south (fire—Notus—salamanders), west (water—Zephyrus—undines), and the north (earth—Boreas—gnomes). The unnamed dread lords for each watchtower are also summoned.

This ritual structure establishes the foundation of the consecrated magic circle within which all the additional rituals of a given working are performed. Both liturgical and magical operations are performed within this magic circle, but we will only concern ourselves with the magical operations. A consecrated magic circle anchors all structures erected within it, ensuring that even a powerful ritual structure like a vortex will not compromise its integrity. It will also keep any energy structures generated within it intact and inviolable, and it can shape and give a geometric structure to energy fields, making them prismatic.

Eight-Node Magic Circle

The four cardinal direction alignment of a consecrated magic circle is too limited, in my opinion, to be used as the base for advanced energy ritual workings. I have developed one that has eight nodes instead. There are four cardinal directions and four in-between points or angles in this re-established magic circle. This structure is placed within the classical Witches' magic circle that keeps it preserved and intact, so we don't need to consecrate that outer circle with eight nodes.

The eight-node inner magic circle allows for the use of more complex ritual structures and allows for a greater variety of geometric shapes to formulate within the circle. Some of these shapes can easily coexist simultaneously. For instance, you could erect a pyramid of power and also a vortex using the eight-node magical circle where both structures would meld and blend together to form a more potent combination of energies.

There is an element-based relationship between the four watchtowers and the four angles, although it varies depending on whether the angles represent a deosil formulation or a widdershins one. If the ritual structure that uses the angles is a vortex, then *each angle takes on the quality of the watchtower to the left.* If it is a normal energy field with a deosil circuit, then each angle takes on the quality of the watchtower to the right. Let me demonstrate this curious fact.

Vortex with widdershins circuit

NE angle—Northern watchtower

SE angle—Eastern watchtower

SW angle—Southern watchtower

NW angle—Western watchtower

Regular square energy field with deosil circle

NE angle—Eastern watchtower

SE angle—Southern watchtower

SW angle—Western watchtower

NW angle—Northern watchtower

That means that if the eastern watchtower is determined in a working to be associated with fire, then in a vortex the southeastern angle would be associated with fire as well. A rule of thumb about setting invoking pentagrams to the circle nodes: A watchtower can be associated with any element regardless of the element ward set to it in the consecration rite in order to accommodate a particular working. Within an established magic circle is complete flexibility that allows for a number of possible combinations to be used within a magical working.

In addition to the eight-node magic circle structure are also three points in the center of the circle. If you can imagine that the center of a magic circle always has a kind of innate pylon operating within it (whether or not it is explicitly drawn), then those three points would represent the zenith, the nadir, and the central point of a magic circle. If you were to stand in the center of the magic circle, these three points would line up with your feet, head, and heart. The midpoint node in the magic circle represents the practitioner, and particularly, their heart center. The other points are the highest and the lowest, or the heavens and the underworld. This should, at least for now, qualify these three points and what they represent in a magical working. The eight-nodes on the periphery and the three in the center make for a total of eleven nodes altogether, making eleven an important number in this kind of ritual work.

Witches' Elemental Toolset

Five Elemental Tools

The five elemental tools (four elements and spirit) are the wand (fire), the dagger (air), the cup (water), and the paten-pentacle or dish (earth). There is a lot of material that is written on these four elemental tools, but for our purpose we can just equate the quality of the four tools with the four element qualities and not have to say much more than that. Each tool has been consecrated and charged in the traditional manner, typically with a combination of lustral water and incense. The wand and dagger (athame) are typically charged between the naked bodies of a female and male Witch in some traditions; but often it is merely a matter of sequestering a tool and then using it for a period of time to make it special, consecrated, and charged.

By contrast, there is less said or attributed to the non-element spirit as a magical tool. In my own workings, I have equated spirit with the crystal. My reason for doing this has more to do with my magical energy work with crystals than any kind of revelatory explanation. Spirit is the quality that integrates the four elements into a singularity—the One. It is ubiquitous and has both an individual and universal dimension, even though they are actually one and the same.

Crystals, particularly rock or glass, can be natural containers of magical energy. I have already covered the topic of crystal magic previously, so here I will state my preference for crystals as a representation of a symbolic tool. After having worked with crystals for many years and noted their qualities as a magical tool, I decided that the quality they most represented was the non-element of spirit. I have been satisfied with that association; others who are not so keen on crystals might find other representatives.

The other two magical tools I work with in energy workings are the sword and the staff. The sword was considered the mark of the rank of Witch-Queen or Witch-King (second degree High Priestess or High Priest) in my tradition, but I have always considered it to be an important tool and have used it as such. The staff was also considered a sign of rank, that of the Magus or elder, which would be third degree by itself, or being a High Priestess who has sponsored the creation of new covens under her authority (a lineage queen). However, I have found the staff (or stang, a horned staff) to be a powerful, excellent, and useful tool as well.

The sword is an extension of the element qualities of the dagger, and so it is associated with air, and represents force, volition, separation, and activation. Lines of force drawn by the sword are more powerful and broader than those drawn with a dagger. The sword is a good ward for spirits, and it can separate sections of the magic circle. I typically use it to draw the consecrated magic circle, but I also use it to draw the watchtowers or angles together in the center of the circle, or to draw a square within a circle (joining the watchtowers or angles).

The staff is an extension of the element qualities of the wand; thus, it is associated with Fire and represents wisdom, mastery, maturity, authority, command, and it is also the physical representation of the magical structure of the pylon. I often use the staff as a visual cue for a pylon that I am building in a magic circle, using its top, foot, and center point to determine the placement of devices when drawing a complex pylon structure. The staff can also summon spirits and powers through its qualities of command and authority that it gives to its owner. I have also used the staff to turn in place and build up an energy field while holding it parallel to the floor and I have used it to anchor a power structure and give it stability.

A wand with a crystal tip is a specialized kind of wand that I have found to be very useful in my magical energy work. I have covered the utility of this tool in the section on crystal magic.

Ritual Patterns Used in Energy Workings

There are some very specific ritual patterns and devices used in ritual-based energy workings. We should cover them here so that they are familiar to you before the rituals are presented for you to view.

Magic Spiral

One of the most basic ritual patterns used in energy workings is the spiral. As a symbol, the spiral is a complex structure related to the circle but also extending beyond it to be associated with galaxies or with a DNA strand. As a magical device, it has two dimensions: direction and vector. The direction is either deosil (sun-wise) or widdershins (anti sun-wise), and the vector is from outside to inside, or inside to outside.

The spiral vector *outside to inside* is where the spiral turns into itself in its center point, which is a kind of winding up or compressing. The vector *inside to outside* is where the spiral expands outward from its center point to its periphery, which is a kind of opening, unleashing, or dissolving. The matrix of spirals using these two dimensions produces four type of spirals.

Typically, Witches are familiar with the spirals that are deosil, *outside to inside* (invoking), and widdershins, *inside to outside* (banishing). But there are two other spirals that are less known, and these are the sealing (widdershins and *outside to inside*) and the unsealing (deosil and *inside to outside*) spirals. Sealing and unsealing spirals are used to freeze and unfreeze an active vortex ritual structure and are used instead of the banishing pentagram device.

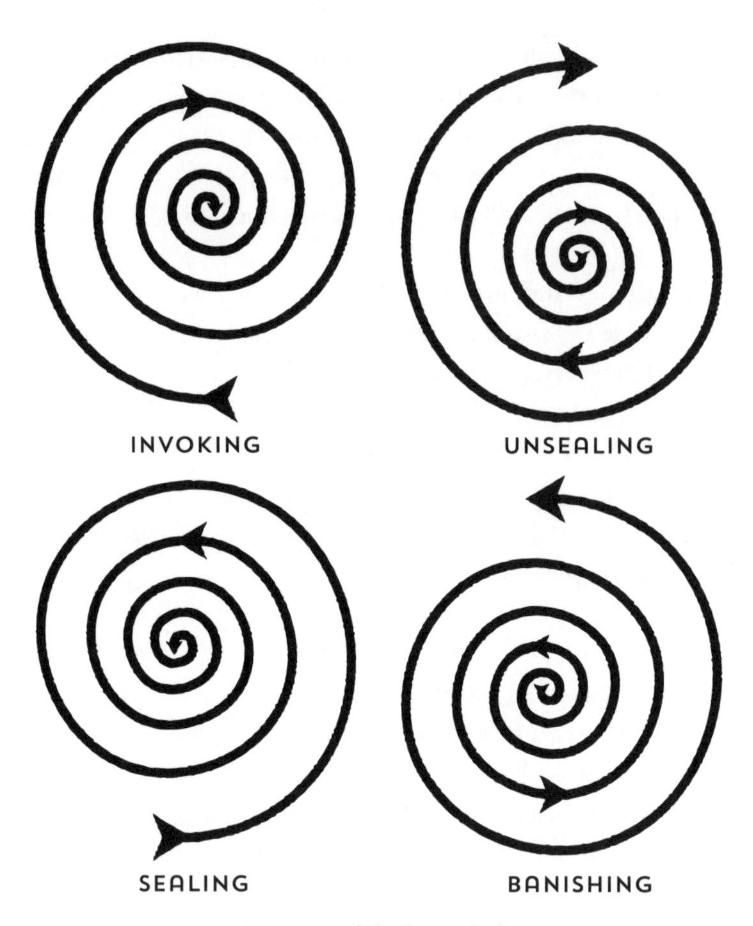

Diagram of the four spirals

When a spiral is used on the floor of a magic circle to either wind-up or exteriorize the energy established there, a different kind of association is applied to the spirals used to perform that operation. A Witch will walk around a circle three times starting in the periphery, slowly spiraling into the center of the circle to fully generate, focus, and wind up the energy in an energy ritual. That would be an invoking spiral being applied to the plane of the magic circle.

To unleash or exteriorize the energy, the Witch will start in the center of the circle and begin to walk widdershins in a circular spiral three times until she reaches the outer periphery of the magic circle, where she will project the energy out to a certain direction. That is a banishing circle, but it doesn't banish the energy as much as it releases or exteriorizes it, which is the other quality of that kind of spiral. It has the same vector and direction as a banishing spiral, but the context is different thereby making its effect somewhat different.

Magical Pylon

Another simple ritual structure is the pylon. This structure is nothing more than a line or loop of force connecting two devices together. Using the dagger to draw a pylon, the practitioner draws a single line of force between two devices that are drawn above in the air and down to the floor. The Witch can draw a single line using a dagger or she can draw a narrow invoking spiral loop between them using the wand. Either method will form a pylon, although the invoking spiral loop will actually produce a stronger field between the two devices because it will be continuously manifesting the connection between the two poles. One other variation is whether the bottom device is joined up to the top, or the top device is drawn down to the bottom. The first is like the ascending wave and the second is like the descending wave used in the centering exercise.

If you want to verify this distinction, just take your dagger, draw an invoking pentagram of any element above your head and then one to the floor, and then join them with a single line of force, going from the top device down to the bottom. Then try the same exercise using the wand—you will notice a slight difference between the two energy fields. The difference might be slight but with practice, you will sense a difference. I would tend to use the wand to perform this operation because the pylon with the invoking loop has a greater emitting force than one drawn with the dagger. And because I distinctly use a transmuter wand to draw all my lines of force and devices used in my ritual workings, variances like these tend to be automatic and internalized.

Western and Eastern Gateways

A set of ritual patterns used in the uncrossing ritual are the western and eastern gateways. These patterns are used to open a doorway into another world within the magical circle. The western gateway is the doorway into the underworld, the domain below the plane of the magic circle, and the eastern gateway is the doorway out of the underworld and into the light of the daylight world. Together, they are the double gateways of the cycle of initiation and spiritual transformation.

A gateway structure is based on the geometric shape of the triangle and conforms to the symbolic qualities of the number three. Most particularly, the idea of mediation, as found in the concept of thesis, antithesis, and synthesis represent the qualities of the magical gateway. In these ritual patterns, the three nodes of the triangle actually represent the mythic Guide, Guardian, and the Ordeal associated with the transit to and from the domain, which are like the basic elements used in the ritualized version of transformative initiation.

For the kind of ritual that we will be employing in the uncrossing rite, we will employ the western and eastern gateways, the gateways that open the practitioner to the underworld (that domain below the plane of the magic circle) and also allow for an exit from that place, ascending to the heavens above the plane of the circle.

The western gateway triangle points to the western watchtower and its legs are in the northeast and southeast angles. The eastern gateway triangle points to the eastern watchtower and its legs are in the northwest and southwest angles.

The practitioner stands in the east facing the west, and draws invoking spirals to the three points of the circle for the western gateway, identifying them as the Guide (southeast), Guardian (west), and the Ordeal (northeast) that must be passed through in order to enter the underworld of the magic circle.

Then the practitioner draws the three nodes of the western triangle together using the hand or wand and imagining lines of power being drawn so that they form a triangle. The person then begins a slow passage from walking from east to west, standing before the western watchtower and performing the pantomime to open a veil or curtain visualized in front of them. The practitioner advances to the watchtower, then turns and proceeds to the center of the circle, imagining a descent to the nadir of the magic circle.

To exit out of the underworld, the practitioner stands in the west facing east and draws invoking spirals to the three points in the circle for the eastern gateway identifying them as the Guide (northwest), Guardian (east), and the Ordeal (southwest) that must be passed through in order to exit the underworld and enter into the world of light. Then the person draws the three nodes of the eastern triangle together and then begins a slow passage from west to east, standing before the eastern watchtower and performing the pantomime to open a veil or curtain visualized in front of them. The practitioner advances up to the watchtower, then turns and proceeds to the center of the circle, imaging an ascent to the zenith of the magic circle.

These two ritual patterns allow for a working to proceed through a double gateway structure that allows for isolation and engagement of the deeper psychic components of the mind, which is how the symbolic underworld domain of the magic circle functions. This is particularly how we will use them in our uncrossing rite, but the double gateway has always represented the doorways of the hero's journey and the transformative initiatory nature of that passage.

Since we have covered all of the tools, techniques, and components for the working of energy-based rituals, we can now examine the basic patterns for the energy-based ritual repertoire.

ROSE CROSS VORTEX RITE

The rose cross vortex is somewhat similar to the ritual of the rose cross in the Golden Dawn system of magic, except that the GD version does not explicitly build a vortex energy pattern. What is required for a vortex is the drawing together of the watchtowers or angles to the center of the circle and a widdershins transit around the circle. The ritual pattern produces a solar vortex, which is a polarized construct because the vortex is a receptive energy field and the rose cross is a creative energy device. Putting them together will create a powerfully polarized field that will hold and contain any energy construct that is generated and built within it.

Other qualities this ritual pattern has is that by itself it will produce a strong healing and protective container. If you are feeling unwell or afraid then this vortex will make you feel protected and provide a healing energy to help you feel better. It can also catalyze the pyramid of power ritual if it is performed within the vortex and allow for a wave form exteriorization when energies are released within it. Tools that are used are a wand or one's hand.

Here is the pattern for this ritual:

1. Using the wand, draw the rose cross device in the northeast angle and project into it a golden colored energy.
2. Proceed to the southeast angle and draw the rose cross device, projecting into it a golden colored energy.

3. Proceed to the southwest angle and draw the rose cross device, projecting into it a golden colored energy.
4. Proceed to the northwest angle and draw the rose cross device, projecting into it a golden colored energy.
5. Proceed to the center of the circle and draw in the zenith a rose cross device, projecting into it a golden colored energy—then draw in the nadir a rose cross device, projecting into it a golden colored energy.
6. Take the sword from the altar and draw the northeast angle to the center of the circle in the nadir. Draw the northwest angle to the center of the circle in the nadir, then draw the southwest angle to the center of the circle in the nadir, and draw the southeast angle to the center of the circle in the nadir. Replace the sword at the altar.
7. Starting in the northeast, perform a widdershins spiral from the outside of the circle and slowly arcing to the center of circle—pass the southeast three times and proceed directly to the center of the circle.

Diagram of the Solar Vortex ritual pattern

8. Stand in the center of the circle facing east, raising the arms so they are parallel to the floor. Stand momentarily, then slowly raise the arms to reach the zenith while slowly inhaling, and pull the energy of the rose cross at that point down to the head, through the body, down to the feet, pushing the energy with the hands until leaning down, exhaling the breath into the floor. Then slowly return to standing erect while inhaling the energy and hold the hands palm to palm before the heart, feeling the energy center at that point.
9. The vortex is now complete. You may continue on to the next ritual or meditate in the center of the circle and absorb the healing energies.

This is the ritual pattern consisting of the movements and actions that are to be performed, but you might want to embellish it with a theme and say something at each of the four angles where the rose cross device is drawn. You would do this also when setting the rose crosses at the zenith and nadir and at the end when the energy field is fully released.

What I would recommend is to focus on the theme of the sun as it cycles through the four hours of the day, starting at dawn and ending at midnight. How to apply this theme will be covered later on in chapter 15, "Preparing for Magical Workings," but for now it is more important to understand the ritual pattern than how to customize it.

The solar vortex has a kind of chthonic quality to it, so ending at the midnight point of the sun would be appropriate. The sun at midnight would be the point in the night that has the greatest danger; but the sun's golden energy would dispel any darkness or evil present, and protect and preserve what is in its embrace until the returning dawn.

ELEMENTAL OCTAGON RITE

The elemental octagon uses the eight-node circle and center points of zenith and nadir to generate an elemental energy field. An elemental energy field consists of a base element and a qualifying element. The base element is set to the four watchtowers using the invoking pentagram device for that element, and the qualifying element is set to the four angles also using the invoking pentagram device for the qualifying element. A pylon is erected in the center of the circle, with the base element set to the foot and the qualifying element set to the head. Then the four watchtowers are joined to the foot of the pylon and the four angles are joined to the head of the pylon.

When the practitioner projects an invoking spiral loop between the head and the foot of the central pylon and draws the energy down from the zenith to the nadir in the center of the magic circle, the elemental energy is established. Because the eight nodes of the magic circle are fused into the center of the circle, the resultant energy generated is a combination of vortex and double squares, making a polarized union between the creative and receptive aspects of the energy field.

All the practitioner needs to do is to imprint the energy field with a sigil placed in a small circle drawn in the center of the circle occupying the base or foot of the pylon structure, and then focusing the intention into it, which is done to mark and emphasize the sigil. The final act is to perform an exteriorization circumambulation spiral of the magic circle, starting in the center and proceeding widdershins outward, passing the northeast angle three times and projecting the energy out through the northeast angle once the practitioner has reached the outer circle at the third pass.

Here is the exact ritual pattern for this working:

1. Proceed to the eastern watchtower and draw an invoking pentagram for the base element with the dagger.
2. Proceed to the southern watchtower and draw an invoking pentagram for the base element with the dagger.
3. Proceed to the western watchtower and draw an invoking pentagram for the base element with the dagger.
4. Proceed to the northern watchtower and draw an invoking pentagram for the base element with the dagger.
5. Proceed to the center of the circle and draw an invoking pentagram for the base element to the nadir with the dagger.
6. Take the sword from the altar and draw the four watchtowers to the center of the circle in the nadir to the invoking pentagram set there. Start with the eastern watchtower, then proceed to the northern watchtower, then to western watchtower, and finally, to the southern watchtower. Then replace the sword on the altar.

7. Proceed to the northeastern watchtower and draw an invoking pentagram for the qualifying element with the dagger.
8. Proceed to the northwestern watchtower and draw an invoking pentagram for the qualifying element with the dagger.
9. Proceed to the southwestern watchtower and draw an invoking pentagram for the qualifying element with the dagger.
10. Proceed to the southeastern watchtower and draw an invoking pentagram for the qualifying element with the dagger.
11. Proceed to the center of the circle and draw an invoking pentagram for the qualifying element to the zenith with the dagger.
12. Take the sword from the altar and draw the four angles to the center of the circle in the zenith to the invoking pentagram set there. Start with the northeastern angle, and then proceed to the northwestern angle, then to southwestern angle, and finally to the southeastern angle. Then replace the sword to the altar.
13. Take the staff from the altar and proceed to the center of the circle. Place the staff in the center of the circle and draw an invoking spiral loop over it. Advance to staff and hold the body close to it while feeling the energy course from the zenith to the nadir, or the head to the foot of the staff-pylon. After holding this position for a short period of time, remove the staff and replace it to the altar.
14. Take the charged and consecrated sigil from the altar and the wand, and then proceed to the center of the circle. Draw a small circle with the wand in the center of the circle, starting and ending in the northeast. Place the sigil in the circle and then draw a sealing spiral over it. Sit and meditate for a short time, then perform the bellows breath to project the energy into the sigil. You can also use the tarot court card to help visualize and then summon the specific Grand Duke spirit, calling its name over and over for a few minutes.
15. Stand and face the northeast angle, and then proceed to walk from the center of the circle in an outward widdershins spiral, feeling the energy intensify as you walk. Draw the energy to you as you make this transit, spiraling until you have made three passes of the north-

east angle—stop there as you make your final pass, walking near the periphery of the magic circle. Then using the wand, project the energy of the vortex field outside the magic circle and into the world.

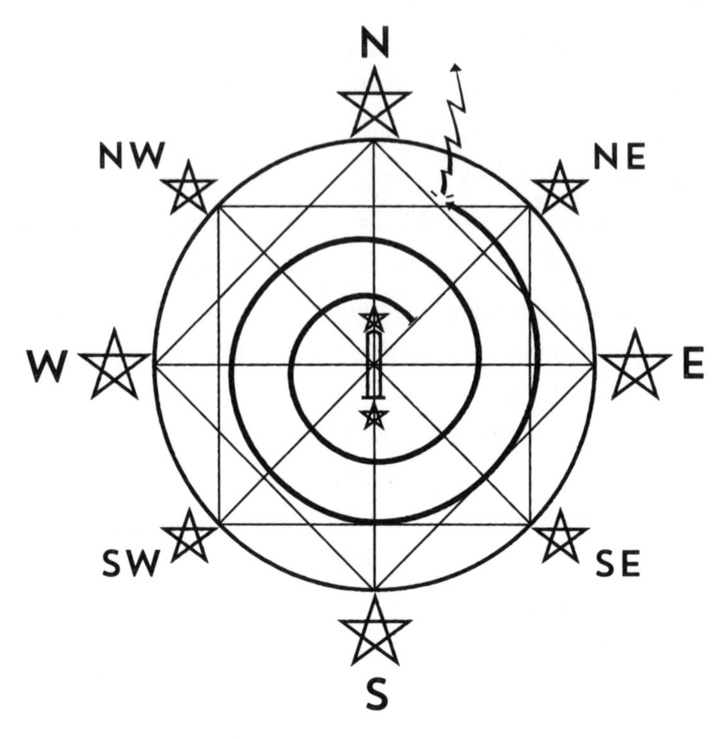

Diagram of the Elemental Octagon ritual pattern

16. Meditate, then ground the energy from your body.
17. Seal the four watchtowers with a sealing spiral, and do the same to the four angles. Proceed to the center of the circle and perform a sealing spiral to the zenith and then the nadir. The rite is complete. (Recall that a vortex cannot be banished.)

I recommend embellishing this ritual with a theme of some kind. In my own collection of rituals, I have used an Arthurian Grail theme, an Egyptian theme, a Greco-Roman theme, and an Enochian magical theme. You can use any other theme that might work for you. Keep in mind that the four angles are aligned to the four watchtowers to the left of them because the ritual structure is a vortex. You should also work on some additional breathing techniques to intensify the ritual, such as using cool breathing when using the sword to connect together the watchtowers and angles, and also when setting up the pylon in the center of the circle. We will cover this task when discussing how to customize the ritual for an actual working in chapter 15, "Preparing for Magical Workings."

In step 14, you could also intone one of the sixteen Enochian Keys for that specific elemental, or use the barbarous evocation for that elemental as found in the book *The Goetia of Dr. Rudd*. Using some kind of powerful words of evocation at that point in the ritual isn't required, but it would add to the drama of the overall rite. You can also use one of the tarot court cards to help you visualize the elemental energy as well as to specifically summon the Grand Duke as an adjunct to elemental energy.

As is the case for all of the rituals in this work, you should embellish them with themes and then practice them until the ritual is practically memorized. You can use a script to read from while performing this rite, but it often becomes cumbersome to manage a script and manipulate the tools and do all of this without halting or having to wait when turning a page, etc. Therefore, there is a balance between embellishing and filling out a ritual with lots of text and verbiage and keeping it simple and easy to memorize.

PYRAMID OF POWER RITE

The Pyramid of Power ritual is used to generate and summon one of the forty qualified powers. This ritual in some ways is more complex than the elemental octagon, but the qualified power it generates is more articulated than the elemental.

The basic pattern for this rite is to set invoking pentagrams of the chosen element to the four watchtowers, starting in the east and ending in the north. This would be the base element of the qualified power. Then once that is completed, the practitioner will join the four watchtowers together in the center of the circle at the nadir using the sword, starting in the North and proceeding widdershins to the west, south, and ending in the east. Then the practitioner will draw a square in the plane of the magic circle connecting the watchtowers to each other, starting in the east and proceeding deosil to the south, west, north, and finishing in the east. The base of the pyramid is now complete.

Then the practitioner will proceed to the center of the circle and draw a pylon device with the wand. He or she will set the base with the invoking pentagram of the base element, then pointing at the apex of the pylon, draw a rose cross device and visualize the symbol of the chosen mystic number and internally summon the associated deity. Then he or she will draw an invoking spiral connecting the base pentagram to the rose cross set to the apex. Finally, the practitioner will use the sword to draw the watchtowers to the zenith of the circle, forming the pyramid structure.

The practitioner will then circumambulate the circle to wind up the power, starting in the east and slowly walking in a deosil arc, passing the east three times while arcing to the center. At the third pass, the practitioner will enter the center of the circle armed with the staff and erect a physical pylon for the magic pylon already there, drawing the power from the zenith through the staff and his or her body to the base. They will recite and visualize the characteristics of the qualified power (colored symbol, keyword) and summon the name of the angelic ruler, repeating it over and over for a few minutes while viewing the associated tarot card as an aid. The pyramid of power is now established.

Once the pyramid of power is built, the practitioner, who is in the center of the circle, will take a sigil and place it before the pylon, charging and connecting it to the base. The practitioner will visualize what he or she wants the power to achieve and perform a short period of bellow breaths aimed at the base to intensify the power.

Then the practitioner will proceed to circumambulate the circle widdershins, holding the staff out before him or her with both hands, starting in the center of the circle and arcing outward until he or she has passed the northern watchtower three times and ends up on the edge of the magic circle facing the north. There he or she will project the power outside of the circle using both hands to project the energy from the tip of the staff outwards and performing a final bellows breath. This will exteriorize the pyramidal energy.

Here is the exact ritual pattern as it should be performed:

1. Take the dagger from the altar, proceed to eastern watchtower, and draw an invoking pentagram of the base element.
2. Proceed to the southern watchtower and draw an invoking pentagram of the base element with the dagger.

3. Proceed to the western watchtower and draw an invoking pentagram of the base element with the dagger.
4. Proceed to the northern watchtower and draw an invoking pentagram of the base element with the dagger, then return the dagger to the altar.
5. Take the sword from the altar and then draw a line from the pentagram in the northern watchtower to the center of the circle at the nadir.
6. Draw a line from the pentagram in the western watchtower to the center of the circle at the nadir.
7. Draw a line from the pentagram in the southern watchtower to the center of the circle at the nadir.
8. Draw a line from the pentagram in the eastern watchtower to the center of the circle at the nadir.
9. With the sword, draw a line from the eastern watchtower to the southern watchtower.
10. Draw a line from the southern watchtower to the western watchtower.
11. Draw a line from the western watchtower to the northern watchtower.
12. Draw a line from the northern watchtower to the eastern watchtower, then return the sword to the altar.
13. Take up the wand from the altar and proceed to the center of the circle. Draw an invoking pentagram into the nadir of the magic circle. Then draw a rose cross in the center of the circle at the zenith. Then draw an invoking loop between the invoking pentagram base and the rose cross shining in the zenith, and step into the center of the circle and perform the descending wave of energy, from above the head down to the feet. Project the image of the symbol for the number qualifier and internally summon the associated godhead.
14. Depart the center and return the wand to the altar.
15. Take up the sword from the altar and proceed to the center of the circle. Draw the base of the eastern watchtower to the rose cross in the zenith. Draw the base of the southern watchtower to the rose cross in the zenith. Draw the base of the western watchtower to the rose cross in the zenith. Draw the base of the northern watchtower to the rose cross in the zenith. Return the sword to the altar.

16. Take up the sigil and tarot card in the left hand and the staff in the right hand from the altar. Proceed to the eastern watchtower and circumambulate the outer circle deosil one time, passing the east, and then arcing in toward the center of the circle, forming an invoking spiral to wind up the power. Perform cool breathing and feel a greater resistance as you proceed ever closer to the center. After the third pass of the east, proceed directly to the center of the circle, facing east.
17. Place the staff standing with you in the center of the circle, then lower yourself to place the tarot card and charged sigil before the staff and draw a small deosil circle around them. Stand fully upright, hold the staff with both hands, and feel the energy moving up and down the staff.
18. Take the right hand and hold it up, pointing to the zenith and visualizing the colored symbol of the qualified power, the tarot card, and quietly reciting the keyword and calling to the angelic ruler over and over for a few minutes.
19. Perform the bellows breath three times, preceded and followed by cool breathing. Then visualize the objective or target that the generated power is to engage.
20. Turn to face the north, then begin to circumambulate with the staff held with both hands and the tip slanting out before you. Perform cool breathing while walking a spiral that is arcing to the outer circle, passing the north three times. Feel a great resistance as you proceed, getting stronger at each step, engage the breath in short bursts of bellows breath every few minutes.
21. At the third pass, turn north, project the power through the staff into the northern watchtower, and expel the breath in a great noisy exhalation or even a shout, then quickly kneel and bow.
22. The rite is complete. Return the staff to the altar and then proceed to the center of the circle to meditate.
23. To clear the working, take the wand from the altar and perform sealing spirals at the four watchtowers and the center of the circle to the nadir and zenith. Deposit the tarot card and the sigil together on the altar. (Recall that a vortex is sealed, not banished.)

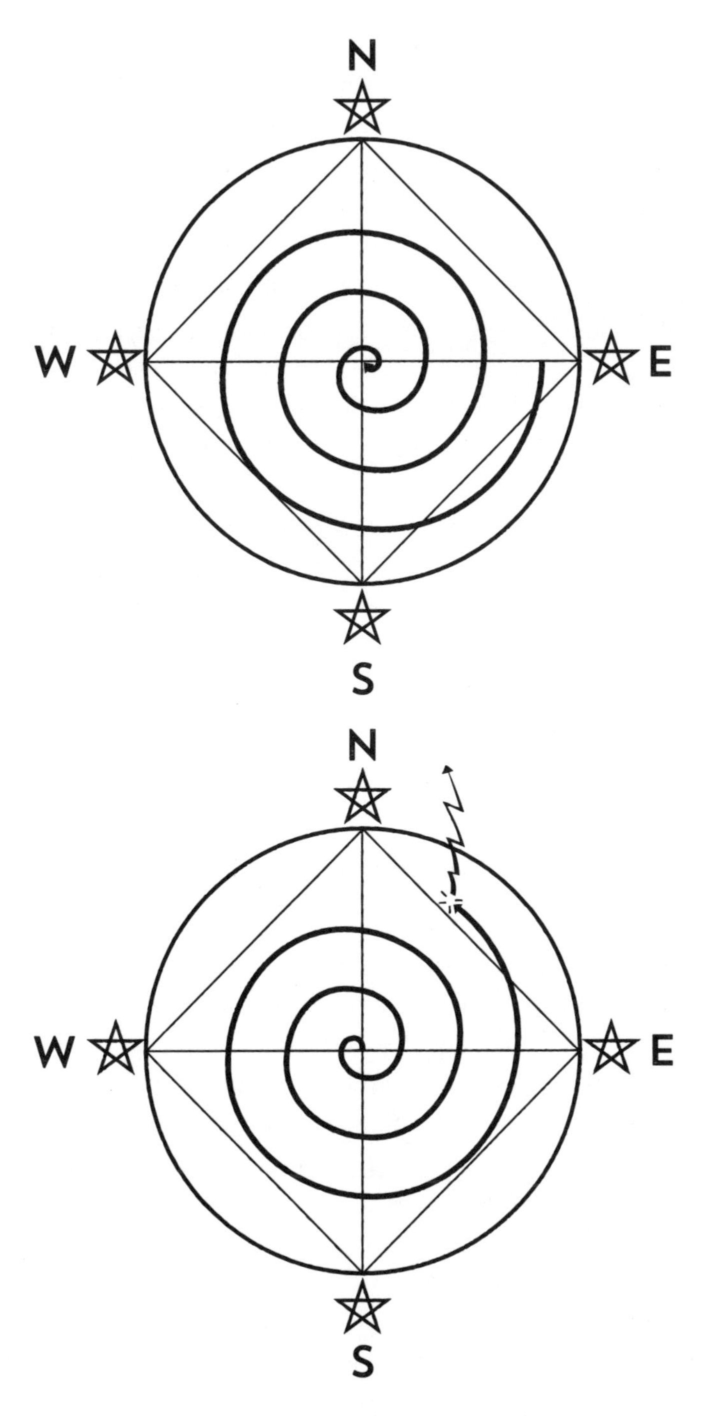

The diagram of the Pyramid of Power ritual pattern

Because the Pyramid of Power ritual has so many steps and is so condensed, I advise you to examine it carefully and practice it in pieces before putting it all together. I have used this ritual in some form or another for more than twenty-five years and have found it to be quite powerful and useful. One thing I would like to note is that this ritual does not generate an explicit vortex like the Elemental Octagon rite. I always set a vortex before performing this rite, such as the Rose Cross Vortex ritual. If this rite is performed but is not enclosed within a vortex, an additional step of performing banishing pentagrams would be required.

Using the tarot pip card as a visualization tool is fairly important to performing this ritual. I have always been very fond of the tarot and grasped it in the very early days when I was a Witchling; being able to work magic using the tarot has always been something that I yearned to do. This ritual answered that yearning, and it opened me up to an energy working that was as effective as any high-blown ceremonial planetary working.

Like the previous rituals, you will need to take this ritual and rewrite it using themes that are acceptable to you, understanding that adding verbiage to the various points in the ritual where they would greatly enhance the rite (steps 1, 2, 3, 4, and 13) should be kept simple to help you memorize it. As stated previously, I demonstrate how this is done in chapter 8, *Preparing for Magical Workings*.

UNCROSSING RITE

The uncrossing rite is an important ritual that is useful if the above energy workings fail to bring about the desired results. Before using this rite, you should know definitively that something is blocking your desired outcome from occurring. The perfect tool used to discover the cause of this failure is divination. I would advise you to perform multiple forms of divination both before an energy working and afterwards for any kind of working just to ensure that the ritual was focused to the correct and clear objective.

Check over the mundane actions that you were supposed to perform along with the ritual working. You should have performed certain mundane actions that would have accompanied the ritual working. These would have been done either before or after the ritual working. You should never work magic for a given objective without also performing mundane actions to increase the overall odds for success. However, sometimes even the best efforts fail, and that is where this working can be deployed to fix things.

An uncrossing rite is used to remove an obstacle that you yourself have unwittingly placed in your way. In most situations, we are our own worst enemies when it comes to fouling up a plan or a good opportunity. If the obstruction is a person or a group of people, this ritual might not work out quite as well, although it is possible that even with such opposition the working will aid you in your quest. If you are facing the opposition of an individual or a group of people for whom you perform the Pyramid of Power rite, I would recommend the 7 of Wands or Fire of Mystery to alleviate or nullify the differences attempting to acquire your objective through a magical working.

When examining the ritual pattern for the uncrossing rite, you will find that it is rather different than the other rituals in this book. I would classify this working as a mystery rite, specifically the mystery of your life at the point of time and the place where this issue is manifesting. To resolve it requires you to undergo a special mystery ordeal; but in this rite, we incorporate fields of energy and a double gateway to achieve these results. We will also focus on the four-element based cosmogonic cycle (creation, golden age, age of death, end times) as well as the eschatological cycle (birth, growth, maturity, death) that represents the curative power of a symbolic death and rebirth, and the associated psychic reset that it would cause you.

To start this ritual, you will first randomly pick five cards from the tarot deck. These are to be given the additional meanings of spirit, air, earth, water, and fire respectively for each card sequentially drawn. These cards will represent the stages (keywords) of the source, beginning, conflict, mitigation, and ending—the five trials that one must undergo. They will be assembled to form a cross, the motif for the ritual.

Additionally, consider taking an herbal bath using High John the Conqueror powder or oil or some other uncrossing magical medicine. This ritual is performed within an already consecrated magic circle, as are all the rituals in this chapter.

This ritual has four stages to it. In the first stage, the practitioner sets a western gateway, passes through it, and then descends into the magic circle-based underworld where a new circle is drawn around the center midpoint. This is the new plane of the magic circle. Once there, a new world is defined through the artifice of building an inverted pyramid structure where the base of the pyramid is on the new plane of the magic circle and the point or apex resides in the center of the circle at the nadir—this is the second stage. There are five invoking pentagrams of creative spirit drawn to the four watchtowers and the center, which are crossed and squared within the circle, and an invoking pentagram of receptive spirit is drawn and projected down into the nadir. A pylon is formed (without using the staff) and the four watchtowers are joined to the nadir with lines of force, forming the lines of the inverted pyramid. Then the practitioner draws a rose cross at the midpoint (the place of the heart) and he or she sits down before it—this is the third stage.

Laying out the five cards in the form of a cross, with source (spirit) in the middle, beginning (air) at the top of the cross, conflict (earth) to the left arm, mitigation (water) to the right arm, and end (fire) to the base. Meditate deeply on each card as you focus on it, draw the invoking pentagram of that element (for spirit, use the receptive left-hand vector), and intone the keyword. Do this for each of the five cards in the cross. Then open your mind to receive whatever messages are in the card. Go through all five cards slowly until the pattern is understandable. You will know what needs to be done to resolve the issue. The sequence of the five elements in the cross matches the pattern of elements as established by Empedocles for the cosmogonic cycle.

When that work is done, close the western gateway and perform the eastern gateway structure to exit out of the underworld—this is the fourth stage. Afterwards, perform sealing spirals to the four watchtowers and the center of the circle at the nadir.

Here is the exact ritual pattern as it should be performed:

1. Perform a mini tarot reading: draw five cards and study.
2. Proceed to the eastern watchtower, face west.
3. Draw invoking spirals to the northeast, southeast, and then the western watchtower—these positions are the Guide, Guardian, and Ordeal respectively—address each when drawing the invoking spiral.
4. Draw lines of force with the right hand, from the northeast angle, to the western watchtower, to the southeast angle, and then back again to the northeast angle. The gateway is established.

5. Proceed to walk slowly from the east to the west, and when arriving at the west, perform the pantomime of opening the veil or a curtain with a dramatic flourish. Step close into the western watchtower and turn to face the east, performing the descending wave.
6. Proceed to walk slowly from west to the east, imagining descending into a chamber. Stop at the center of the circle.
7. Turn to face the west, then with the right hand, project a line of force and draw a circle around the center at the midpoint, starting in the west, moving widdershins around and completing in the west. Visualize the new plane of the magic circle at chest height.
8. Take the dagger from the altar. Proceed to the eastern watchtower and draw an invoking pentagram of creative spirit.
9. Proceed to the southern watchtower and draw an invoking pentagram of creative spirit.
10. Proceed to the western watchtower and draw an invoking pentagram of creative spirit.
11. Proceed to the northern watchtower and draw an invoking pentagram of creative spirit.
12. Proceed to the center of the circle and draw an invoking pentagram of creative spirit at the midpoint. Return the dagger to the altar.
13. Take the sword from the altar and draw the four watchtowers together on the plane of the magic circle to the center at the midpoint, starting with the north and proceeding widdershins to the west, south, and finishing with the east.
14. Draw the four watchtower pentagram devices together into a square, starting in the east. Proceed south, then west, then north, and complete in the east.
15. Return the sword to the altar and take up the wand. Proceed to the center of the circle and draw an invoking pentagram of receptive spirit into the nadir, projecting it below the plane of the magic circle. Then draw an invoking spiral loop connecting the center invoking pentagram at the midpoint to the invoking pentagram in the nadir. The inverted pylon is now established.

16. Return the wand to the altar and take the sword. Proceed to the center of the circle and draw the lines of force from the watchtower-invoked pentagrams down to the invoked pentagram in the nadir, starting at the north and proceeding widdershins, to the west, south, and east. The sides of the inverted pyramid are complete. Return the sword to the altar.
17. Take up the five tarot cards and proceed to the center of the circle and stand there, using the hands to feel the midpoint plane of the magic circle and then project them down to the nadir. Sit facing the west and place the five tarot cards in the form of a cross. The first card is placed in the center, and the other four are arranged one at the top of the cross, one on the left, and one on the right and the other on the bottom arms of the cross. This should be done in the sequence in which they were drawn.
18. Draw an invoking pentagram on each of the five cards formed in a cross. Start with the center (Source—receptive spirit), then the top of the cross (Beginning—air), the left arm (Conflict—earth), the right arm (Mitigation—water), and the bottom (End—fire). Then meditate for a while on each card. Seek to understand the nature of the issue and how it will be resolved. Do this until everything is made clear.
19. Stand up facing west, and proceed slowly to the western watchtower. Perform the pantomime for closing and sealing the curtain and then turn to face the east.
20. Draw invoking spirals to the northwest, southwest, and then the eastern watchtower—these positions are the Guide, Guardian, and Ordeal respectively; address each when drawing the invoking spiral.
21. Draw lines of force with the right hand, from the northwest angle, to the eastern watchtower, to the southwest angle, and then back again to the northwest angle. The gateway is established.
22. Proceed to walk slowly from the west to the east, and when arriving at the east, perform the pantomime of opening the veil or a curtain with a dramatic flourish. Step close into the eastern watchtower and turn to face the west, performing the ascending wave.

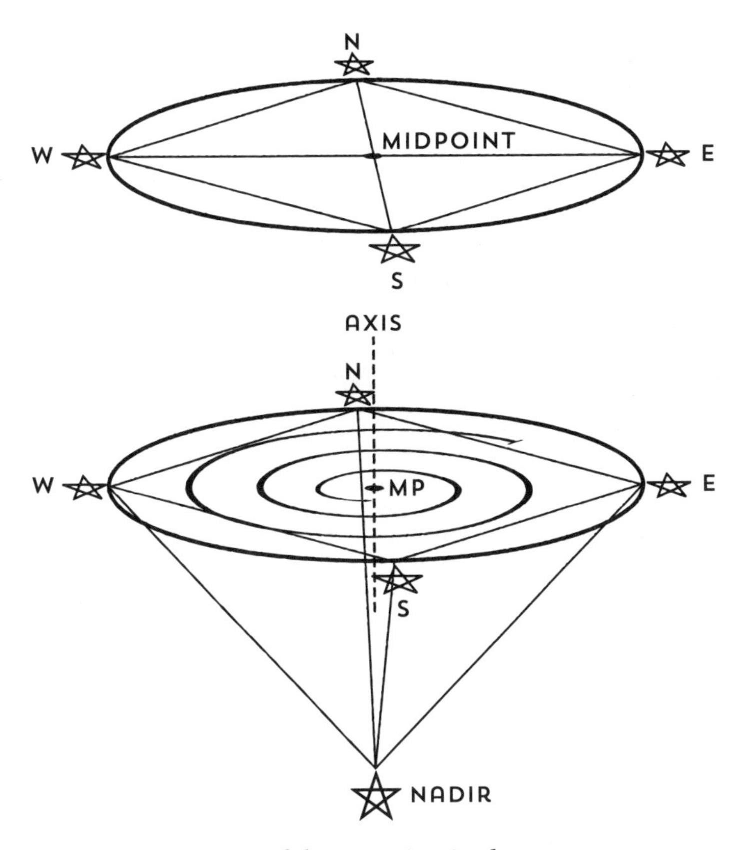

Diagram of the uncrossing ritual pattern

23. Proceed to walk slowly from east to the west, imagining ascending out of a dark chamber—stop at the center of the circle and visualize a beautiful dawn.
24. Draw sealing spirals over the four watchtowers, the center midpoint and nadir—the rite is complete.
25. Take a notepad and proceed to where the five tarot cards are laying. Write down all of your observations and insights for each card and a synopsis of the reading.

The uncrossing rite is actually a kind of initiation passage since it follows the initiation pattern of the Hero's Journey, so I would classify it as an ordeal proper. However, energy workings are not considered to be ordeals unless they address a very strategic objective in the life of the Witch or represent a challenge such as invoking all sixteen elementals over time.

Now that we have covered all of the devices, tools, and ritual patterns, we should learn how to integrate all of these components together to forge magical workings incorporating the extended energy model of magic.

Chapter Thirteen

SPIRIT CONJURING FOR WITCHES

> Those that can heal can harm; those that can cure can kill.
>
> —Celia Rees—*Witch Child*

Since we have covered most of the material that is a part of this book, I would like to discuss what you can do to merge the lore of *Spirit Conjuring for Witches* with the lore in this book. There are a number of inclusions and trade-offs that will assist both energy magical workings and spirit evocations to be even more empowered and successful.

If you have a copy of *Spirit Conjuring* and look at pages 57 through 60, you will find that I briefly touch on the topic of energy magic being used to power a conjuration. I don't actually give much in terms of details, and I don't reveal where in a conjuration it would useful to place an energy working.

However, now that we have completely gone over the basics of energy magic, I can provide some pointers that will show you how to add an energy working to a conjuration. The whole purpose is to create an energy field or envelope into which the spirit can appear, giving it greater tangibility and a more potent capability to affect the material plane.

First off, I would recommend using the elemental octagon to generate an elemental field that would be aligned with the energy component of the spirit to be conjured. You can make this match by comparing the characteristics of the spirit with the qualities of the elementals, or if there is a specific alignment to a direction or an element, work with that to find a match. It doesn't have to be a perfect match. Just imagine the kind of energy you would like that spirit to possess and find the best one. Immersing a spirit through an energy field will likely make it more apparent to your senses, allowing for a greater communication and also making the conjuration a more visually fulfilling experience. Of course, you would omit naming and summoning the elemental spirit so as not to confuse it with the spirit that you are evoking. Just setting up the energy-based ritual working should suffice to empower the evocation.

Secondly, the place where you would perform this elemental energy working would be between setting the Rose Ankh vortex and performing the western gateway opening. What you want to do is to create an energy layer that the vortex will hold, and then perform a gateway that will allow you to unify the underlying structures and establish a new level in the evocation. Placing a gateway between workings allows you to unify existing layers and to then ascend to the top and to establish a new layer.

Using the western and eastern gateways in this manner will allow you to perform multiple workings over time, whether they are conjurations or energy workings. Because the Rose Ankh vortex contains whatever is generated within it, you can use this structure to build up many layers of magical energy and then release them at a strategic moment. You won't release the energy in a vortex until you trigger a climax, so if you seal the vortex in place, you can return at a later date to add more layers to the magic. The magical energy in the vortex will continue to build up, layer by layer, until you finally trigger a climax and release it all.

The secret to this kind of working is to set the Rose Ankh vortex, perform an energy working, and then unify the layers and establish a new level through the western gateway. You can perform the eastern gateway if you wish to resolve what is established in the vortex, but the energy won't be released until you trigger a climax—that is, the part of the ritual that exteriorizes the energy field. Therefore, you can perform the elemental octagon or the pyramid of power, or any combination, to build up many layers of magical energy until you release it. Each energy field will be set with a specific goal and a magical link, so in this situation you could multiplex a complex goal and it would be successful when the energy is released. The trick is that you would perform a single exteriorization ritual action within the unsealed ritual complex (widdershins arc, inward to outward) to trigger all of the enclosed vortex energy fields.

In *Spirit Conjuring*, the core technique was the summoning and assumption of your personal godhead. This was explained as a method to contact and link up with a practitioner's higher self, which was done to empower and protect the Witch as she conjured spirits within her own magic circle. For *Elemental Powers*, the core technique is performing an energy working to empower the practitioner with an element-based energy. If these two core techniques are merged into one technique, where the practitioner assumes his or her personal godhead and also performs an energy working for self-empowerment, the result could easily supercharge the practitioner to make difficult magical objectives more likely to occur. In other words, the application of the godhead assumption could bend probabilities even more than what might be achieved using an energy working by itself.

Merging these two techniques could certainly make your magical workings far more powerful and successful than omitting the godhead assumption. I would say that the possibilities are nearly endless in that regard, and certainly performing all energy-based magical workings under the influence of a charged godhead assumption would certainly be a very potent and a highly energized addition to normal energy workings. This is something I have incorporated into all my workings with much success for energy-based outcomes, and I would recommend it for you to try and see what it does for your magical workings.

Let me sum up how combining the operations in *Spirit Conjuring* and *Elemental Powers* can be used to enhance the workings of both.

1. Add the elemental octagon ritual after the Rose Ankh vortex ritual and before performing the western gateway opening. This will greatly empower the magical evocation of a spirit and give it a more material substance.

2. Use the Rose Ankh ritual before the elemental octagon ritual or the pyramid of power ritual working and then perform the western gateway opening afterwards to establish the energy layer in the vortex.
3. Energy workings in the Rose Ankh vortex followed by the western gateway will produce multiple energy layers as long as the trigger climax is omitted, the vortex is sealed, and the gateway closed after the energy working (for that session) is completed.
4. Layered energy workings can have their own singular objective and magical link that is either separate or grouped with an overall objective.
5. Releasing many layers of energy will produce an enormous output of energy, but each layer will be applied to a singular outcome, and the many waves of released energy will ripple through the fabric of the consciously imbued material reality.
6. Merging the godhead assumption and the self-empowerment techniques will unleash your personal godhead to greatly aid all of the operations for energy workings, from the initial divination to the final outcome.
7. Performing a detailed conjuration of the spirits associated with magical energies, such as elementals and qualified powers, will greatly enhance the magical workings. It will contact the intelligence behind the energy to aid and assist in achieving your magical objective. This two-prong approach to energy working will help to make the magical operation potentially even more successful.

Using the components of both spirit conjuring and energy workings together can make both methodologies more effective and successful. Developing the expertise at combining both systems of magic will confer upon whoever accomplishes this task the truly earned title of a Witch and Pagan Magus. Mastering both systems will fully empower your abilities to work any kind of magic, and it will give you a base upon which to build even more detailed, elaborate, and successful workings.

Chapter Fourteen

THOUGHTS ABOUT PRACTICAL MAGIC

> Every problem has a solution, although it may not be the outcome that was originally hoped for or expected.
>
> —Alice Hoffman—*Practical Magic*

A pious man went to synagogue every Sabbath, fervently prayed, sang psalms, gave alms to the poor, and observed every good orthodox practice that one could possibly do. In his prayers, he earnestly asked the Lord to help him win the lottery because he felt that his need was great and his purpose just. But every time there was a drawing, the man didn't win, and he became despondent. He said: "Lord, I am a good man, pious and righteous. My need is great and unselfish; certainly I should be favored to win the lottery, yet still I haven't won. Why have you forsaken me?" Then he heard a voice from on high say to him: "Saul, give me a break. Go buy a lottery ticket!"[31]

31. This is my rendition of an old joke that doesn't have a specific author, usually referred to with the moral saying, "You got to be in it to win it." It is part of the popular Yiddish folklore.

In my many books and articles about practicing the art of ritual magic, I talk about how the discipline of ritual magic always requires extensive mundane actions being simultaneously performed when one is working magic for a specific end, especially for some kind of material change. I guess you could say that I have made that point to an excessive degree, but I believe that it's fundamental to successfully working magic.

It represents the fact that magic is not a phenomenon that miraculously manifests the object of one's desire for the benefit of the practicing Witch. Magic has a fundamental problem when summoned to manifest unearned fortune or fame—it typically fails. What magic does accomplish well is set in motion a powerful potentializing force that requires practical non-magical actions and focused work in order to realize that potential.

Working magic and then doing nothing afterward is like the joke about the pious man who begs God to make him a lottery winner. He does everything right except he doesn't buy a lottery ticket, thus making it completely impossible for him to win the lottery. While I don't advocate working magic and testing it by purchasing a lottery ticket, some have used this approach with varying results. My approach to practical magic is very … well, practical!

How do I define mundane actions? What exactly does that mean? It means being certain of yourself and your capabilities, shrewd, open to all possibilities, and able to act on multiple plans of action while knowing that one of them will pay off while others may not—and all for different reasons. By being shrewd, I mean that you should always seek and establish goals that are not only likely and achievable but can also lead to other possibilities that help you gain even greater potentials for advancement. Never be too desperate, too tied to one outcome, or too inflexible. Always try to know where your life is leading you and always plan for the unforeseeable and the unexpected. You may not know what may befall you, but you are mentally prepared for the fall.

From the hardest and largest tasks to the most minor and insignificant, all things are accomplished in stages. We proceed and achieve our end in stages, so all goals should be achievable in their time and place. It's also important to know yourself. That means to really know who you are, what you are capable of accomplishing, and most importantly, what you really want and how badly you want it. You must be able to realize when opportunities arise and then strategically take advantage of them. Having more plans and backup plans, all carefully thought out and worked to some degree of detail is also critically important. Never approach a problem with only one possible solution, since life is never that restrictive or narrow. You should also be aware that making plans doesn't necessarily guarantee that any of them will work. Seeking something that is way beyond your ability or nearly impossible to realize will only add to your problems and difficulties.

The most important consideration, as I have said, is to know yourself: know who you are and what you are capable of, and then establish your goals in an incremental manner. Let one accomplishment play into another. Does this sound too complicated or too difficult? Break it down into tasks that are simple and manageable. Big changes that benefit you don't usually happen overnight, but catastrophes do happen quickly, so you need to be aware of what might be coming.

All of these considerations are what I call measuring and determining your base, which is *yourself* in the present time and place. You are the question that must be answered, and perhaps one of the greatest tools for determining the answers to that question is divination. As a practicing Witch, you should master more than just one method. In other words, you should know multiple methods of divination and use them at different times and compare their results.

For instance, ask the tarot, the runes, and the *I-Ching* the same question and see how the results from each system agree and also expand on their derived knowledge. It is a truism that knowledge is power, but the Witch has resources of occult knowledge that go far beyond what the normal person has, *if* they are effectively used. Perform divination to establish who you are, your desires (and why you want them), and your current potential for realizing them. Are your objectives things that are within your grasp or are they far beyond your capabilities at the present time?

Here's another example: Let's say that you want to become the president of the company that you just got hired on in the recent past. If you aren't already very high up in the corporate hierarchy, the chances that you will be made president of that company in the near future are not very good. Working magic to realize this goal will probably produce little or no results, and in fact could harm you by creating unrealistic expectations. It might also make you behave in an arrogant and self-important manner and give birth to personal delusions.

If instead, you carefully study the company where you are working, look at how others have successfully climbed up the ladder of promotion, you might discover the secret of how such an ambition may be realized—incrementally and at various strategic points in your career.

Seeking and desiring something does not make it so, and working magic will not somehow miraculously change the nature of the game to favor you. It has to be approached in a shrewd manner and examined carefully over time. It's a process that must be accomplished in stages or not at all.

Also, if after you have looked over the various individuals who have succeeded in being promoted to the top, and the corporate culture is such that only cronies and relatives get advanced then this company may not ever be able to help you in realizing your ambition. In such a situation, you will have to be open to all possibilities, including being promoted to a higher position within another company. If you are seeking a lofty objective then it must be approached carefully, decisively, strategically, and you must be open to all possibilities, including moving on to other more profitable and rewarding situations.

A similar logic also applies to other objectives, whether they involve your material situation, social situation, relationship status (or lack thereof)—all of these needs must be determined in the same methodical and coldly rationalistic manner. If you have needs or something is lacking in your life, then it is possible that the circumstance of that need has not yet been examined in an objective and careful manner. You should always ask: "Do I really want this to happen? What am I willing to do to make it happen? Is it something that I am capable of doing? Is my life situation amenable to allowing this thing to happen? Do I have fears, negative opinions of myself or my abilities, etc.?"

A Witch should engage in a great deal of soul searching and divination before deciding to use magic to change the equation in her material or mundane situation. Most importantly, she should have already determined the various steps and actions required to make this happen. Without a shrewd and practical approach to resolving her problems in life and achieving success, all efforts—magical or mundane—will be for naught.

What this does, in a nutshell, is dispel the notion that by working magic to make something happen, it will automatically and miraculously happen. I have never seen this approach to magic achieve any degree of sustainable success. Even engaging in positive affirmations, while laudable, or maintaining a positive attitude (no matter what happens) will not in themselves produce the result that one is seeking to make happen.

Errors Associated with the Law of Attraction

There is a terrible mindset afflicting occultists and many in the New Age arena that causes them to believe merely projecting positive and empowering sentiments and beliefs is all that is required to miraculously attract success to oneself. This is an illusion, and one that is terrible in its effects. It produces not success but delusion and inhibition. I could characterize this mind state by saying that no matter how big of a lie you believe about yourself, ardently believing it doesn't make it so.

This is a misuse of the New Thought's basic psychology of self-empowerment creed, called the Law of Attraction. I won't get too deep into this system of belief (you can easily get information by performing an internet search on the term "Law of Attraction") but suffice it to say that the Law of Attraction states that a person's thoughts powerfully determine their reality. There might be some truth to that statement, but the reverse is also true—reality has a powerful impact on a person's thoughts and beliefs. In fact, I would wager that the opposite to the Law of Attraction is far more likely to occur.

As a Witch, I would have to agree that this so-called law seems outwardly plausible and rational. However, knowing yourself thoroughly is one of many ways to addressing how you can achieve the realization of a specific desire (or not). Still, you can't change yourself by simply using affirmations and positive thoughts and nothing else. Attempting to "fake it until you make it" doesn't usually work because often situations are more complex and require a lot more internal work to fully realize success. You have to take positive actions, make plans, and seek to implement them. You have to understand the scope of what it is you are trying to achieve and then use all practical means in achieving it. If you fail, shift to plan B or plan C. Each failure is an invitation to learn what you are doing wrong and how to correct it.

For instance, let's say you need a better paying job. You put together your resume, determine what you are capable of doing, and then figure out how to convince others that you have that ability. Perhaps you work magic to help empower yourself. You also seek out others to help you objectively judge whether you have all of the various points nailed down. Maybe they put you through a job interview rehearsal. You have all the right qualifications and good references.

Let's say you go through an interview and after the second stage, they decide to hire someone else. Instead of being dejected, you should contact them and find out how they saw you, what were your strengths and weaknesses. If your approach is one that is open to all possibilities, your expectations will not be unrealistic. So not getting the job won't be seen as some kind of failure. Plan B is the next interview with the next company, and you will continue to gain more information and adjust your approach until you are successful.

You may also need to have other options, such as another resume for another kind of work, and use that one as well. You should also cold call companies and gather information about what jobs are available, who's hiring, what kind of people are they looking for. The more information that you are able to gather, the more empowered you are. In such a quest, you never give up, you never stop trying, you don't let small failures put you off course. You should maintain the highest flexibility and openness to whatever happens.

Trust me when I say that this kind of approach will make you indomitable! You will succeed, and not merely as a matter of chance, especially when having so many possibilities to choose from. Life consists of infinite possibilities, it's just that only a few of them are likely. A wise Witch is able to divine the one opportunity that leads to many more.

Does Magic Have a Cost?

I would also like to address the popular belief that magic has a cost. It would seem that when people make this statement, they are saying that working magic or being on the receiving end of it requires some kind of sacrifice. In other words, you have to give up something in order to gain something, a sort of zero-sum game. This theme came into the popular mindset from the TV show *Once Upon a Time*. Perhaps the odd counterpoint to that fantasy TV show is that the evil queen is able to do all sorts of magical mayhem to all of the other characters in the cast and nothing ever happened to her. Where is the cost that she must pay for using magic? Is the implication that when evil people work evil magic the cost is neutral because evil is cool?

I can understand this clever idea as a plot device in a TV show script because it adds some spice to the fantasy magic deployed (and some polish to the Rumpelstiltskin mythos), but from the standpoint of actual magical workings, this concept makes very little sense.

Like any other action, magic does have consequences. Yet even doing nothing has consequences! Does magic typically have bad or undesirable consequences baked into it? Well, that depends on what is being done through the artifice of magic and the Witch's competence. Of course, such logic can be applied to any act or refusal to act in any given situation. If I refuse to pay my taxes or just forget about filing them, I am sure that some kind of negative consequence will manifest for me at some point via the IRS. Yet this is not a magical operation—it's just taking some of kind action.

However, magic can and does produce unexpected consequences and sometimes these can be wonderful or quite unpleasant, depending on the context of the magic. Catastrophic good fortune is very, very rare but not impossible, just as is catastrophic misfortune. Often accidents can happen to just about anyone, but very seldom is any kind of magic attached to them. A simple insight to all of this is that all actions have consequences, including magic. That is probably all that anyone can say about magical effects.

In all of the years that I have been practicing ritual magic, I have never experienced anything like a *cost* associated with either using or benefitting from magic. As an occultist, Pagan, and Witch, I have noticed a social cost if I am not quiet about my beliefs and practices, but that represents the errant prejudice in others I have experienced from time to time. All I have to do to ensure that my neighbors and acquaintances don't give me any grief for what I believe and practice is to just be quiet about them. So, the consequences for being public about my beliefs or being indiscrete has consequences. It says nothing about my magic or that I am somehow hindered because I am a Witch.

Now that we have gone over this obvious practical methodology, it should be apparent that you can't work magic by itself to obtain a result; conversely, maybe the need to work magic is completely superfluous. Indeed, millions of people achieve success in their undertakings every day and they are not Witches nor do they work any kind of magic.

I never said that magic will make all of these material things realized. What I am saying is that for those of us who must work magic, we may use it to change our material situation and that doing so does not confound our magical and spiritual obligations. We are Witches—it's our spiritual way and our path. Other folks have their beliefs and practices and follow them as well.

Magic does not provide the answer to every issue or situation that a Witch might experience; in fact, often magic can cause more problems than it solves. But it is our way and our path, and so we use it to find a greater happiness and satisfaction in our lives.

I would like to make a final note on this line of consideration and ask the question: What kind of magic does a Witch work to affect the material plane? Do we invoke deities, angels, demons, project energies—what kind of magic do we do? There is a huge variety of different kinds of magic to choose, from folk magic to ceremonial magic. In addition, there are many techniques for working this kind of magic that can engage magical powers in many different formats, such as energies, magical objects and substances, magical places, many different kinds of spirits, or a combination of some or all of them.

Any magical working that is going to have a very immediate impact on the material plane should likely consist of energies and entities that are close to the material plane. This would include elemental spirits of the air, water, earth, and fire; deities of the specific geographic locality or under the earth; and entities in the underworld. I believe that only forces and beings engaged in the earth plane and its constant changing outcomes could be helpful in making changes in the material world. This is of course my opinion, but it is based on working magic for decades.

For those who want to stay within the arena of traditional Witchcraft with reasonable additions then I would recommend working with the sixteen elementals and the forty qualified powers. I would also use astrology and the phases of the moon to determine the auspicious timing of such a working, and I would incorporate lots of divination, especially before and even after the working.

I would also use all of the possible mundane actions and steps necessary to ensure success for any magical endeavor. Doing all of these things and remaining flexible, practical, and insightful will help to make you a successful magical practitioner... and there is nothing like success to help empower you and assist you to achieve your goals.

Chapter Fifteen

PREPARING FOR MAGICAL WORKINGS

> Excellence without effort is as futile as progress without preparation.
>
> —William Arthur Ward

The next topic that we should cover are the preparation steps that are required to perform any kind of workings. These preparation steps consist of two sets of tasks. The first task is to adapt the ritual outlines (covered in chapter 12) to a specific theme or ritual system so that the ritual outlines are filled out to become part of your personal magical ritual system. You don't actually need to do that work, but the purpose of building a magical system that uses the advanced energy workings is to personalize it. Customizing the rituals is an important step to making these rites a part of your own personal magical tradition. The second task is actually doing the preparation work that underlies a ritual-based energy working. This chapter will cover both tasks.

My main purpose for writing this chapter is to show how one would prepare these rituals for three different hypothetical workings and then undergo the preparation steps for performing them. These three workings (appearing in the next chapter) will demonstrate how you could approach these tasks in a practical manner and use these rituals to perform workings for yourself.

Once we have the rituals written up so that they meet our tastes and expectations, we need to plan for an actual working, perform divination, create and charge the sigil for the magical link, and determine the best timing to use. I will need to show you how to clarify the intention and reduce it down to its simplest form. I have already discussed some of these points earlier but not in the context of actually doing a working. I think it is useful to put the preparation steps in the context of getting ready to perform a working.

What we have covered in the previous chapters represents quite a body of lore for the Witch who seeks to add the repertoire of the energy model-based magic to her workings. It is a lot to consider and integrate into an existing magical system. This I know from prior experience. You will doubtlessly find the additional tools, breathing techniques, and other elements of this magical methodology easy to co-opt; but what will be more challenging will be to take the ritual patterns and dress them up with themes so that they will fit into your repertoire of rituals.

It is true that the published Gardnerian Book of Shadows appears to contain few of the actual magical rituals used to change the material world. The seasonal liturgical rites, initiations, and the Witches' Laws seem to dominate the occasional trifling spell or recipe. That lack is often (but not always) filled in by the coven organization and the initiatory line from which it descends.

If you are lucky enough to have a body of rituals to work magic in addition to a certain tradition of deities and demi-gods, myths, heroes and heroines, you probably should use that tradition for the themes you would use to flesh out the ritual patterns for the rituals in this work. If you don't have an established body of liturgical lore in your current body of rituals or find the theme used in those rituals to be unappealing, you can devise your own tradition and build up themes in the rituals presented here.

We Alexandrian Witches have a tendency to play around with different cultural themes in our magical rituals. While the Welsh Pagan tradition, as depicted in Evangeline Walton's rendition of the *Mabinogion,*[32] was a staple for Alexan-

32. Evangeline Walton, *The Mabinogion Tetralogy*: "The Prince of Annwn," "The Children of Llyr," "The Song of Rhiannon," "The Island of the Mighty" omnibus edition (London: Overlook Press, 2013).

drian covens, many of us were not Welsh, nor did we know (or care to know) the Welsh language. We had to learn to pronounce the names of deities and other mythic persons using a language that was never pronounced as it was spelled; it was unnatural to our clumsy American English-speaking tongues.

Therefore, once a Witch had gained the second degree and graduated out of basic coven workings, they would turn to other cultural and Pagan-based themes. Egypt was a favorite, as was the Greco-Roman period. Some became involved in Nordic or Saxon Pagan cultural themes, or a Paganized King Arthur Grail mythos; still others played around with Sumerian, Minoan, Canaanite, or even Slavic themes. A single coven supported a few of these themes, or at least chose one that was not Celtic. Because I came out of a coven that supported the idea that anyone could appropriate whatever theme they wanted to use and then share the results of their work with the coven, we had as many themes as advanced members. Some even took the approach of creating a comic book-based theme, such as Superman or Conan the Barbarian, or sci-fi based themes of Frank Herbert's *Dune* or Robert A. Heinlein's *Stranger in a Strange Land*.

When I founded the Order of the Gnostic Star many years ago in Kansas City, we developed four themes: the first was based on a Paganized Arthurian Grail tradition, the second was ancient Egyptian, the third was mythic Enochian, and the fourth was very much a sci-fi-occult (with a smattering of Lovecraft) kind of theme. I supplied the group with the ritual patterns based on my years of practice and elements distilled from own personal rituals, and we took those ritual patterns and built up theme-based workings that were quite aesthetically appealing. We all had a hand in this work (at least at first), and the results were some very useful and workable rituals. The ritual patterns presented in this book are based on those same patterns with some adaptive modifications. So, what I am expecting you to do is to follow the same course that my friends and I followed many years ago to build up the rituals of the Order.

Rewriting the Ritual Outline

Writing up rituals is definitely an art form, and if you do it from scratch, you will find that it will require experimentation with some revisions until you get it just right. The theme won't be as important to you as much as the steps used to build up and complete the working so that it is workable. However, if you have a ritual pattern based on a previously written successful ritual working then you will already have the steps determined. You will just need to write it up with some kind of theme to it make wholly your creation.

Now this task might at first sound a bit daunting, but I can give you the formula for doing it and also show you the few correspondences that you will need to build your own rituals out of these ritual patterns.

Ritual Themes and Incorporating a Pantheon

In the following example, I am going to use the Egyptian theme to build out the rituals for these three workings; to keep things easily memorized, I won't add a lot of verbiage to each ritual. There is a balance between adding a lot of verbiage to the rituals or very little; I think having to read a script of papers during a ritual is awkward and interrupts the flow of actions that make up a good ritual working. Less verbiage is probably better and easier to memorize. Secondly, I will strategically modify the four basic rituals that will be used in these workings, showing exactly where they can have features added that will customize them. Let us start this work by examining each of the four rituals.

OCTAGON ELEMENTAL RITE

We will focus on the four watchtowers and the four angles set with the base element and the qualifying element. For each of these nodes in the magic circle we will want to choose four creative deities and four receptive deities. At the center of the circle, we will select the archetypical masculine and feminine attribute of the unified deity to facilitate the visualization of the joining and fusion of these two polarized energy attributes.

Eastern Watchtower: Thoth (Tehuti)

Southern Watchtower: Horus the Elder (Heru-Behutet)

Western Watchtower: Osiris (Ausar)

Northern Watchtower: Set

Center of the Circle—Nadir: Geb

Southeastern Angle: Hathor (Het-hor)

Northeastern Angle: Seshat

Northwestern Angle: Nephthys (Nebet-Het)

Southwestern Angle: Isis (Aset)

Center of the circle—Zenith: Nuit (Nut)

Joining of Geb and Nuit is Neteru—the One God

The theme is represented by the eight qualities of the deities establishing an archetypal sexual polarity and a union. The pairs do not need to be mates, but it facilitates the working if they are.

Rose Cross Vortex

The Rose Cross Vortex is a paean to the sun and its diurnal cycle from dawn, noon, dusk, to midnight. The theme is the sun at midnight when its light is most crucial to the dispelling of darkness, fear, sickness, and despair. It represents the exaltation of light amidst the perilous time of absolute darkness and night. This is a kind of Egyptian sun salutation.

There are five deities that are summoned at these four points of the diurnal cycle and the center of the circle.

Northeastern Angle: Ra (Dawn)

Southeastern Angle: Hathor (Noon)

Southwestern Angle: Tum (Dusk)

Northwestern Angle: Khepera (Midnight)

Center of Circle: Amun-Ra (Ra to the Zenith, Amun to the Nadir)

Pyramid of Power

The Pyramid of Power symbolizes the great pyramids of Egypt that were erected as resurrection monuments to the Ba godhead of the great pharaohs, and so the theme would follow the idea that the pyramid is a structure of god-like power in the material world.

There are five nodes in the pyramid—the four watchtowers and the center midpoint. I would qualify these points with the four sons of Horus, and the center would be qualified by the goddess Maat. However, the pylon apex would use one of ten Egyptian gods that would personify the ten mystic numbers. Where we have put Greek gods in association with the ten numbers, I will supply the ten Egyptian gods here. You can look back at chapter 8 to examine the section on the Pythagorean system of the ten numbers to see where I have applied a deity attribute to each of the definitions of the ten numbers. The choice of deity to number is my own invention and might differ from yours, and that's completely acceptable.

Five Nodes of the Pyramid (Sons of Horus and Maat)

Eastern Watchtower: Tuamutef

Southern Watchtower: Imset

Western Watchtower: Qebhsennuf

Norther Watchtower: Hapi

Center of Circle Nadir: Maat

Ten Mystic Numbers and Egyptian Gods

1. Neteru
2. Nuit
3. Ra
4. Isis-Maat (Creation-Order)
5. Horus (the Elder)
6. Osiris
7. Thoth
8. Hathor
9. Amun
10. Set

In addition, each of the thirty-six numbered tarot cards (2 through 10) would align with the thirty-six Egyptian decan gods, and the four remaining cards (the four aces) would align to the four deities of the primal elements: Shu, Tefnut, Geb, and Nut.[33]

As you can see, if you want to thoroughly work through a specific cultural pantheon, you would have to go through each of the deities associated with the various correspondences of the four elements, sixteen elementals, and forty qualified powers and replace the place-marker deities there with the ones in your elected pantheon.

Doing this task is like creating a kind of symbolic key of correspondences that you could use to qualify all of your rituals, and it is one of the components that you would probably need to create if you wanted to work with your own pantheon. You would need to know some of the mythology for your chosen pantheon and employ it into the ritual themes, as I am doing here. This would work with the Egyptian and Greco-Roman pantheon, but not so much with other pantheons that are not as well-known or with a smaller set of deities.

I have performed some research to find out what is already known in order to fill these categories, at least for the Egyptian pantheon; but for everything else, it is just a creative process that ultimately becomes your own personal system. You only need to justify it to yourself. On the other hand, you can leave the spirit names that are already in this book and go with them.

While it might be counterproductive to load up the text in the rituals with all the background information associated with the themes and the deities, it would be a good idea to do research and write up notes that will help you get a much deeper and thorough knowledge of these important attributes to your ritual work. In fact, if you are using a particular pantheon, it would be wise and efficacious to also engage in various periodic liturgical rites to establish an actual relationship with each of those deities—doing so would certainly add a considerable amount of power to your magical work.

UNCROSSING RITE

Since this ritual is an underworld journey then the characteristics of the chosen cultural pantheon and associated mythology would greatly qualify this ritual. I have drawn upon the New Kingdom tomb-painted-inscribed book the *Amduat*

---

33. For a quick list of these decan gods, see "Decans" at *Egypt—Astronomy/Astrology* (accessed May 18, 2020): http://ib205.tripod.com/decans.html. See also Stephen Skinner, *The Complete Magician's Tables* (Singapore: Golden Hoard Press, 2006), 125–126.

(things or happenings in the underworld) that depicts the passage of Ra through the twelve hours of night and his rebirth in the dawning of a new day.[34]

Since we don't need to get into massive detail associated with this book, the following approach is an abridged version that gives us a flavor of this important text, representing as it does the regeneration and rebirth of the sun through the underworld in its daily passage. We can look at the first gate (entrance into the underworld) and the twelfth gate, the final hour where the sun as Ra is reborn.[35] This will be the theme of this working for an Egyptian version of the rite, but any other cultural variation would follow a similar pattern, representing death and the ordeal of rebirth.

We will begin with the western gateway into the underworld, using the Amduat to color that transition.

Guide, Guardian, and Ordeal of the Western Gateway

Guide: Sia (God of the mind) and the double Maat (total justice)

Guardian: Wepwawet (opener of the ways)—serpent key that opens the gate and then seals it afterwards

Ordeal: Atum (God of the western gate) and the ordeal of the serpent named "That Which Swallows All"

Five nodes of the inverted pyramid (the underworld)

Eastern Watchtower: Khepri (God of rebirth and eternal renewal)

Southern Watchtower: Anubis (God of embalming and guide of the dead)

Western Watchtower: Selqet (Scorpion Goddess—magical protector)

Northern Watchtower: Set (who defeats the serpent Apep)

Center of the Circle—Nadir: Osiris (Lord of the underworld)

Center of the Circle—Zenith: Ra-Khnum (Underworld Ra)

---

34. Theodor Abt and Erik Hornung, *Knowledge for the Afterlife: The Egyptian Amduat—A Quest for Immortality* (Zürich: Living Human Heritage Publications, 2003). The book covers in detail the Amduat with colorful plates and pictures.

35. Ibid., 24–30, and 140–145.

Guide, Guardian and Ordeal of the Eastern Gateway

Guide: Isis and Nephthys

Guardian: Serpent "Encircler of the World"—passage through rebirth from tail to mouth

Ordeal: Khepri (sacred scarab of eternal rebirth) and Shu (god of air who lifts up Ra to the sky)—these two gods facilitate the rebirth of the sun as Ra, leaving behind the mummy of Osiris in the underworld

Now that we have covered the rewriting of the rituals that we will use in the three example workings, I can discuss how you would go about preparing yourself for a magical working. There are a few things that you will need to know that haven't been discussed in this context.

Ritual Preparation

Before you try to perform a magical working to make some kind of material change in your life, you need to perform the preparatory steps. These would include divination, sigil work, determining the kind of energy to use in a working (which would also determine the ritual or rituals to be used), determining the date and time, and any basic preparatory work such as purification and preparing the mind and temple. These steps would be followed for each and every working performed. I will present each one to make certain that you understand what is needed to perform a working.

Divination

Ritual workings are not planned and performed in a vacuum. They are part of a continuous process of religious and magical practices, meditation sessions, research, and above all, divination.

Divination is to the Witch and a magical practice as the eyes and vision are to the body. It is important to know where we have been, where we are, and where we are going. We need to know if our quests and our magical exploits are prudent and fruitful or foolish and empty. We also need to know when we are accurately seeing the world as it really exists or if we are acting under a terrible bias of delusion and unfounded opinion. Divination can help us see the world around us, know ourselves, and understand our life's path at the present and in the future. Without divination, we are blind and subject to delusion. Not only does divination show us our path, but it can also tell us when we need to do something.

The techniques of divination are many, but the competent Witch should have at the very least for her use the following techniques:

Tarot: Since I have introduced the tarot as the repository of all occult and magical symbolism in this work, it is therefore both a system of doing divination and performing magic. I recommend mastering this system thoroughly, because with the introduction of advanced energy workings, it is the very stuff of your magical workings. The tarot will show you the sequence of events of the past, present, and the probable future. However, it cannot tell you exactly when something should be done or might occur.

Astrology: This technique can tell you not only when something will occur and give you an idea of the potentiality behind the combination of your personal latent abilities (the natal chart), it can also reveal how you will work with or respond to current stimuli (transits) and how they will affect what you choose to do. You can also cast a horary chart to get an answer to a question or an elective chart to determine the most auspicious time for a very important working.

While you can get a huge amount of data from examining a number of different charts, I have found that it tends to be overkill for an energy working. Individuals who have knowledge and a taste for astrology can use it but keeping things simple is better. For energy workings, I look at the lunar phase and do the working at a convenient time during the night. As stated previously, you can actually perform energy workings at any time, day or night.

Dice or knucklebones: When you need a quick yes or no answer, or something to help you zero in on a hunch or intuition, the use of dice is a very effective technique of divination.[36] To get answers based on random chance effects is the power of using dice to determine an outcome.

36. A more thorough explanation for using dice or knucklebones can be found in *Spirit Conjuring for Witches*, 183–185.

Pendulum: This device helps you discover locations and directives, but it can also be used to answer yes or no questions. I have found that using a template or a map as the base for pendulum work will produce the best results.

Crystal or mirror gazing: Scrying is probably one of the more difficult techniques to master since it requires you to be able to still your mind or come close to stopping it altogether. Thoughts crowd out the ability to ask a question and observe an image that answers it, so you will need to discipline your mind to become quiet as the session is performed. It also requires some innate psychic abilities, such as clairvoyance.

Other systems: I have also used geomancy, the *I-Ching*, and runes to perform divination; the results are often quite good. The key is to be able to use multiple techniques of divination and not get locked into just one or two. It is important to push yourself outside of your comfort zone in order to get useful insights and shrewd perceptions out of a divination session.

Sigil Work

After performing enough divination to determine what magical action is required and the most desired outcome that you might be seeking, it is time to fashion the sigil link for that working.

We have already covered how to build up a sigil and also how to informally charge it, but more importantly is the work that you would do to simplify the magical objective. This is where you will clarify the objective of the working by eliminating all extraneous interests and desires from it, to hone it down to that one singular powerful thing. I can tell you from experience that there is nothing more distracting and nullifying than having too many objectives mashed together into one big objective. The more complex your objective, the less likely it will be realized.

It is therefore important to remove conflicting desires and reduce multiple paths to a single path. You can always perform multiple workings on multiple objectives, but it is a waste of time to try to bundle objectives together into a single working. Establishing a magical link should have a single target and purpose. While it is the fad these days to multitask, energy magic just doesn't work that way. If you want your magical working to have a lot of impact, you need to pare down your objectives to one single thing. Doing so will ensure that your working will supply the maximum amount of energy to your objective, eliminating the possibility of a cross-purpose occurring or for the energy to be diluted along multiple pathways.

The same steps to build a sigil—that is, reducing the characters in a phrase to just the basic holistic forms—also applies to your objective. Break down what you want the magic to do into the most basic structure, and then base your sigil on that alone. I can guarantee that a reduced and simplified objective will be much more powerful than a complex one.

Getting down to this simplified level might take some meditation and even some divination, but the sigil work is not done until the objective is clear and simple and the sigil is built using that as the source text. I also recommend that the sigil work should be done in a relaxed and unhurried manner, like an artist painting a great work of art. Focus on this work and never worry about the time or the effort, because until you have the sigil completed, you aren't going to be able to plan the working or perform it.

Choosing the Energy

Once you know what you want to do and have produced a clear and precise objective with a corresponding elegant sigil, you must determine what kind of energy you want to use. Since we have defined in this work three basic methods, you can use a simple mechanism to make that determination.

Here is the logic I would use to make this determination. Look over the qualities and keywords in chapters 7 for elementals and 8 for qualified powers. You will also need to ask yourself some questions about what you intend to do:

1. Do you want to apply this energy to something that is wholly internal to yourself and is not based on any external circumstances or situations? If the answer is yes, what you will want to do is use the simple energy working method to generate and ingest a specific element energy. You won't need a ritual or ritual working to make this happen and you can do it at any time and any place as long as you are alone and will not be disturbed for about an hour or two.

2. Is the objective based solely on your emotions or is it a combination of emotions triggered by an external circumstance?
3. If it is solely emotional, choose an elemental working using the elemental octagon.
4. If it is emotional and has specific circumstances attached to it then you will choose a qualified power using the Pyramid of Power ritual.

Differentiating between an objective that would use an elemental versus one that would use a qualified power might be subtle, so I think that a few examples should be discussed here. Firstly, elementals are typically absorbed internally and will affect the outward emotional response of the practitioner. For instance, if you want to empower yourself with a certain kind of energy, perhaps to attract a lover, impress potential employers, or do well during an exam, using an elemental would be key. However, if you want to address an outward situation, such as dealing with deceitful friends or lovers, overcoming a strategic material loss, wanting to turn competitive foes into friends, or seeking legal justice for criminal actions done against you, a qualified power would be your choice.

If you choose an elemental, you will have to select a specific one. You can do this by breaking up your magical objective to fit in one of the four categories. Fire is for knowledge and insight—wanting to actively know something. Water is for feelings and emotions—wanting to feel something or make someone else feel something. Air is for action and change—wanting to motivate either yourself to make something happen or motivate someone else. Earth is for money, health, and material success—a desire to better your material situation, receive healing energies, or find your way in the world. Once you have determined the base element, you can check the description of the elemental qualities to refine your selection to a specific elemental. You can do this kind of magical working for yourself or for someone close to you, as long as you have some kind of a bond with them.

If you choose a qualified power, the selection process will require a bit more searching because you are not only matching the element but also the circumstance. The element category is the same for an elemental but the ten mystical numbers represent circumstances; you will need to look over each card to see if it fits your situation. Not only do the ten cards represent a certain circumstance, they can also help you to resolve that situation if applied in that manner with your magical objective. Once again, reviewing chapter 8's descriptions of qualified powers will help.

For instance, if you were trying to deal with a circumstance where it seemed that you were fully and completely opposed and unable to find any way out of a difficult situation, summoning the qualified power of 10 of Swords could help you overcome what might be considered overwhelming odds, even though the image is one of complete defeat. The 5 of Swords might present an alternative to such a situation, since your negative outcome might have more to do with your alliances and associations rather than your actions. These are based on the meanings of the qualified powers found in chapter 8.

After choosing the energy that matches your objective, it is still important to meditate on this choice and perhaps even perform divination on it. If the tarot card of the energy that you have chosen appears in the reading, it could be a clear indication that you have chosen the correct energy.

Timing—Place and Time for the Working

The beauty of energy work is that you can do this kind of magic at any time of day or night, season, or phase of the moon. There are no limitations to successfully performing your working. If what you are doing is neither strategic nor critical, I would say do the working when you have everything together to do it. There should be nothing holding you back.

However, if this working is strategic or critical, you will want to look into other considerations to maximize the potential of your working—these kinds of workings do need to be worked during a certain lunar phase, season, and time. While I have worked powerful magical workings in the middle of the day, I really prefer to do them at night when the overall energy fields of consciousness are quieter and less filled with emotional spikes and the mass concerns of the local populace.

We all know that the lunar period has four phases: new, first quarter, full, and last quarter. The moon waxes and wanes over a twenty-eight-day cycle. If we take those four phases and break them into eight sub-phases, we will have defined the lunation cycle. If you study the subject of lunar astrology, you will learn that the phases of the moon occurring during a month are also passing through a specific season as the sun passes through a specific sign. A full moon in June (called the Strawberry Moon) will be different than the full moon in January (called the Wolf Moon); in addition, the full moon in a specific zodiac sign when it is full is always the zodiac sign opposite the sun: for example, the Taurus full moon occurs when the sun is in Scorpio. Consulting an astrology book that characterizes the phases and the zodiac signs for the lunar energy qualities would be very helpful.

Although all these qualities will have to be factored into an energy working for a strategic or critical life objective, we will concern ourselves with just the lunar cycle. Since the powers of the moon are either waxing or waning, positioning an elemental working would be best during the waxing of the moon, on or before it reaches the full moon.

Here is the table of the eight phases of the lunation cycle:[37]

Lunation	Interval Degrees	Key Word	Description
New Moon	0–45	Emergence	Subjective, impulsive, novelty
Crescent	45–90	Expansion	Self-assertion, self-confidence
First Quarter	90–135	Action	Crisis in action, strong will
Gibbous Moon	135–180	Overcoming	Clarification, revelation, illumination
Full Moon	180–225	Fulfillment	Objectivity, formulation, manifestation
Disseminating	225–270	Demonstration	Disseminator of ideas, populism, education
Last Quarter	270–315	Re-orientation	Crisis in consciousness, inflexibility
Balsamic	315–360	Release	Transition, seed-state, germination

As you can see, the best phases of the lunation cycle are between the end of the first quarter (keyword "action") and the end of the gibbous phase (keyword

37. Dane Rudhyar, *The Lunation Cycle: A Key to the Understanding of Personality* (Santa Fe: Aurora Press, 1986), 50–56. I have used the text to distill the entries in this table.

"overcoming"). The balsamic phase (keyword "release") is best for divination, and the full phase (keyword "fulfillment") is good for completing a working and sending it into the world. What you want to do is to tie your working with the waxing energy of the moon and see that it is fully exteriorized on or just before the full moon. Since energy workings consist of typically a single evening of work, they would still have to be scheduled around a typically busy work week. Even so, you would still find a range of days where doing such a working would be both auspicious and convenient.

Final Preparation

The preparation for a magical working is started once a date and time are determined. Of course, you would already have your rituals customized and practiced to the point where working them would be easy and mostly (if not completely) memorized. You would also have plans in place to be undisturbed and either alone or with those who would help you with the working. The space where you would do the working must be ready at this time, with the candles, incense, wine (for grounding afterward), consecrated sigils, tarot cards, and all the regalia for the work prepared and ready for use so that nothing can interfere or disturb your calm approach to this event.

Start out with a nice relaxing bath—while immersed, try to empty your mind of all material cares and concerns. You should focus on the work, looking forward with pleasure at doing this magical working. Once done with bathing and anointing yourself with perfumed oils, don your robe and start out with a period of sitting meditation for no less than thirty minutes, though a full hour would be better. Once everything is ready and you feel clear-headed and rested, you may begin the work.

For energy work, it is not necessary to pay attention to the planetary hours or any other astrological considerations other than the phase of the moon, and only when that is required. Since there is little or none of the planetary factors at play in an energy working, you don't have to pay attention to them. Some people like to use the planetary hours and notice the transits occurring during the hour of your working, but it's not necessary to do so. The energy working abrogates all time and space; in a sense, the working occurs within the eternal Now with only the lunar phase having any effect on the working at all.

To start the working, perform the circle consecration ritual that is part of your traditional working rites. If you are so inclined, you could write a new circle consecration rite using the same themes and pantheon as your advanced energy rituals. However, the energy work proper begins once the circle consecration ritual has been completed. It is important to start with a proper magic circle that is properly defined, consecrated, and warded.

Chapter Sixteen

THREE ENERGY WORKINGS: TALES OF POWER

> But the artist persists because he has the will to create, and this is the magic power which can transform and transfigure and transpose and which will ultimately be transmitted to others.
>
> —Anaïs Nin

I thought that it would be useful to present three workings with customized rituals that could be used by example to aid writing up the rituals and also performing magical workings. We already covered how to customize the rituals and prepare for a magical working, so now we need to show three examples. Although purely hypothetical, these workings represent the kind of workings I myself have done over the years. These are my three magical tales of power; like the best stories, they are based on facts and provable techniques.

What follows can show you how workings can be used to resolve issues and to achieve goals through the use of magical energy workings. They might detail something that you have or will experience, or perhaps not. What they are useful for is showing how to work energy magic to assist and empower you to achieve what you desire in the material world.

Scenario 1: You are in a competitive bid to get a new job with an excellent company. They have accepted your résumé; the position and pay, if you get it, would greatly help you to live in a more comfortable economic level than you have previously. You are scheduled to spend an entire day of interviews and meetings with various members of staff and management for this job position.

This is a strategic change, and you seek magical help to empower and enhance your abilities to present yourself in a constructive and positive light. After performing some divination, you have chosen to use an elemental to help you settle and energize yourself for this important appointment. The elemental you have chosen is Earth of Air to give you a disciplined mind, self-control, the ability to show decisiveness and planning abilities, and that you are disciplined and able to set and achieve goals. You already have these abilities, but presenting them under pressure is not an easy thing to do, so the elemental will help you out. When you attend this day-long interview, you will have the sigil hidden away in your wallet.

Scenario 2: You are presently very single and have not had much luck lately finding a long-term lover. This is a situation both involving the emotions (love) and also a circumstance you haven't had any opportunity to change. You aren't desperate yet, but it has been a while since your last relationship.

You have looked at yourself objectively and you affirmed that you don't have any social issues, emotional hang-ups, lingering biases, and believe you are a normally attractive person who has a decent job. You have checked a couple of divination readings, and nothing appears to be out of the ordinary. Your state of being single is just your present circumstance, and you appear to be ready for finding someone. You have also talked to your friends and asked them for their advice; they have truthfully told you that if you found someone, you wouldn't have any problems building a relationship.

This is a strategic change in your current situation, and you want magical help to increase your odds in finding someone. You are being ethical, so you aren't aiming your magic at anyone in particular. You are socially engaged with friends and acquaintances, so there are possibilities for you to meet someone.

After performing some additional divination and spending some time in seated meditation, you have chosen a qualified power to help resolve your situation. The obvious choice, of course, is the 2 of Cups, also known as the love card, whose element quality is water of creation and whose symbol is the blue light. This is also the first decan of Cancer, and it is ruled by the angel Methraush.

Scenario 3: You have worked a series of magical workings to attract a mate, but they have completely failed. It has been almost a year since you first started these workings, and you are starting to get desperate. These magical workings didn't produce any bad results, they just produced nothing. You aren't socially disconnected and have plenty of friends, so there is nothing wrong with you as far as you can tell. Your last relationship was a disaster, however, and you were deeply hurt and devastated by the breakup. Your friends tell you that your former partner was a very negative person with a lot of problems and that you deserved better. You understand that quite well, and you even spent time with a psychologist to try and understand why you chose someone who was not a good fit with your family and friends, and your emotional needs. Speaking to the therapist helped you clarify your issues and separate them from your partner's. You believe you received clarity and closure from therapy.

At this point in time, you know why you got into that bad relationship and believe that you learned a lot about yourself. You are ready for new romance and are pretty certain that it won't be like the last one. However, you spent some time doing a number of readings on yourself along with periods of meditation and asked friends to help you analyze some of those readings and insights. You have discovered that you are actually of two minds about finding a new lover. One side of you is positive and excited about finding a new lover, but the other side is deeply afraid of being hurt and humiliated again. You are at cross-purposes, and the magic that you worked has been short-circuited and blocked from manifesting anything.

You basically have two paths available to explore regarding relationships: you can give yourself more time to heal and get over your former failed relationship, or you can work magic to try and internally unite yourself by breaking off the past and opening yourself to new possibilities. You decide on taking the initiative and making a break with the past, so you plan on working an uncrossing rite to help you make that change.

We have now covered the three scenarios I wanted to share as examples of workings that you might find yourself working someday. These examples will also show how the advanced energy model of magic works to empower and assist you with everyday situations and circumstances.

Scenario 1: Getting the Job Done While Self-Empowered

You have done all of the preparation work and produced the following sigil. You are ready to do the work. (Using the Career Success sigil.)

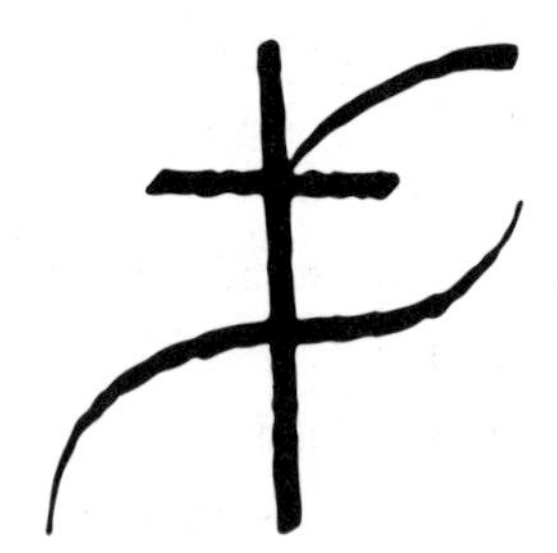

Image of magical sigil for scenario #1

Here is the customized ritual pattern you will use to perform this working:

ELEMENTAL OCTAGON

Proceed to the eastern watchtower and draw an invoking pentagram for air using the dagger. Say: I invoke you, Tehuti (and imagine Thoth before you).

Proceed to the southern watchtower and draw an invoking pentagram for air using the dagger. Say: I invoke you, Heru-Behutet (and imagine Horus before you).

Proceed to the western watchtower and draw an invoking pentagram for air using the dagger. Say: I invoke you, Ausar (and imagine Osiris before you).

Proceed to the northern watchtower and draw an invoking pentagram for air using the dagger. Say: I invoke you, Set (and imagine Set before you).

Proceed to the center of the circle and draw an invoking pentagram for air to the nadir using the dagger. Say: I invoke you, Geb (and imagine Geb before you). Return the dagger to the altar.

Take the sword from the altar and draw the four watchtowers to the center of the circle in the nadir to the invoking pentagram set there—start with the eastern watchtower, then proceed to the northern watchtower, western watchtower, and finally to the southern watchtower. Then replace the sword on the altar and pick up the dagger.

Proceed to the northeastern watchtower and draw an invoking pentagram for earth using the dagger. Say: I invoke you, Seshat (and imagine Seshat before you).

Proceed to the northwestern watchtower and draw an invoking pentagram for earth using the dagger. Say: I invoke you, Nebet-Het (and imagine Nephthys before you).

Proceed to the southwestern watchtower and draw an invoking pentagram for Earth using the dagger. Say: I invoke you, Aset (and imagine Isis before you).

Proceed to the southeastern watchtower and draw an invoking pentagram for earth using the dagger. Say: I invoke you, Het-hor (and imagine Hathor before you).

Proceed to the center of the circle and draw an invoking pentagram for earth to the zenith using the dagger. Say: I invoke you, Nut (and imagine Nuit before you). Return the dagger to the altar.

Take the sword from the altar and draw the four angles to the center of the circle in the zenith to the invoking pentagram set there. Start with the northeastern angle, then proceed to the northwestern angle, the southwestern angle, and finally to the southeastern angle. Then return the sword to the altar.

Take the staff from the altar and proceed to the center of the circle. Place the staff in the center of the circle and draw an invoking spiral loop over it. Advance to the staff and hold the body close to it while feeling the energy course from the zenith to the nadir, or the head to the foot of the staff-pylon. After holding this position for a short period of time, remove the staff and return it to the altar.

Take the charged and consecrated sigil from the altar and the wand, and then proceed to the center of the circle. Draw a small circle in the center of the circle with the wand, starting in the northeast and ending in the northeast. Place the sigil in the circle and then draw a sealing spiral over it. Sit and meditate for a short time, then perform the bellows breath to project the energy into the sigil. Visualize the Princess of Swords (or Page of Swords) tarot card. Say: I invoke the Grand Duke Camuel who serves Carmasiel, Lord of the East. Say his name over and over for a minute or two.

Stand and face the northeast angle, and then proceed to walk from the center of the circle in an outward spiral, feeling the energy intensify as you walk. Draw the energy to you as you make this transit, spiraling until you have made three passes of the northeast angle. Stop there as you make your final pass, walking near the periphery of the magic circle. Using the wand, project the energy of the vortex field outside of the magic circle and into the world. As you do this, visualize complete calm, competence, and self-assurance. Project this energy from the core of yourself into the material world. This moment in the ritual has to be one where you feel as though your hair is on fire—you feel the power deeply and visualize it changing your world. What you feel is a glowing sense of self-confidence that grows in your mind and takes root in your heart.

Meditate, then ground the energy from your body.

Seal the four watchtowers with a sealing spiral, and do the same to the four angles. Proceed to the center of the circle and perform a sealing spiral to the zenith and then the nadir. The rite is complete. Take up the sigil and feel it resonating with magical powers. Keep it in a safe place until it is time to leave for your interview, at which time you place it carefully in your wallet.

Diary: Ritual working was quite successful and you felt empowered and really together. You performed this ritual two days before the scheduled interview and meetings. Once at the interview, you felt completely at ease. It seemed like the people who interviewed you were impressed with your ability to clearly and calmly answer their questions. You even surprised them by asking some very insightful questions about their company that they were only too happy to answer. They have invited you back for a second visit, and you have found out that no else was asked to come back.

Scenario 2: Sending Out Waves of Love

You have done all of the preparation work and produced the following sigil. You are ready to do the work. (Based on the phrase FIND A LOVER.)

Image of magical sigil for scenario #2

Here are the customized ritual patterns you will use to perform this working. You will first perform the rose cross vortex ritual and the Pyramid of Power ritual for the 2 of Cups. You are using the rose cross vortex with the pyramid of power so that when the energy is released, it will produce waves of energy instead of a bolt.

ROSE CROSS VORTEX

Using the wand, draw the rose cross device in the northeast angle and project into it a golden colored energy. Say: I invoke you, Ra, Lord of the Dawning Sun.

Proceed to the southeast angle and draw the rose cross device, projecting into it a golden colored energy. Say: I invoke you, Hathor, Lady of the Noon Sun.

Proceed to the southwest angle and draw the rose cross device, projecting into it a gold colored energy. Say: I invoke you, Tum, Lord of the Setting of the Solar Disk.

Proceed to the northwest angle and draw the rose cross device, projecting into it a gold colored energy. Say: I invoke you, Khepri, Lord of the Midnight Hour of the Sun.

Proceed to the center of the circle. In the zenith, draw a rose cross device, projecting into it a gold colored energy. Then draw in the nadir a rose cross device, projecting into it a gold colored energy. Say: I invoke you, Ra-Khnum, standing in his solar boat; and I invoke you, Amun, hidden mystery of continual rebirth.

Take the sword from the altar and draw the northeast angle to the center of the circle in the nadir. Draw the northwest angle to the center of the circle in the nadir, the southwest angle to the center of the circle in the nadir, and the southeast angle to the center of the circle in the nadir. Return the sword to the altar.

Starting in the northeast, perform a widdershins spiral from the outside of the circle that slowly arcs to the center of circle. Pass the northeast three times and proceed directly to the center of the circle.

Stand in the center of the circle facing east, raising your arms so that they are parallel to the floor. Stand momentarily and then slowly raise your arms to reach the zenith while slowly inhaling. Pull the energy of the rose cross at that point down to the head, through the body, and down to the feet, pushing the energy with the hands until leaning down, exhaling the breath into the floor. Then slowly return to standing erect while inhaling the energy. Hold your hands palm to palm before the heart, feeling the energy center at that point.

The rite is complete. Meditate for several minutes, and then begin the next rite.

PYRAMID OF POWER

Take the dagger from the altar. Proceed to eastern watchtower and draw an invoking pentagram of water with the dagger. Say: I invoke you, Taumutef, Great Son of Horus.

Proceed to the southern watchtower and draw an invoking pentagram of water with the dagger. Say: I invoke you, Imset, Great Son of Horus.

Proceed to the western watchtower and draw an invoking pentagram of water with the dagger. Say: I invoke you, Qebhsennuf, Great Son of Horus.

Proceed to the northern watchtower and draw an invoking pentagram of water with the dagger. Move to return the dagger to the altar, but before replacing it upon the altar, say: I invoke you, Hapi, Great Son of Horus.

Take the sword from the altar and draw a line from the pentagram in the northern watchtower to the center of the circle at the nadir.

Draw a line from the pentagram in the western watchtower to the center of the circle at the nadir.

Draw a line from the pentagram in the southern watchtower to the center of the circle at the nadir.

Draw a line from the pentagram in the eastern watchtower to the center of the circle at the nadir.

With the sword, draw a line from the eastern watchtower to the southern watchtower.

Draw a line from the southern watchtower to the western watchtower.

Draw a line from the western watchtower to the northern watchtower.

Draw a line from the northern watchtower to the eastern watchtower, then return the sword to the altar.

Take up the wand from the altar and proceed to the center of the circle. Draw an invoking pentagram of water into the nadir of the magic circle. Say: I invoke you, Maat, Goddess of Justice and Order.

Draw a rose cross in the center of the circle at the zenith. Then draw an invoking loop between the invoking pentagram base and the rose cross shining in the zenith, and step into the center of the circle and perform the descending wave of energy from above the head down to the feet. Project the image of the symbol (Light) for the number qualifier and internally summon the associated godhead (Nuit.) Say: I invoke thee, Nuit, Goddess of Light and Creation.

Depart the center and return the wand to the altar.

Take up the sword from the altar and proceed to the center of the circle. Draw the base of the eastern watchtower to the rose cross in the zenith. Draw the base of the southern watchtower to the rose cross in the zenith. Draw the base of the western watchtower to the rose cross in the zenith. Draw the base of the northern watchtower to the rose cross in the zenith. Return the sword to the altar.

Take up the sigil and tarot card (2 of Cups) in the left hand and the staff in the right hand from the altar.

Proceed to the eastern watchtower and circumambulate the outer circle one time, passing the east and then arcing in toward the center of the circle to form an invoking spiral to wind up the power. Perform cool breathing and feel a greater resistance as you proceed ever closer to the center. After the third pass of the east, proceed directly to the center of the circle facing east.

Place the staff standing with you in the center of the circle, and then lower yourself to place the Tarot card and charged sigil before the staff and draw a small deosil circle around them. Stand fully upright, hold the staff with both hands, and feel the energy moving up and down the staff.

Take the right hand and hold it up, pointing to the zenith and visualizing the colored symbol of the qualified power (Blue Light), the tarot card (2 of Cups), and quietly recite the keyword (water of mitigation) and call to the angelic ruler. Say: I invoke you, Methraush, ruler of the first decan of Cancer. Repeat the name Methraush over and over for a couple of minutes.

Perform the bellows breath three times, preceded and followed by cool breathing. Visualize the objective or target that the generated power is to engage. In this case, it would be to charm yourself with powerful radiant lights of love that permeate every fiber of your body and saturate your mind with love. Focusing and immersing yourself into a pool filled with this love would be a good image to project. Since you have been preparing for this rite for days, you will experience the full realization of your emotional pitch and the depth of your feelings. Take time to fully process these feelings and thoughts.

Turn to face the north, then begin to circumambulate with the staff held in both hands and the tip slanting out before you. Perform cool breathing while walking in a widdershins spiral that arcs to the outer circle, passing the north three times. Feel a great resistance as you proceed, getting stronger at each step. Engage the breath in short bursts of bellows breath every few minutes.

At the third pass, turn to the north, project the power through the staff into the northern watchtower, and expel the breath in a great noisy exhalation or even a shout. Then quickly kneel and bow. Feel the culmination of all of the emotions captured in this working. Drive the feelings of love, passion, and sexuality to a point of ecstasy as you reach the end of the spiral.

The rite is now complete. Return the staff to the altar and then proceed to the center of the circle to meditate and feel the powerful forces of love that are centered in yourself and projected out into the world, giving you an intuitive thrill of future amorous possibilities.

To clear the working, take the wand from the altar and perform sealing spirals at the four watchtowers and the center of the circle to the nadir and zenith. Deposit the tarot card and the sigil together on the altar.

Diary: This ritual working was an exciting and emotional experience for you, because you felt that by taking this action that you were going to have a wonderful experience. Falling in love is a truly wonderful miracle, but making it into a long-lasting relationship may require some further energy work on yourself. The day after this working, you found yourself skipping around, feeling almost giddy with happiness—but others didn't perceive you as fake or silly; it just seemed like you were very positive and upbeat. Four days later after your friends had noticed the new you who was happy and fun to be with, you got two strongly interested parties and one solid date request. The good feelings appear to be continuing now days after your working.

Scenario 3: Owner of a Broken Heart

You have done all of the preparation work and produced the following sigil. You are ready to do the work. (Based on the phrase "BROKEN HEART?" where the question mark stands in for the word "why.")

Image of magical sigil for scenario #3

Here is the customized ritual pattern that you will use to perform this working.

UNCROSSING RITE

Perform a mini tarot reading: draw five cards and study them. In order: XIV–Temperance, 2 of Wands, 5 of Swords, XI–Strength, Queen of Wands.

Proceed to the eastern watchtower, face the west.

Draw invoking spirals to the northeast, southeast, and the western watchtower—these positions are the Guide, Guardian, and Ordeal respectively. Address each when drawing the invoking spiral. Say: I summon the Guide, Sia, God of the Mind; the Guardian Wepwawet, Opener of the Ways, who will open the gateway and seal it after I have passed; and the Ordeal of Atum, God of the Gateway, who shall send us through the ordeal of the serpent named "That Which Swallows All."

Draw lines of force with the right hand from the northeast angle, to the western watchtower, to the southeast angle, and then back again to the northeast angle. The gateway is established.

Proceed to walk slowly from the east to the west. When arriving at the west, perform the pantomime of opening the veil or a curtain with a dramatic flourish. Step close into the western watchtower and turn to face the east, performing the descending wave.

Proceed to walk slowly from west to the east while imagining you are descending into a decorated burial chamber. Stop at the center of the circle.

Turn to face the west. With the right hand, project a line of force and draw a circle around the center at the midpoint, starting in the west, moving widdershins around, and completing in the west. Visualize the new plane of the magic circle at chest height.

Take the dagger from the altar. Proceed to the eastern watchtower and draw an invoking pentagram of creative spirit. Say: I invoke Khepri, God of Rebirth and Eternal Renewal.

Proceed to the southern watchtower and draw an invoking pentagram of creative spirit. Say: I invoke Anubis, God of Embalming and Guide of the Dead.

Proceed to the western watchtower and draw an invoking pentagram of creative spirit. Say: I invoke Selqet, Scorpion Goddess of Protection.

Proceed to the northern watchtower and draw an invoking pentagram of creative spirit. Say: I invoke Set, who defends the solar boat against the serpent Apep.

Proceed to the center of the circle and draw an invoking pentagram of creative spirit in the midpoint. Say: I invoke Osiris, Lord of Kenti Amenti, the Underworld. Return the dagger to the altar.

Take the sword from the altar and draw the four watchtowers together on the plane of the magic circle to the center at the midpoint, starting with the north and proceeding widdershins to the west, south, and finishing with the east.

Draw the four watchtower pentagram devices together into a square, starting in the east, and proceed to the south, the west, the north, and completing in the east.

Return the sword to the altar and take up the wand. Proceed to the center of the circle and draw an invoking pentagram of receptive spirit into the nadir, projecting it below the plane of the magic circle. Then draw an invoking spiral loop connecting the center invoking pentagram at the midpoint to the invoking pentagram in the nadir—the inverted pylon is now established. Say: I invoke you, Ra-Khnum, the Solar-Ba that is to be Reborn.

Return the wand to the altar and take the sword. Proceed to the center of the circle and draw the lines of force from the watchtower-invoked pentagrams down to the invoked pentagram in the nadir, starting with the north and proceeding widdershins, to the west, south, and east. The sides of the inverted pyramid are completed. Return the sword to the altar.

Take up the five tarot cards and proceed to the center of the circle and stand there while using your hands to feel the midpoint plane of the magic circle and then project them down to the nadir. Sit facing the west and place the five tarot cards in the form of a cross. The first card is placed in the center, and the other four are arranged one at the top of the cross, one on the left, one on the right, and the other on the bottom arms of the cross. This should be done in the sequence that they were drawn.

Draw an invoking pentagram on each of the five cards formed in a cross. Start with the center (source, receptive spirit, XIV–Temperance), then the top of the cross (beginning, air, 2 of Wands), the left arm (conflict, earth, 5 of Swords), the right arm (mitigation, water, XI–Strength), and the bottom (end, fire, Queen of Wands). Then meditate for a while on each card. Seek to understand the nature of the issue and how it will be resolved. Do this until everything is made clear.

Stand up facing west and proceed slowly to the western watchtower. Perform the pantomime for closing and sealing the curtain. Turn to face east.

Draw invoking spirals to the northwest, southwest, and then the eastern watchtower—these positions are the Guide, Guardian, and Ordeal respectively. Address each when drawing the invoking spiral. Say: I summon the Guides Isis and Nephthys, who renew life; the Guardian serpent named "Encircles the World" who is the passage into rebirth from tail to mouth; and the Ordeal of

Khepri and Shu, they who make Ra-Khnum reborn and who lifts him up into the sky to complete the deliverance in the newly forming dawn.

Draw lines of force with the right hand from the northwest angle, to the eastern watchtower, to the southwest angle, and then back again to the northwest angle. The gateway is established.

Proceed to walk slowly from west to east. When you arrive at the east, perform the pantomime of opening the veil or a curtain with a dramatic flourish. Step close into the eastern watchtower and turn to face the west, performing the ascending wave.

Proceed to walk slowly from east to the west, imagining ascending out of a dark chamber. Stop at the center of the circle and visualize a beautiful, brilliant dawn.

Draw sealing spirals over the four watchtowers, the center midpoint, and the nadir. The rite is complete.

Take a notepad and proceed to where the five tarot cards are laying. Write down all of your observations and insight for each card and a synopsis of the reading.

Diary: This was a very difficult working that produced waves of grief, crying, and anger. You could feel all of the bad things and all of the hard emotions that you thought had been purged out of you. All of this happened after crossing the western gateway and building the inverted pyramid. You had to stop at a couple of points to let the emotions pass over you. The reading, however, has shown you the way—that much you understood before even starting the ritual. When you got into the center of the inverted pyramid and set up the tarot card reading, you felt your emotions center—all of grief and pain just disappeared.

The reading told you what you have intuitively known and understood all along in that bad relationship (5 of Swords—earth, conflict). It was almost psychic the way that you knew what your partner was doing behind your back. Yet you gave up your inner power and allowed yourself to be dominated and continuously gaslighted (5 of Swords). However, your internal source is about expressing and communicating and knowing the truth (XIV–Temperance), and you have passed into a state of emotional balance (2 of Wands). What is required is self-empowerment

(XI–Strength) for mitigating any remaining obstacles. The end result is the Queen of Wands, the fully empowered person that you need to be. You need to internally resolve your issues in order to be both free of the past and ready for the future.

Based on this reading and powerful feelings of self-love, healing, and resolution, in addition to the voices of your friends and parents positively affirming your personal qualities, you have determined that you need to work elemental magic on yourself before you try to do any further love magic. You believe that in the lunar cycle after the next one, you should be able to resume your romantic pursuits and be of one mind. For the next magical working, you will invoke the elemental water of earth to soothe and heal your emotions.

The three scenarios shown above with diary entries are probably a bit optimistic, but not too much. I have had similar experiences using these rituals in this manner and the outcomes were positive. Some of my acquaintances have also used similar ritual workings to make strategic changes in their lives and experienced positive outcomes.

Chapter Seventeen

EMPOWERING WITCHCRAFT

> Believe in yourself and all that you are, know that there is something inside you that is greater than any obstacle.
>
> —Christian D. Larson

We have now covered the basic knowledge that you will need to practice advanced energy workings. Everything that you need to make this kind of magical work a part of your repertoire can be found in this book. However, having reached the final chapter, you should know that it is not the end of this kind of study—it is just the beginning. What I have done is to give you the basic foundation. Upon that you can build a whole new magical system with endless possibilities. How do I know that this is true? It's simply because it is the path I followed many years ago.

Using the basic structures found in this book I have fashioned a system of magic that rivals and exceeds what the most advanced magical orders and the hosts of ceremonial magicians possess. It took me many years to build this foundation and then extend it even further, but now you have it in a single concise work. So, you are more fortunate than I because I have shared with you this foundational knowledge that I had to build from scratch over many years.

If life were somehow fair, and the people in the world were compassionate and believed in equality, and everything that you tried to do met with a successful outcome then there would be no need for this book, or perhaps even magic. Yet even for the very fortunate and lucky few life is still a struggle and things happen that are challenging and difficult to resolve. For the rest of us, life presents to us some profound challenges and difficulties that would seem almost insurmountable.

The One Thing

Energy magic is used to empower an individual so that they can at least feel that they have a chance of dealing with difficulties and adversity. It also gives the practitioner methods to address specific deficiencies or to counter adverse circumstances with positive ones. Energy magic is used to build up the self and turn potentials into realized goals. Energy magic specifically focuses on the material world because it is the basis for all that occurs in our life and colors our experiences, and because the world is not fair, we need something to help us turn the world slightly to our advantage.

Energy magic is used to solve problems within yourself and the circumstances of your life in the material world. It is not only a body of magical rituals and techniques—it is also the way to approach a problem to resolve it. There are several steps that are followed when approaching a solution to a given desire or need, and these can be used to also sort out and pinpoint the *one thing* that will open up your possibilities and resolve whatever issue you were facing. It reminds me of the brilliant dialogue in the movie, *City Slickers*, between the characters Curly and Mitch, and I include it here for your study and amusement.

Curly: Do you know what the secret of life is?

Curly: This. [holds up one finger]

Mitch: Your finger?

Curly: One thing. Just one thing. You stick to that and the rest don't mean shit.

Mitch: But what is the "one thing?"

Curly: [smiles] That's what you have to find out.

The secret to a successful working is reducing what are frequently multi-tiered and multi-tasked goals of life into a sleek and simple objective—the "one thing." It doesn't mean that you should only have a single goal in your whole life; instead, it means that you need to simplify and clarify your magical goal and desire down to just one thing. Do one thing at a time and you will be far more successful with your magic than if you tried to empower some elaborate plan. That bit of wisdom is probably the most important part of energy work, and it is often the stumbling block for both experienced and novice magical practitioners. A cluttered or scattered goal will fail to create results.

Once again, here are the steps you need to execute in order to assemble a successful magical energy working; of course, these steps are covered more than once throughout the book.

Define a desire or a need and simplify it down to that "one thing."

- Perform divination to determine if working energy magic is the correct approach, whether there are any blockages, and also whether the goal is within the realm of possibilities.
- Build a sigil, draw it on parchment, and bless and charge the parchment.
- Select the energy components that are needed for the work, whether they are just self-empowerment, emotional-based, or emotions and circumstance.
- Determine the timing, if any—elementals and qualified powers work best using the lunation cycle if the change is strategic.
- Perform the working at the elected time and place.
- Write up diary entries and perform post-working divination.

You can also use the energy working by itself to draw and ingest energy into your body to help empower yourself. Doing this on a regular basis is beneficial for a number of reasons. You can use it to heal your body and your mind by generating a specific element energy and drawing it into yourself. You can also use this technique to empower tools and other items.

In addition to working rituals to project outwardly a magical energy to make something happen, you can project the charge into an object instead, creating a kind of energy talisman or amulet. You can also take the sigil that was used in a magical operation and hide it on your person when you are out in the world. The kind of energy talisman or amulet is one that is made of metal or contains a crystal, for obvious reasons. A crystal can be used to store many layers of magical energy and function as a kind of battery. Wearing a piece of jewelry with a gemstone or crystal mounted on it is probably the very best example of a device used to contain and discharge energy whenever required.

A Pagan Magus

A Pagan Magus is a special kind of a Witch who would be a rare commodity these days; they would be able to work many advanced and different kinds of magic, having a nearly endless repertoire of rituals and techniques to use. The last one that I am aware of was Alexander Sanders, the father of the Alexandrian tradition of Witchcraft. What he did was what Gerald B. Gardner could only dream about—incorporating traditional grimoire magic and other forms of magical occultism into the foundational practices of the Witchcraft tradition. Alex's flamboyant style and his ability to merge many kinds of magical techniques and systems into his Witchcraft lore was breathtaking and certainly amazing.

A while back, I ordered a copy of what had once been a rare British film that had been produced and released in 1969. That film was a documentary with the curious title of *Legend of the Witches*, which was produced by an obscure British film company (Border Films Ltd.) and written and directed by Malcolm Leigh. You can find it on YouTube and watch it there; I recommend it.

The modern Witches depicted in this ninety-minute black and white documentary were from the primary coven run by Alex and Maxine Sanders. While it's not unusual today to find videos of Witches on YouTube, at that time it would have been quite astonishing for a practicing Witch coven to allow a film crew to document actual Witchcraft practices. However, considering the fact that Alex Sanders already had a notorious reputation as something of a gratuitous public promoter of Witchcraft, such a revealing film is somewhat less amazing than it might seem.

This entire documentary showed that the Witchcraft practiced in 1969 was highly experimental and creatively motivated. Modern and traditional methods were seamlessly incorporated to produce the most effective results. Lore and liturgy were appropriated from other traditions, but the essence of what was done was still within the pure spirit of the original creed of modern Pagan Witchcraft.

Since the lore originating with this tradition of Witchcraft (Gardnerian) was sparse and likely from questionable sources, replacement lore was developed and used to fill out that tradition so that it had a more complete and comprehensive praxis. This is not any different than what others later did with their original but sparse traditions, particularly those that evolved into the many forms of modern Paganism and Witchcraft today. Gaps in the lore and supposedly lost methodologies required the incorporation of new perspectives, regardless of their source. We saw this described in chapter 3, where I discussed the three threads of the magical tradition and their passage through time.

The final result was a wholly new system and praxis, incorporating both traditional and new elements. While this documentary is quite dated and obviously promoting myths and self-serving beliefs instead of historically verified facts, the resultant creativity was neither compromised nor made spurious by this association. By viewing the film, we get to see Alex engaging in a very creative approach to his beliefs and practices. He was not yet an Alexandrian Witch, but he had already broken away from those who represented the Gardnerian Witchcraft orthodoxy of the time.

Alex Sanders was in the process of creating a new tradition and praxis by merely allowing his creative imagination to have the opportunity to freely associate ideas, experiment, and explore new ground.

Perhaps the most interesting thing about this obscure documentary is that it shows us all how to be a Pagan Magus, by depicting the experiments and exploits of one of the better-known Pagan Magi of our time. Alex Sanders passed away in 1988 but left behind a considerable legacy, even though he never wrote or published any of his thoughts, beliefs, or practices. Instead, he used the media to document what he was doing. He left it to his followers to write his biography and to present to us his legacy, such individuals like me.

While it might be true that Alex didn't have the gift of writing himself, it is through the writings of others that he was able to leave behind his many different perspectives and beliefs. There is also an entire tradition of Witchcraft called the Alexandrian, which Alex bequeathed to his initiates, although it wasn't either his purpose or desire to create a new tradition. Alex and Maxine called themselves "Witches" with no other descriptive adjective; it was only their later followers who distinguished themselves as Alexandrians, in honor of both Alex and Maxine.

Using Alex as an example, it is important to understand that the lore and practice of Witchcraft is neither complete nor all-encompassing. There are many areas where the traditional lore is sparse or nonexistent. The typical Book of Shadows has to be augmented with lots of lore, and even the existing lore had to be reorganized and rewritten. What is missing, of course, are all of the songs, traditions, recipes, and even a cultural perspective and a traditional language. All these elements have been developed since the days of Gerald B. Gardner in order for Witchcraft to function as a quasi-folk religious tradition. When it comes to the practice of magic, we are left—like Alex Sanders—to borrow and steal from other traditions and practices to build up our lore. Even then, it doesn't create a seamless whole because all of the systems of magic are basically different, and some are incommensurate.

What I have proposed to do with my two books, *Spirit Conjuring* and *Elemental Powers,* is assemble a body of lore that would easily fit seamlessly with any of the many different traditions of Witchcraft, so long as there was a need and a desire to perform magical workings. I hope that these books will help individuals develop their own extended and more advanced Witchcraft magical lore so that they, too, might function as a Pagan Magus.

Though the task is not impossible, it is one that requires a fair amount of effort, discipline, and—above all—lots of practice. Still, some of the other qualities that are needed are curiosity, openness, and flexibility. If a Witch is a hidebound traditionalist who is neither curious nor open then exploring these new worlds would not be appealing to her, and it is doubtful whether such a person would purchase my books.

It is my hope that these two books will act as a stimulus, a guide, and an inspiration for further magical work on the part of the Witchcraft community. What I would like to see is a resurgence of magical practices where individuals and groups once again break new ground and become the new wave and cutting edge of magic in the western world. I don't need to see or hear about people using my ritual methodologies. I just want to see magic become the focus of Witchcraft once again, and for practitioners to explore all the avenues, experiment, share, and publish new rituals and techniques.

As a final note, I would like to give the web address for my blog: frater-barrabbas.blogspot.com. There you'll find hundreds of articles that are mostly indexed by subject on the left bottom side of the webpage panel. I have written articles about nearly every subject in the area of Witchcraft and ritual magic that you might find interesting or useful. I hope that you visit my blog from time to time to read all of the articles I have posted there.

May the gods and goddesses of all the pantheons bless and keep you well.

Frater Barrabbas

BIBLIOGRAPHY

Abt, Theodor, and Erik Hornung. *Knowledge for the Afterlife: The Egyptian Amduat —A Quest for Immortality*. Zürich: Living Human Heritage, 2003.

Bardon, Franz. *Initiation into Hermetics: A Practice of Magic*. Wuppertal, DFR: Dieter Ruggeberg, 1971.

Crowley, Aleister. *The Book of Thoth*. New York: Samuel Weiser, 1972.

Decoz, Hans, and Tom Monte. *Numerology: Key to Your Inner Self*. New York: Perigee, 2002.

Duquette, Lon Milo. *Tarot of Ceremonial Magick: A Pictorial Synthesis of Three Great Pillars of Magick*. York Beach, ME: Weiser, 1995.

Frater Barrabbas. *Spirit Conjuring for Witches*. Woodbury, MN: Llewellyn Publications, 2017.

Frater U∴D∴. *Practical Sigil Magic*. St. Paul, MN: Llewellyn, 1990.

Hornung, Erik. *The Egyptian Books of the Afterlife*. Ithaca, NY: Cornell University Press, 1997.

Kingsley, Peter. *Ancient Philosophy, Mystery, and Magic: Empedocles and Pythagorean Tradition*. New York: Oxford University Press, 1995.

Maanasvi, Manoj Kumar. *Principles of Pythagorean Numerology*. New Delhi, India: EduCreation Publishing, 2018.

McEvilley, Thomas. *The Shape of Ancient Thought: Comparative Studies in Greek and Indian Philosophies*. New York: Allworth Press, 2002.

Peterson, Joseph H. "Theurgia Goetia," 1998. Last updated September 14, 2020. http://www.esotericarchives.com/solomon/theurgia.htm

Phillips, David A. *The Complete Book of Numerology: Discovering the Inner Self.* Carlsbad, CA: Hay House, 2015.

Regardie, Israel, ed. *Gems from the Equinox*. Newburyport, MA: Weiser Books, 2007.

Skinner, Stephen, and David Rankine. *Goetia of Dr. Rudd (Sourceworks of Ceremonial Magic)*. Singapore: Golden Hoard Press, 2010.

Skinner, Stephen. *The Complete Magician's Tables*. Singapore: Golden Hoard Press, 2006.

Stratton-Kent, Jake. *The Testament of Cyprian the Mage*. London: Scarlet Imprint/Bibliotheque Rouge, 2014.

Underwood, Ron, dir. *City Slickers*. 1991; New York, Warner Brothers Pictures.

INDEX

D

E

F

I

K

L

M

O

P

To Write to the Author

If you wish to contact the author or would like more information about this book, please write to the author in care of Llewellyn Worldwide Ltd. and we will forward your request. Both the author and publisher appreciate hearing from you and learning of your enjoyment of this book and how it has helped you. Llewellyn Worldwide Ltd. cannot guarantee that every letter written to the author can be answered, but all will be forwarded. Please write to:

Frater Barrabbas
℅ Llewellyn Worldwide
2143 Wooddale Drive
Woodbury, MN 55125-2989

Please enclose a self-addressed stamped envelope for reply, or $1.00 to cover costs. If outside the U.S.A., enclose an international postal reply coupon.

Many of Llewellyn's authors have websites with additional information and resources. For more information, please visit our website at http://www.llewellyn.com.

To Write to the Author

If you wish to contact the author or would like more information about this book, please write to the author in care of Llewellyn Worldwide Ltd. and we will forward your request. Both the author and publisher appreciate hearing from you and learning of your enjoyment of this book and how it has helped you. Llewellyn Worldwide Ltd. cannot guarantee that every letter written to the author can be answered, but all will be forwarded. Please write to:

Frater Barrabbas
℅ Llewellyn Worldwide
2143 Wooddale Drive
Woodbury, MN 55125-2989

Please enclose a self-addressed stamped envelope for reply, or $1.00 to cover costs. If outside the U.S.A., enclose an international postal reply coupon.

Many of Llewellyn's authors have websites with additional information and resources. For more information, please visit our website at http://www.llewellyn.com.